THE AGE OF DESIRE

THE AGE
OF
DESIRE

*Reflections of
a Radical
Psychoanalyst*

JOEL KOVEL

 Pantheon Books   New York

Grateful acknowledgment is made to the following for permission to
reprint previously published material: Macmillan Publishing Co.,
Inc,. for lines from "The Second Coming" from Collected Poems
by W.B. Yeats. Copyright © 1924 by Macmillan Publishing Co.,
Inc., renewed 1952 by Bertha Georgie Yeats. Also reprinted by
permission of A.P. Watt Ltd.

Library of Congress Cataloging in Publication Data
Kovel, Joel, 1936–
The age of desire.
Includes bibliographical references and index.
1. Psychoanalysis—Social aspects—Case studies.
2. Psychotherapy—Social aspects—Case studies.
3. Desire—Social aspects—Case studies.   4. Marx, Karl,
1818–1883—Case studies.   I. Title.
RC455.K68   616.89'09   81–47198
ISBN 0–394–50818–1   AACR2

Manufactured in the United States of America

First Edition

To Molly, with her transcendent praxis

Bring me my bow of burning gold!
Bring me my arrows of desire!

—WILLIAM BLAKE, *Milton*

I then asked Ezekiel why he eat dung, & lay so long on his right
& left side? he answer'd, "the desire of raising other men into a
perception of the infinite: this the North American tribes
practice, & is he honest who resists his genius or conscience only
for the sake of present ease or gratification?"

—WILLIAM BLAKE, *The Marriage of Heaven and Hell*

CONTENTS

Preface   xi

Acknowledgments   xv

PART ONE: INTRODUCTION   1

   1   *The Lamentation of Quesalid*   3

   2   *Almost a Memoir*   5

   3   *Babel: A Fantasy*   7

PART TWO: CASE STUDIES IN HISTORY AND DESIRE   35

   4   *Love and Money*   37

   5   *Concerning Totality*   52

   6   *Desire and the Transhistorical*   61

   7   *Rich Girl*   86

   8   *Desire and the Family*   108

   9   *The Vigilante*   133

   10   *The Administration of Mind*   167

   11   *The Mending of Sarah*   202

PART THREE: THE RECAPTURE OF DESIRE   229

   12   *Desire and Praxis*   231

   13   *Transcendence and Universality*   242

Postscript   261

Appendix   265

Notes   270

Index   277

A Note About the Author   283

PREFACE

For nearly twenty years I have worked as a psychiatrist and psychoanalyst—seeing patients, teaching, writing, being involved in the profession, even playing some small role in administering it as director of a residency training program.

I have also been engaged in radical politics since my youth. Here my involvement has taken a complex course: intense though unfocused during college in the torpid fifties; suppressed throughout medical school, as professionalism took hold; rekindled during the midsixties, but again unfocused; and, for the past decade, increasingly centered on the development of a body of radical theory. I have also taken a number of forays into radical action.

And so I am a Marxist psychoanalyst, and have to define just what this means. I did not plan it so; indeed, I could not have planned it so, as there was nothing of the sort to foresee when I began my career. Perhaps I was unconsciously motivated by a premature exposure to Blake's dictum, from *The Marriage of Heaven and Hell*, that "Without Contraries is no progression," for there are few things so contrary as Marxism and the intractably bourgeois pursuit of psychoanalysis. In any case, things having turned out eccentrically for me, they seemed worthwhile to pursue. At the least, I found myself with a superabundance of noble tradition. Although my work as a psychoanalyst was maddeningly problematic, it nonetheless contained a glorious truth that could not be ignored. And as for Marxism, for all that it has tended to be defeated when virtuous or oppressive when victorious, it was inconceivable that anything worthwhile—or even interesting—in the human sphere could be worked out without engaging it. But the reasoning behind my persistence went beyond the particular merits of each doctrine, inasmuch as the central flaws of each body—the subjectivism of psychoanalysis, the hidden positivism of Marxism—seemed to match up, like an immense jigsaw puzzle, with the strengths of the other: Marxism's grasp of historical reality, psychoanalysis' contact with spontaneity and the roots of imagination, what we will be calling desire.

And so I have stewed happily in the juices of contradiction and prepared this work as the outcome of my reflections. Its primary aim is to recast the main issues of psychiatry-psychoanalysis (the relationship between the two will be developed in the text) along the lines of radical social thought, particularly Marxism, while its subsidiary goal is to indicate certain lines of development open to Marxism by virtue of a psychoanalytic appropriation of the mental depths. Of the two goals the one that is secondary here is much the more important so far as the future goes, for Marxism, despite all that has wracked it and the many radically different interpretations to which it has been subjected, remains the principal alternative open to humanity and the one philosophy around which world history will turn. However, the development of Marxist theory in the present work has taken a back seat for the very commendable Marxist reason that theory should be organically linked with social practice, or *praxis*; and since my main praxis is that of a psychiatrist/psychoanalyst, it is upon the reconstruction of the theory of this sphere that the work dwells. The result may therefore seem somewhat narrow and parochial for the Marxist vision, and needlessly preoccupied with states of mental disorder that are but the raw materials of a practice hemmed in by bourgeois assumptions. Nonetheless, I have striven to delineate what is universal and historically crucial in madness. This the best I can do from the vantage of my praxis. Limits are inevitable in any work; and the most one can expect is what I have tried to offer here, namely, limits well suited to be transcended.

The present study belongs to an already developed tradition of Marx-Freud works, something of which can be tracked in the occasional footnotes I have provided to orient the reader. However, no attempt has been made to deal with the literature exhaustively.[1] If I have not explicitly considered the Marx-Freud tradition it is because I wanted ideas to flow organically from actual life, and so have chosen to portray certain individuals as the substratum from which the theory develops. Although a certain amount of scholarly detail has thereby been lost, it perhaps has been compensated for by the sense of conviction that accompanies thought grounded in actual experience. In any case, the figures who have influenced me the most—Blake, the young (Hegelian), Marx, the later (Marxian) Sartre, Reich, and Marcuse—will be apparent in what follows.

If the name of Freud does not appear in this roster of influences it is because Freud has been more than a mere "influence" on me. His figure has defined not only my thought but my identity and the way I have brought bread to my table these last twenty years. The present work may be read as an extended argument with Freud or, rather, with the Freud I have assumed. If I have found much to quarrel with, the reader will also recognize the depth of attachment from which the quarrel springs. For all that I find his shortcomings integral to the socially backward position of the mental-health professions as a whole, Freud has always seemed, compared to the others who have periodically tried to improve upon him, like a mighty oak amidst a tangle of sumacs. To me, Freud is not simply the discoverer of a new psychological system, nor the developer of a new psychotherapeutic technique, as psychoanalytic orthodoxy prefers to see him; rather, he is the last great bourgeois thinker, the one to have drawn the contradictions of an age to their sharpest degree and thus to have provided radical discourse with its launching point.

The reader will perhaps be struck by the rather peculiar form in which this work has been cast. Once I decided, as would a proper Marxist, to situate theory with praxis, I was faced with an interesting predicament following from that praxis proper to psychoanalysis. One cannot work as a psychoanalyst without strict confidentiality. Though this demand is historically conditioned, being rooted in the privatization of personal life under capitalism and therefore closely related to the bourgeois nature of psychoanalysis, it must be respected as rational within the world as we live in it. Consequently, I could not write directly about my practice; it had to be fictionalized, specifically, by my composing each figure out of a number of real clinical occurrences with different patients, patched together with material from my own life and with some material that is simply fabricated. And if the patients have to be made up, so must I be myself. It occurred to me that a weakness in my discourse—the fact that I could not use undisguised clinical material—could be turned to advantage. Since I was not an omniscient figure behind the text but a fictionalized one within it, then I might as well construct a persona for myself, and people the work with figures who could concretely embody the various ideas I wanted to set forth. In this way I could have at my disposal multiple levels to represent the complexity of reality and my relation to it. In sum, inasmuch as I make so much of the imagination as a historical force, I thought it might be a sound principle to use my own. Upon further reflection, I do not see how any discourse whose truth is predicated on grounding theory organically in praxis can avoid an imaginative elaboration. It seems to me that there can be a truthfulness in using the imagination, and falsity—or, at least, a fore-shortening of the intricacy of life—when it is avoided. In any case, I found it more enjoyable to write in this manner, as well as being con-sistent with a theory that demands respect for desire.

One final word. It may be tempting to look for specific individuals represented, or even parodied, in my portrayal of the so-called mental-health professions. This would be understandable but incorrect. I am concerned herein to represent ideas allegorically, and the figures chosen for this purpose are not intended to portray any individual persons. There is one exception, a man now dead, to whom I try to pay some homage, though his figure is somewhat distorted.

ACKNOWLEDGMENTS

Thanks to Wagner Bridger, Byram Karasu, and Pedro Ruiz for essential support in the finest tradition of academic freedom; and to the residents in psychiatry at the Albert Einstein College of Medicine, who have given me heart by their efforts to transcend the profession of psychiatry. Richard Serra, Joe Kennedy, and Peggy Leo gave essential environmental support. Stanley Aronowitz and Jessica Benjamin painstakingly read the manuscript and gave me the benefit of their reflections. Thanks also to John Broughton, Lizzie Borden, Jean Elshtain, Howard Gadlin, Adrienne Harris, Arnold Kaufman, Richardo Zuniga, Ed Sullivan, Howard Gruber, and Millie Lopez-Garriga for more of the same. And to radio station WBAI-FM for playing Paul Robeson.

Three individuals stand out as having been particularly significant in the development of this work. Ethel Levine typed and bore witness with cheer and wit to the pangs of its gestation. Philip Pochoda gave salutary editorial guidance from the very beginnings of the project. He is that kind of editor who cares enough not to fear disagreement with a temperamental author, and has the authority and judgment to work his points through the latter's narcissism. Finally, and in a class by herself, there is DeeDee Halleck, about whose relation to this work a whole other book needs to be written.

Part One

INTRODUCTION

1

THE LAMENTATIONS OF QUESALID

Lévi-Strauss writes of the Kwakiutl Indian Quesalid, who did not believe in the power of the shamans of his tribe.[1] In his desire to expose them, he began frequenting their meetings until one day he was invited to join the group. And so Quesalid began a four-year apprenticeship, during which he convinced himself by direct learning that the sorcerer's power was based on trickery and illusion, and the suggestibility of the patient. Instead of genuinely assuming the patient's illness, as he professed to do, the shaman would resort to such tricks as spitting out a bloody piece of goose down that had been secreted in his mouth and that he then identified as the material embodiment of the disease. "His worst suspicions confirmed," Lévi-Strauss continues, "Quesalid wanted to continue his inquiry. But he was no longer free," for his skills had become known and his services were in demand. Gifted at what he knew to be fraudulent, Quesalid nonetheless acquired a reputation as a healer and became socially indispensable. Unable to transcend his own contradictions, he came to believe in them, or at least to rearrange his disbelief. He turned his critical faculties to the differentiation between types of what he called a "false supernatural," and "was led to conclude that some forms were less false than others—those, of course, in which he had a personal stake and whose system he was, at the same time, surreptitiously building up in his own mind." In short, he became adept at exposing the baser techniques of his colleagues in neighboring villages. By making his fellow shamans look ridiculous, Quesalid brought down the scorn of the community upon them and so deprived them of the basis of their authority. Meanwhile, he himself grew great in prestige

3

and healing power. "Quesalid, rich in secrets, pursued his career, exposing the imposters and full of contempt for the profession. . . . He carries on his craft conscientiously, takes pride in his achievements and warmly defends the technique of the bloody down against all rival schools. He seems to have completely lost sight of the fallaciousness of the technique which he had so disparaged at the beginning."

Could this have been otherwise?

2

ALMOST A MEMOIR

Some years ago—never mind how many—I disembarked before a gigantic buff-colored building and commenced the study of medicine. Over the portico of this structure had been chiseled the words "Of The Most High Cometh Healing"; and so for the next four years I let the gentle rain of medical wisdom fall down upon me, baked myself under the hot sun of clinical experience until I became tough and leathery, and endured the long cold nights spent by the side of the sick and dying. At length I was pronounced fit to enter the ranks of medical professionals.

But I am a vexatious sort, and was no sooner in the real world of medical practice than I became embroiled in crisis. What had seemed fascinating within the protective confines of school became repellent and dehumanizing once it was the substance of daily work. I found myself particularly depressed by the domination that technology seemed to hold over every practice. Its icy grip molded the contours of disorder itself, so that the very diseases brought before our clinical gaze became those of machines, or at least of organisms that seemed to have long since given up on life. Longing for work that would bring me closer to the real life of my patients and anxious, too, to re-establish connection with what in college had been called the "humanities," I suddenly veered from the pursuit of traditional, "organic" medicine and entered the more ambiguous but also more intriguing pursuit of psychiatry and, later, psychoanalysis.

I did so not without trepidation, remembering that my worst medical school grades had been in psychiatry, the product of an aggravating habit of thinking I knew better than my teachers, for which I had paid on a number of occasions. This habit, no doubt deeply rooted in a rebellious character structure, had been fueled by the contrast between expectation and reality. I had commenced medical training fresh from a reading of Freud's *Interpretation of Dreams*. Inspired by that prodigious work, I looked to psychiatry for more of the same insight and depth, but found instead banality and ennui, comfortable men prating of "adjustment reactions" or the "cardinal signs of schizophrenia." The subject enthralled me yet seemed encased in a thick wall of theoretical jelly. As yet I had no grasp of why this should be so and too much youthful arrogance to care much about finding out. Consequently, I became bored and sullen, or occasionally sarcastic, and eventually lost interest in the whole matter, intrigued as I was by the mysteries of positive medical science.

After my disillusionment and the return to what proved to be my true vocational love, lingering doubts about how I would fit into the world of psychiatry plagued me. Though often submerged by the demands of the work, which had indeed brought me closer to the real lives of people and opened, too, onto the wider world of human affairs, these doubts never completely went away. Instead, I learned to live with them, to analyze out their filaments in my own infantile history, to adopt, however uneasily, that ideology which accepts and tolerates the imperfectibility of the world.

My malaise, however, endured, and took strength from my own growing success. As I grew in the world of psychiatry I could no longer hide behind the irresponsibility of the inexperienced. I felt the obligation to offer an opinion that others were seeking; the need to take something of a political stance that, however unpopular at large it may be, seemed to me an inescapable interpretation of reality; and, perhaps, a sense that time was passing, and that the moment to declare myself would come but once.

But ideas are practices, and practices are practiced by other men and women. The longstanding doubts from my student days would have to be confronted. Was this peevishness? Was I but another Quesalid, forced by the social order to turn a critical capacity into mundane advantage? There could be no telling unless I spoke out.

I decided to have a go at it.

6

3

BABEL: A FANTASY

Having learned enough of the secrets of the mental healers to pass among them as one of their own, I decided to further my knowledge by attending their national convention. The leading mental experts of the day would be there to exchange the most up-to-date conceptions and to seek the truth about the puzzles of the mind. The accumulations of more than a half-century of scientific labor had been concentrated in a few hotels of a large midwestern city. Literally hundreds of scientific papers were to be delivered at dozens of symposia, and scores of special lecturers brought good-sized crowds of professionals to gilt-walled conference rooms. There were even national political figures speaking to the throng about the "incalculable loss in dollars and human suffering wrought by mental illness," and the plans government had for dealing with the scourge.

My heart quickened as I checked into the hotel and saw the professionals gathering, chatting amiably among themselves, striding purposefully from here to there, or just relaxing. I had not known psychiatry had claimed so many. Few relaxed for long. I was struck by the attention to detail shown by the convention organizers. Leisure time itself was administered, and thoughtful care was taken that all members of the family would be profitably occupied. As I crossed the magenta carpet of the hotel lobby I nearly collided with a convoy of wives headed out the door. It was one of the special "spouse events," in this case a guided tour, in the words of the elegant program, of the "Negro District, with its rich and varied history."

On the check-in line for the hotel I received another agreeable surprise when I looked at the badge of the florid, aquiline doctor in front of me and immediately recognized the name of one of the most prestigious departmental chairmen in the country, a man of legendary

7

dynamism and sire to scores of brilliant careers. A bearded young man with sad eyes and a formal Eastern European accent deferentially approached the great man, informed him that he would be moving to this very city to work in a Veterans Administration hospital (the young doctor had evidentally been on the staff of the great doctor's department of psychiatry), and listened for the older doctor's benediction. It was slow in coming but wondrously effective all the same. A long pause, then in evenly measured cadences and scarcely an inflection, the simple words "I wish you well," said with chin high and followed by a barely perceptible nod. "I guess from now on we will meet only at conventions," the young man dolefully replied and then quietly padded away. Impressed, I decided to begin my explorations with the keynote lecture to be given that afternoon by the great doctor.

The great doctor's lecture was titled "The Crisis of Psychiatry" and was to be held in the hotel's largest meeting room, the Grand Imperial Ballroom. By the time I arrived, some four hundred professionals had already gathered. Most stayed through to the end, and those who left were steadily replaced with newcomers. The patriarch began his talk by graciously acknowledging the encomiums delivered by the conference chairman, himself a distinguished psychiatrist. Ruddy and vigorous in his later years, the great doctor had earned the right to reminisce. He told of his lineage, back to the great Adolph Meyer and even to Freud himself, who had analyzed his own analyst. He talked of the thirties, when psychiatry was smaller and still under the shadow of neurology departments in medical schools; of the forties, when his own career began in the army, and of how the world war had contributed to putting psychiatry on its feet as a major profession. He then went on to the fifties, the halcyon years of psychoanalytic psychiatry. During these times he launched his own department and began training the generation that now ruled the profession. And they were years of seemingly unlimited expansion, a growth that continued into the sixties, when the government began getting into psychiatry in a big way with its Community Mental Health Centers. The seventies became even more exciting. To the psychological and social insights of previous decades had been added a veritable renaissance of biological thinking: new drugs, new neuronal pathways, new hormonal relationships. The pace of discovery was exhilarating and bid to unlock the age-old secrets of the human brain. In sum, psychiatry had, from the angle of its own standards of professional knowledge, achieved a truly impressive level, not the complete synthesis of which science had dreamed for centuries, but certainly some progress in that direction.

There was, however, another angle, he reminded the audience, from which the sense of progress induced by these developments could be misleading. Like so much of the suddenly remote era of a decade ago, what seemed psychiatric prosperity could also turn into inflation. Carried away by excitement, the profession had promised too much and had to retrench in the face of public skepticism and tightened federal money. The public, the government, and the profession alike had lost faith in the hypertrophied guarantees of those years. Psychiatry had to show *results*, not just hopes and fancy ideas. Today, with insurance companies and the government bearing an increasingly larger share of the burden of payment, public agencies were also going to have an increasingly larger share in determining what gets done. This is not necessarily a drawback, although the profession must redouble its efforts to maintain confidentiality and the integrity of the doctor-patient relationship. But the people in government were not faceless bureaucrats. He had trained a number of the top ones himself and knew at first hand that they were as humane as any practitioner in this very audience. It was time, therefore, for the profession to start confronting realities, realities that included, besides the growth of government regulation, the enormous proliferation of nonmedical practitioners—psychologists, social workers, and therapists of all kinds. It was necessary, he claimed, for psychiatry to face up to its true identity as a part of medicine without, of course, relinquishing its special role among the mental-health professionals, a role earned by the unique discipline of medical training, which added the rigor of the biological sciences to the compassion and caring required of the therapist.

The profession, as this doctor saw it, suffered from an embarrassment of riches incurred at a time of crisis in public confidence. Psychiatry had to stand proud, but it had to stand humble as well to recognize that the complete understanding, much less cure, of mental illness was still eons away, that psychotherapy was not all that effective by conventional standards of measurement, and that the right combination of drugs had not yet been found except in a minority of cases. Our task as a profession was to hold on to what we held dear and to convince the public and the government that more, not less, research and training were required. To do this psychiatry must pull together, bury useless theoretical squabbles, uphold the best scientific standards, and focus on those activities for which tangible results could be demonstrated. In short, it had to redefine itself as a vital part of medicine. In recent years there had been an ominous decline in the number of medical students applying for psychiatric residency training. Students were staying away because psychiatry had been unable to represent its riches to them in a coherent way. It was in a sense the profession's fault that this was happening; but it was a fault only, not a deep flaw. Basically, psychiatry was healthy, expanding, and socially indispensable. The next period could be its Golden Age if only it would recognize itself.

I left before the applause died down and wandered among the throng until I found myself before the ornate door of a somewhat smaller but still substantial hall. I was just in time to hear a symposium by three of the most distinguished psychoanalysts of the day on a topic of great scientific and therapeutic interest, "The Borderline States and the Narcissistic Personality." The session promised to be especially exciting, since each of the speakers represented a major school within contemporary analysis. The panel moderator reminded the audience that the existence of such scientific controversy contradicted the beliefs that psychoanalysis was a closed system or that it had long since stopped generating new ideas. And there could be no doubt of serious divergences here. At times, disputations among these schools had resulted in adherents of one or the other being forced out of particular analytic institutes. All regarded themselves as true descendants of Freud, as good clinical psychiatrists, and as scientists whose thinking was organically tied to their method of data gathering. Yet they disagreed—albeit politely—on so much.

The first speaker, Dr. A, reminded the audience that there was a large group of patients seen nowadays who did not suffer from discrete symptom neuroses, such as phobias, obsessions, et cetera, or from chronic neurotic character patterns. Such individuals were somehow "worse" than neurotics without yet having the fixed dislocation with respect to reality that characterizes psychosis. These patients —whose number seems greater now than in former years, although that was not a matter upon which he felt qualified to pass judgment— suffered from diffuse impairment in their self-feeling and their ability to relate to others. They were detached, fragmented in their interests and activities, and incapable of forming lasting love relationships. Sexually they performed adequately but seemed to drift, being more preoccupied with immediate pleasure than with in-depth feeling. Also they seemed to vacillate between various perversions without much sense of guilt or shame. Nonetheless, they generally felt empty, bored, and without worth, despite a façade of fairly good social adaptation. Of course, such a very complex group of people seemed to defy classification. At one end of the spectrum were well-functioning types who suffered mainly from inner feelings of estrangement, while at the other were chaotic individuals who had lapses of psychotic thinking or were psychopathic, with amorality and major difficulties in controlling their impulses. Nonetheless, it was essential for purposes of scientific advancement that some kind of classification of these disorders be attempted. Only thereby could the psychoanalytic community arrive at the underlying mechanisms of the psychopathology and so develop rational therapeutic strategies. In other words, we must be able to accurately diagnose these disorders—which might be called *borderline*, in that they stood between neurosis and psychosis; and *narcissistic*, in that a more or less diffuse impairment of the self was involved. And we had to go beyond the relatively anecdotal usage of these terms.

Dr. A, who was a lanky, nattily dressed man, was now coming to the meat of his talk. As if in anticipation he paused, took off his prominent tortoise-shell glasses, and ran his fingers along the edges of his neatly trimmed beard. We knew that his man had taken part in major psychoanalytical research and waited expectantly for the denouement.

Dr. A continued by reminding the assembled professionals that the most essential psychoanalytic insights had to do with the persistence of childhood and infantile modes of thinking in the adult, i.e., with what analysts termed a genetic and developmental point of view. Modern neurology began with the insight of Hughlings Jackson that brain structure existed in a hierarchy in which the older, more animal elements are overlaid and controlled by more biologically recent "human" ones. Just so did Freud's great discovery consist—in simplest terms—of the animal id beneath the human ego, or, from another angle, of the primary process of thinking beneath the secondary one of ordered logical discourse. It was found that what was "older" phylogenetically and more primitive in terms of structure also corresponded to what had transpired during the childhood of the individual and was persisting in the adult. Unearthing these structures was the secret of psychoanalytic therapy and theory alike.

So much was ingrained wisdom, Dr. A asserted. Why not then use this principle to make a precise and detailed morphology of the borderline and narcissistic conditions? Psychoanalysis had at its disposal a recently discovered treasure trove of research into the mother-infant relationship. Work of this sort had been a major force in the psychoanalytic life of the past generation and had substantially revitalized the field. Now, since it had been established that the human self was made in this matrix, was it too great a leap to postulate that disorders of the self, such as borderline and narcissistic pathology, would be best approached through developmental concepts? Accordingly, Dr. A argued, vicissitudes of the mother-child dyad could be correlated with vicissitudes of self-pathology (psychoanalysts love to use the word *vicissitudes*) in a rigorous develpmental sequence. And so he proposed to distinguish the borderline conditions, proper, from the narcissistic ones. The former were more disturbed and resulted from lesions in the "undifferentiated" phase of development, when self and other, i.e., mother, were not distinguished in the infant's mind. If psychosis resulted from the combination of a biological defect with severe impairment in mothering, the borderline state was the product of maternal impairment alone. Because the mother was not reliably "there" (which, of course, meant more than being just physically present) when the infant needed her to differentiate himself, he never developed a secure sense of reality; hence, he was always prone to regressive reactivation of this weak spot. The narcissistic states, on the other hand, reflected lesions at a more developed stage of the progression, that of "rapprochement," when the infant had achieved self-other discrimination but had to return frequently to his mother for recognition and other types of emotional refueling. Here, inconsistency, coldness, or other defects in the mother would produce lacunae in the child's self-recognition, and would be compensated for by feelings of grandiosity, omnipotence, or detachment on the child's part. We would thus be on the road to narcissistic personality pathology. At higher levels of development, Dr. A went on, the self-system could be presumed intact, and the classic neuroses would take root out of the essential Oedipal configuration. In other words, the Oedipus complex is between a whole child and his whole mother and father. The impulses are toward them as separate people and the consequences, including the fantasy of castration, would be suffered by the child, who stood in this way to lose his phallus, but not himself, in the Oedipal triangle.

Dr. A concluded by pointing out the necessity for further scientific research, particularly to isolate distinct subtypes of the borderline/ narcissistic conditions and to correlate them with particular developmental vicissitudes. He emphasized that the ultimate test was therapeutic validity, since the analytic situation remained the alpha and omega of our investigation. Indeed, it was precisely the response of particular patients to interpretations aimed at particular developmental levels that confirmed his belief in the validity of the proposed schema. And with this conclusion, Dr. A stepped down.

Dr. B had attained a legendary reputation for theoretical sophistication and for his iron rule of a major private hospital. He physically contrasted with Dr. A, being portly, clean-shaven, and somewhat acerbic in manner, and lost no time in launching a major attack on his colleague's views. There was, of course, much with which he had to agree: the need for precise diagnosis, for example, and the ultimate test provided by clinical experience. But it was precisely this latter standard that made him differ so heatedly with Dr. A. To extrapolate from adult data into an infantile schema of such linear simplicity was impermissible; moreover, it smacked of that bugbear of psychology, reductionism, the boiling down of a complex and overdetermined intrapsychic system into a few principles that can easily—all too seductively easily—be correlated with overt behavior. Such thinking was all right for ethologists, behaviorists, and other simplistic types. But the subtlety of intrapsychic mechanisms does not permit psychoanalysts to fish in shallow waters. No analyst doubts the determinative value of infantile experience; but to admit this should not lead us onto a primrose path where human complexities are correlated with fixed sequences of mother-infant interactions. Our science (one could not help observing that the more learned psychoanalytic theoreticians took a proprietary air toward their discipline) has reached maturity; sermonizers may clutch at big simple answers, but those who seek the truth need to eschew hopes for closure in favor of concentrating on the multiple pathways by means of which vicissitudes of drive and ego development interact with external reality to produce the infinitely complex states of normality and pathology. Dr. B hoped it was not necessary to remind his audience that we are dealing with two instinctual formations, libido and aggression, each of which, deriving from the id, develops with some degree of independence, and invests both self and object representations. These representations in turn are but subsystems of the ego, which has its other apparatuses as well: for example, reality testing, defense, and the synthetic-integrative functions. Finally, we have the great and, as yet, imperfectly understood system of the superego with which to contend, also invested with instinctual as well as partially de-instinctualized energy, particularly from the aggressive source. While it is apparent that borderline and narcissistic states manifestly consist of pathologic self-representations as well as self-object boundary distortions, it would seem from a theoretical standpoint that the malignant invasion—if Dr. B could be permitted for purposes of exposition such colorful language—might penetrate the self-representation from any one of a number of foci within ego, id, or superego. In short, we had to attend to the possibility of *intrasystemic* conflicts, i.e., within one of the three great mental organizations, as well as that of *intersystemic* conflict between them. Dr. B then proceeded to show how the narcissistic pathology of a number of patients could stem from a number of different mechanisms. He ended his talk with a passionate plea for theoretical agnosticism and sophistication. It was essential, he said in conclusion, for psychoanalysis to earn the respect of other sciences, within medicine and without, if it was one day to realize Freud's dream of mastering the secrets of human nature, including the promise, as yet unfulfilled, that a physiological basis would ultimately be found for psychology. And we could do this only by recognizing the complex and multifactorial determination of behavior.

Now it was Dr. C's turn. He was a somewhat stout but genial and elegant man whose vaguely European accent added authority to his words. The audience was especially attentive to his comments, inasmuch as his particular school of analysis was considered the most avant-garde within the profession. Indeed, some feared, while others hoped, that it would soon split from or be forced out of the main body of the discipline. So far the central organization had avoided imposing this fate, which had befallen so many pioneers-turned-heretic in the past; and Dr. C, as well as others within his group, could generally count on adequate representation on panels at the major conventions. Nonetheless, one never knew whether fireworks would take place when Dr. C spoke, especially when it was in conjunction with Dr. B, who was both his nemesis and *bête noire*.

Dr. C began his remarks by reminding the audience that we were more than three quarters of the way toward the twenty-first century. Why, then, did psychoanalysis still remain so yoked to concepts of the nineteenth century, as revealed, for example, in the work of his learned colleague B? Freud we may forgive for this, inasmuch as he was a man of his times who could not jettison his mechanistic inheritance. But how long must we ape Freud in his clumsy theorizing? Let us abandon this vain biologism, which sees instincts, energies, and apparatuses at work beneath the surface of behavior! We are clinicians above all, and our clinical science, psychoanalysis, affords us a tool of great precision. What this tool unearths is no biological instinct but the self itself—or, as he would call it, the Me—fused with yet invariably differentiated from its objects. Our guide must always be the various transferences developed in analytic work, that is to say, the structured patterns of interaction manifested by the patient as he repeats the essential themes of his life in the analytic situation. Only transferences are real for us as analysts; everything else is speculation, be it Dr. A's oversimplified dragging of mother-child phases into adulthood (here he had to agree with B's critique), or B's obscurantist mystification derived from Freud's archaic metapsychology. The vicissitudes we seek are not of somatically based instinctual processes but of the Me itself. The normal individual has this process of self-realization within him: it is the summation of his life processes and his way of being-in-the-world. (Dr. C here interjected that he hoped his audience would not take his use of this term as any kind of endorsement of existentialism, an antiscientific philosophy foreign to the spirit of psychoanalytic inquiry.) Let us drop the useless nitpicking over the "ego" that has dominated psychoanalysis for two generations (from the standpoint of ego psychology, the self was merely a "subsystem" of ego, an organ within an organism), and concentrate on the Me as the leading term of psychoanalytic theory. We could then focus on secondary disorganizations of a primarily intact Me, in other words, the classical neuroses; or alternatively, on primary disorganizations of the Me, that is, the narcissistic disorders, borderline states, and psychoses.

A great advantage of his system, Dr. C pointed out to the audience, was its assimilation into a more forward-looking therapeutic attitude. The classical approach, from Freud right on to Dr. B, emphasized the unearthing of buried id derivatives, i.e., repressed instinctual wishes, such as the urge to kill father, have sex with mother, and so on, which stemmed from the childhood neurosis and clogged up current adult functioning. However, from the standpoint of a psychology that postulated a primacy to Me development, to accentuate material of this sort would be to impose negative self-images at the expense of a more holistic attitude; in other words, it would be analytically false and would work to delay Me integration. Technically speaking, then, C's system implied a more friendly, supportive attitude on the part of the analyst, worked to reduce guilt and shame, and tended to make people more accepting of themselves. Only when this happened could further Me growth occur. Thus, it shortened analyses and made them more successful, no mean boon considering the increasing influence that insurance companies and other third-party payers are wielding over analytic practice.

The discussion was about to begin and it promised to be a lively one indeed. Dr. A was taking it all rather calmly, but smoke was fairly coming from Dr. B's collar as he girded himself for battle. Yet, for all that I enjoyed controversy, I decided to leave. I was getting depressed and wanted some time to sort things out.

What troubled me was the thought that it did not much matter whether the ensuing discussion succeeded in bringing the three points of view I had just heard closer together or farther apart. Something else was wrong with them, something that could not be more than vaguely sensed but that cut deeper into their discourse than any debate on the terms so far advanced could address. And until I figured out exactly what terms to use in order to account for my malaise, further attendance at that panel would only add to the confusion.

So close and yet so far! But were A, B, and C far from each other, as they themselves held, or were they rather equivalently far from the reality they were engaging, and in that respect close to each other? And here I was troubled by the awareness that I shared so much with these men and, for all my criticism, respected their intellect and clinical skills. And I knew as well how deeply the psychoanalytic tradition they represented had sunk into my own bones, knew that I could not help feeling loyal to it. Perhaps I too suffered from Freudolatry, was another case of the fatuous father worship that had so often made psychoanalysis ridiculous. No, that had been worked out. The loyalty was based on something better. I recalled my youthful reading of The Interpretation of Dreams and the sense of scales falling away, the sudden realization of the radical profundity that Freud's vision provided. I could not formulate it explicitly then but realized in later years that the encounter had forged a lifelong promise to seek the same vision. It was not the image of Freud the father—that querulous, jealous, Saturnine figure—which held me but rather that of the heroic explorer and liberator, the deep-sea diver, the archeologist of the soul, the demystifier and the social critic. This

Freud was not to be worshipped, for that would deny what was emancipating and critical in his genius, but to be emulated in truth telling, even at the cost of isolation.

I now began to make some sense out of my malaise, could already feel the depression melting into anger. It was not that Doctors A, B, and C were drifting apart from psychoanalytic discourse but that they were using it in a formally correct way yet utterly without that spirit of emancipation and critique which had infused Freud's great works. The smugness, the academicism, the pedantry experienced in that room, weighed more heavily on me than I had first thought. It was not just the stale smoke that had made the atmosphere stifling but the smell of the discourse, something about the way language had been used.

I could not yet fathom this something, but I knew it was there and could begin to appreciate how it sclerosed the work and made it— despite the original promise of psychoanalysis—repressive. A's developmental sequence, for instance: Was it not a piece of conformism, a nice yardstick by which to measure people, this stage following that in lockstep, so that those out of line—the "sick"—could be shamed with their immaturity? They used to blame it on the Devil; now, with "health ethics," it was a case of arrested development. And what were A and his ilk doing but providing a map for all the little boys and girls to follow, presumably "natural" but inevitably man-made and so reflective of an imposed order? And man-made indeed. Why did so much psychoanalytic writing, even the most seemingly abstract theory, read like a string of complaints directed by a boy against his mother: the subject always a "he," the offending parent, who does too much or too little, a "she"? It was not enough to pass off such usage as a necessity imposed by language or reflective of actual social structure. The analysts were always trying to do this, on those rare occasions when they bothered to think at all about the broader implications of their work, but what they never began to consider was the active aspect of language and society. For them these were givens that encompassed a firmament in which was inscribed whatever they said, thought, or did. Bemused by the privileges and claptrap of "science," they thought themselves dispassionate observers and not social agents. Lost in an ideology of passive contemplation, they saw social practice as an automatic fixed structure, not as a dialectical play of forces within which their own activity and the choices they made sustained one side or another. And one side that analysts always seemed to sustain was patriarchy: the vector of their work invariably pointed to a "nature" represented by woman who nourishes the human represented by the male and against which he is to struggle and eventually dominate. Most analysts considered themselves moderately progressive and had been sufficiently influenced by bourgeois feminism to disclaim any intention to fetter women. But it was there, sunk deep into their practice and anchored to a biological mystique of development, so that any analyst, for example, who advocated something as mild as day-care did so uneasily, knowing he was going against the grain of his profession's wisdom.

Then there was Dr. B. How often had I heard those Jesuitical tones, those arid inquisitorial splittings? Each step in the reasoning followed from the last, Thomistically, and like the prodigies of the Church Fathers, were designed not for enlightenment but for domination. Forget the real world, in which analysts were a highly rewarded if somewhat beleaguered class. Attend rather to theoretical mysteries in which the criterion of truth was respect for the master. I remembered scenes of my training, the younger analysts fawning on the illuminati, those elder training analysts with seerlike access to privileged code words: "intrasystemic," "aggressivized energy," "deneutralization." (They also had access to privileged patients and made choice referrals to their favorites, but that was not discussed.) The main issues were complexity and a sterile field. Analysts should do nothing else but analysis, and analysis was nothing but a fantastically subtle and complex technical pursuit that related to nothing else in the world and was utterly incomprehensible to the uninitiated, i.e., the whole population except for a thousand or so properly certified professionals. Thus was the outside kept out and the inside in.

At times psychoanalysts would condescend to admit that they had something to say to the world. They would climb down from their tower to lecture to the rabble or might even take exquisitely measured positions on "issues of public policy." Often these would be carefully screened by the appropriate committee of the national organization to ensure that they emerged with the appropriate degree of sobriety; but this was not really necessary, the painstaking schooling and exposure to masters like Dr. B having long since stamped a timid circumspection on the analytic mind. And one knew which way these canons pointed, recalled the blue-ribbon colloquium years before on the "Psychological Roots of War, with Particular Attention to Vietnam." I remembered it well: it was held in a hotel as elegant as this one, at the apex of the nightmare; a bunch of analysts and Ivy League social scientists, all sleek and dressed like brokers, sat around a mahogany table trying to figure out Indochina. I had introduced the question of U.S. imperialism, thereby inducing one of the social thinkers, a particularly learned man from Harvard, to bristle and snort. But the latter never had to rejoin, because the analytic theoreticians got there first with their scientist line, reminding the group of how complicated things were, how singular explanations were simplistic and never got to the heart of a human situation, how the analyst above all saw the complexities, the conflicts, the ambivalences, all those intricacies that grown-up thinkers recognized for truth. And, sure enough, the discussion turned to the vicissitudes of idealization as revealed in the U.S. policy maker's attitudes toward LBJ, and remained, despite my protest, on a nice, safe psychological plane. I began to wonder then whether "psychology" had not been created in order to trivialize history. Perhaps it had been made into a discrete sphere in order to blind people to a larger truth, in which case the convolutions of Dr. B's theorizing would take on an added, even more dubious value than the preservation of narrow professional privilege.

But B, for all his awesomeness and influence within the profession, belonged to an old guard that was passing. It was Dr. C who held the fascination of the younger generation with his skillfully tooled combination of chic and respectability. C left no doubt that you still had to be one of the analytic cognoscenti to get the point and to really help people, that is to say, the right kind of people. Yet he had at the same time elegantly erased everything critical and problematic from Freud's vision of humanity. B had done something of the same, he and his colleagues having encased the radical vision with their rigmarole of an ego. But this had at length become unwieldy, cluttered, so obviously academic and sterile as to lose appeal. C, on the other hand, had a better idea: simply march a holistic Me front stage and have it block everyone's view into the darkness that Freud had momentarily illuminated. This was not exactly original, as Fromm, Horney, and a number of others had worked out pretty much the same approach decades ago. But C had so far succeeded in keeping his Me system within the ambit of official psychoanalysis; and because this was an international organization with ties to medical institutions and other centers of influence, C might well deserve some credit for his innovation. But what a pallid reification it was once stripped of the fancy jargon! One even preferred the reifications of B, with all their ponderousness, to those of C, with their false lucidity. If one is going to reify, to make a "thing" out of a relationship, it should be done with the "ego." At least the ego is a theoretical construction that retains the potential of being formed by negation. "Ego" always leaves something behind, something deeper than itself. If there was, as Freud showed, something inherently problematic about us, then the ego/id split, for all that it had come to be used biologistically and in the interests of positive thinking, gave one hope of entry into the mystery. And instinct theory, though callused from being used to beat down the possibilities for human change, also could help keep one's eyes open to the truth that there was something inhuman about us after all—not "animal," for that would be an insult to other species, or "aggressive," for that would be to put a lid on activity and outrage, but "unspeakable," "abominable," "unfathomable," "ineffable," and "wondrous," all those words that, lacking theoretic rigor, were somehow truer and deeper than the rigmarole of psychoanalytic theory: truer and deeper, but not true or deep enough, it having been Freud's farthest reach to recognize that the psyche, though it generated language to know itself and the world, had a reality beyond, or beneath (or neither, all spatial indications failing) language   unlanguaged   thinglike   unconscious. Language could be shaped toward the description of anything in the world; but when it tried to account for its own ground, it broke down. And so the self, which one wanted to retain in theory, was always problematical, never accountable in positive terms. There was the radical insight, which permanently demolished positive social theory; and here was Dr. C oozing respectability and surrounded by an adoring clique of foppish young professionals, with his puffery of a Me: just the thing to reassure those who might otherwise wonder whether life in bourgeois society had no meaning. These uplifting messages, one knew, eventually fell of their own weight, to be replaced by the next sales pitch. Before Me Theory, there had been Ego Identity; before that, something else; afterwards, who knows what? Meanwhile, one had to endure the boredom of bad theory, possibly the ultimate judgment to be passed on it. Was there not something better to do?

Maybe it was true, as one had often heard bruited around the profession, that psychoanalysis, long the linchpin of American psychiatry, was washed up, a shell of its former self, superseded by better therapies and more scientific approaches to human disorder. Certainly there had been a crescendo of such attacks during the last decade. As the shabbiness of today's discourse provided these newer ventures with an automatic legitimacy, and as the convention, in its catholic wisdom, had provided a forum for almost all existing points of view in contemporary psychiatry, I decided to round out my day's edification with some more sessions. By perusing the fat, glossy program I was able to select two talks of a diametrically opposite bent, united only by their protest against psychoanalytic hegemony. Indeed, the reactions moved in such drastically different directions as to suggest the products of fission flying from a disintegrating nucleus. Like a human cloud chamber, I might be able to discern a deeper unity beneath the fragmentation. And who knew whether Protestantism, here as in religion, might have fruitful consequences?

The first talk, given in the Mirabeau Room and titled "New Ventures in Authenticity," was infused with the fervent conviction that psychoanalysis had betrayed human potential by hiding behind a fig leaf of scientific detachment. The speaker, a youthful-looking man in his mid-forties, had been a rising academic star: top medical school, top residency program, years of analysis—a smooth climb up the ladder. Only fifteen years ago he had been a Young Turk at the same meetings. His paper on "Systems Theory and Psychiatric Management" had stirred a lot of interest for its brash, almost presumptuous bid to integrate mind, body, and society. Then he discovered family therapy, which had a natural fit with the Systems Theory Approach, and, following that, some of the sophisticated encounter-group techniques. A new career unfolded. He became a major figure on the lecture circuit, a kind of traveling road show, doing lucrative workshops two or three times a month in which he would demonstrate the latest techniques in family therapy from a systems-encounter perspective. The intoxicating idea was that, with the change in therapeutic structure, new and liberating therapeutic vistas had opened up. No longer tied to one-on-one intrapsychic exploration, we were now free to experiment with novel forms of interaction. The reality, here and now, of immediate family experience would replace the sluggish and distant intellectualizations of individual analytic therapy. Action and expressiveness replaced words and reflectivity. What counted was to stir up real, gut emotions in the sessions. By way of proving his liberation from the old ways, the doctor started to bring accounts of his own family experience, and then the family itself, into his presentations and therapeutic practice. One memorable day his own father joined him onstage. Confessing his "distancing," he approached the old man and humbly asked forgiveness. The two hugged and wept; and the audience, moved, did not easily forget the experience.

The doctor began his talk by reminiscing about that time. People thought him crazy then, he said; there was talk about having him run out of the professional societies, even of having him delicensed. But those antics were not the end, only the beginning of a whole new series of insights. What he had learned was that immediacy was all. As great as making contact with his father had been, he knew that the most essential feature of the encounter was its uniqueness, its surprise. He could never follow it up without introducing some anticipation, hence guardedness and, eventually, jadedness. So the therapist had to search for perpetual revolution in his practice. Therapy was pure creativity, novelty its only sure feature. All was flux; one could never stand in the same stream twice. Such was reality, and therapy had to capitalize on it, make it a conscious program. In the pioneering spirit that made America great, psychological people had to pull up stakes and launch themselves into the new world. And without guideposts, without those Freudian theoretical strait jackets that got in the way of real feeling. Therapy could not rest with any closure or explanations. If words were used, they must only set up paradox, trick the patient into that point beyond which no explanation could hold. Only then could real change set in. And to accomplish this in the modern world, one had to be extremely light on one's feet, given the incredible wealth of techniques. The perfect therapist would learn them all—existentialism, Zen, Gestalt, psychosynthesis, Rolfing, est, primal, bioenergetics, and a host of others—not to mimic any but to stay ahead, to combine the n therapies into $n+1$ and then, once the $n+1$ had been used, to combine them with n so as to get $n+2$, and so on, happily, to infinity. Just now, for example, he was happily experimenting with a bioenergetic variety of the est technique. The insights were fantastic, right up to the limits of human potentiality; but they were all the more beautiful for being evanescent. Like therapeutic butterflies going off into the sun, they would leave behind a space for even greater insights to follow. Because human potential was infinite, we were made holy, in the Creator's image, and only complete, restless innovation would begin to tap these riches, i.e., start the job of potential maximization ("infinitization," he called it); that was our mission in life. The only constant feature required of the therapist-innovator was realness, sheer authenticity. One had to be a psychological athlete to do the job properly; it meant pulling out all stops, not hiding behind that rigid analytic posture of phony verbiage and abstinence. And that is why he had just founded his Institute for Authenticity, where appropriately qualified professionals could learn all the existent techniques for growth enhancement and, at the same time, go through a gut-wrenching program, staffed by personally trained disciples, designed to bring about total openness. He thanked the organizers of the convention for allowing him, an old apostate, to make this plea for a new vista, and hoped that they would join him in his quest for human realization.

The second talk, conveniently held in the adjacent Bonaparte Suite, was given by an equally flamboyant avatar of newness in psychiatry. Charisma, erudition, and shrewdness had propelled this doctor to the top of his generation. No one could match his track record for grants (in this talk, as contrasted with the others, people took notes): his curriculum vitae had hundreds of entries to certify his productivity. Even if 98 percent of the articles were written by research fellows under his tutelage, the figure was still pretty impressive. With his slight stature, bright eyes, and bow tie, he looked like an eternal schoolboy up there on the podium. He was a great favorite of the convention, and the room was packed for the lecture. I could barely get a seat in the rear.

The doctor's constant smile and callow appearance was belied by his formidable toughness of mind. As though he too had been listening to the other talks and preparing a rejoinder, he opened with a broadside. Psychiatry, he began, had too long suffered from lint-headed humanists who shackled the scientific spirit with their mystical mumbo jumbo. Nobody, of course, was against talking to patients; but talk never proved anything, only quantifiable measurement did. Freud started it all when he broke with the scientific tradition to introduce his fairy tale of psychoanalysis, which emphasized meanings over facts, psychic reality over real reality. Since meanings were inherently arbitrary and always rested in the eye of the beholder, psychoanalysis cleared a path for any snake-oil salesman who came along peddling one sleazy ideology or another. In fairness we must credit Freud for keeping a gateway to science open with his insistence that some day the ultimate physioloigcal cause of behavior would be found. At least the psychoanalytic profession had, by keeping itself medical, retained a toe hold in science. This was indeed the reason why he himself had gotten his analytic training, back in the days when such was a virtual passport for academic advancement. But his analyst friends, good doctors as they might have been, had not gotten the message or, rather, messages, which, at the risk of seeming patronizing, he was going to give once more. First, that analysis did not work, at least in any provable sense, investigators having shown that while all therapy worked a little, no therapy in itself worked better than any other. Moreover, the only thing that mattered was the personality of the therapist. Fine, well and good; but if such was the case, why bother with high-powered training or theoretical squabbles? Why not just go to your grandmother or some cheaply trained and poorly paid social worker who could hold the patient's hand? And the second message was this: that whether analysts or psychologists liked it or not, Freud's hope was being fulfilled. Science, having recovered from the nonsense game of meanings, had gone back to material substance and was putting together the big brain synthesis that would once and for all explain behavior neurologically. While analysts were grubbing about and looking at their navels, real scientists had gathered the threads revealed by the discovery a generation ago of antipsychotic drugs, and aided by more precise diagnostic criteria, were following them into the recesses of the brain. Not since the discovery of DNA and the double helix had such a big synthesis loomed in the medical world. Imagine, a fulfillment of man's age-old dream to master his own nature! For once moods, feelings, and thoughts could be precisely allocated to neural networks or structures, then pharmacodynamic control could be rationally developed. In other words, Aldous Huxley's soma was just around the corner. Within the span of our careers, he predicted, a euphoriant drug without side effect or toxicity would be developed. This potion could not only eliminate mental disease; it could attack neurotic suffering, and normal unhappiness as well, thus ushering in a golden age of humanity. Even now we had many of the components in place. The behavioral expert, no longer forced to burrow blindly like a mole for hidden meanings, could turn his attention to the growing armamentarium of psychotropic drugs. By skillfully blending drugs into cocktails, the psychiatrist could cancel out side effects and play on various dysphoriant moods—anxiety, jealousy, guilt, shame, and so forth— thereby bringing the patient more in line with rational standards of happiness. The doctor, appropriately trained, would become a virtuoso of behavioral management. He would, in fact, play on the patient, bringing all the untapped human capacities to the fore. While drugs would be a leading—and perhaps ultimate—instrument for him to use, we had to remember that much else could be employed to manage behavior: for example, all the recently developed wisdom of behavior modification and cognitive psychology, even some of the principles of psychoanalysis. The important thing was to put all this power into the proper context, away from wishy-washy soft-headed thinking and in the direction of hard science. Thus would science, by fulfilling its principles of rational control, effect the elimination of human disease and unhappiness.

It was necessary, however, to plan for the step. We had to move positively, not just eliminate soft-headedness. Obviously, a highly trained professional cadre would have to administer these changes and provide responsible leadership no less than vision. This was why he was setting up a consortium of departmental chairmen and foundation heads who would plan for the future, bringing together the finest minds in academia, the drug corporations, and appropriate governmental bodies. The best, he concluded with measured understatement, was yet to come.

My spirits had been declining precipitously throughout this talk, and at its end I stumbled out of the room in such a daze as to almost bump into an elderly man standing with his back to me. I began to apologize, then stopped with an exclamation of delight. It was R, one of my favorite teachers and a man I never expected to see at meetings of this sort. As if to anticipate my wonderment at his presence, the old man began to speak first.

"Don't worry, I haven't gotten senile yet. It's just that my granddaughter is graduating from a college here in town, and I figured I could write off the trip as a tax deduction by checking into this zoo. After a few hours, though, I'm beginning to think it's not worth it. Might as well let Uncle have the money. [One wondered whether R had been to the previous lecture.] It's been twenty years since I was at one of these things, and the only thing I learned today is that horseshit piles up over time. We used to have some real doctors in this trade; now they're all technicians or P.R. men. Maybe they just can't admit there hasn't been a good idea in the business since 1923. But then, if they did, where would be their power? Anyhow, all I see is recycled trash. To think I played a role in training this generation of fakers! Well, the best ones stay at home taking care of their patients, which is right where I'm going as soon as the kid gets her sheepskin, or whatever plastic they use these days. I learn all I want to know from my patients. That, plus what Freud wrote about analysis in 1912, is enough of a guideline for me. But here I go, lecturing again;

maybe I am getting a little flaky, narcissism of the aged, you know. So why don't you tell me what's happening at your end?"

I uttered a few pleasantries, then excused myself. I liked R immensely but could not be distracted with reminiscences just then. Too much was churning. Still, it was good to have met the old man, I mused as I left the hotel and headed for a nearby park where I hoped to find enough solitude to spin out the filaments of my disjointed musings. R reminded me of what I could overlook at times like these when the clash of abstract ideas was likely to remove people from their concrete actuality. He made me think how much more complicated it all was than just the play of ideologies, and of how my long experience—or should I say complicity?—in these matters made it impossible to write of them from an ordinary, detached perspective. For though I despaired of my profession—of professionalism in general—I had to contend with the reality of life in the creatural world where there were, in fact, "good doctors," that is to say, some I had worked with, learned from, taught, liked, and felt indebted to, only individuals to be sure, but what was more real than the individual in whom history was concentrated? And it was just as well to have to contend with such a complication, since it might offset my penchant for grand generalization. I knew these people outside the net of sociological abstraction, as particular individuals—friends, rivals, students, teachers. I knew their faults, which could be somewhat glibly summed up under the rubric "bourgeois"; but I knew that virtues, too, could be found distributed among them: steadiness, reliability, shrewdness, good humor, tolerance, and above all a capacity, not universal, to be sure, but not totally lacking either, to *care* for patients, to enjoy being with them and to be able to stay with the afflicted, not to give up or to judge, but to be there, accepting. And I knew as well that though some systems, such as Freud's psychoanalysis, appealed to me greatly more than others, the virtues of practitioners have precious little relationship to the theory they espoused, and virtually no relationship at all to whether they were physicians or some supposedly lesser breed. I had, in fact, to check the tendency within myself, born no doubt of bad conscience, to come down particularly hard on physicians; to remind myself that the good ones should not be faulted simply because they had managed to get a few extra crumbs off the table. True, their fat fees kept their good qualities above the common herd. But one could not simply dismiss this contradiction with a sneer. If these doctors did well along with doing good, it was only an indication that they failed to transcend the immense burden of social class. Yet they had risen to the top of their class, if not above it, not so much monetarily as qualitatively. And of how many could more be said? The same professionalism, in other words, that had spawned such depressing examples of theory and practice as had been inflicted on me this day could also reproduce the higher achievements of the bourgeois era. There was a split between historical role and personal characteristic that both vexed and fascinated me. Obviously, the two were related, but they also went their own ways so that an individual's qualities were never fully determined by circumstances or even by what was idly called the "interaction" of circumstances with heredity. Psychology had somehow fallen into this crack. Although I wanted to pull it out, I simply bowed before the fact. In any case, I knew that I would rather put someone close to me in the hands of one of these liberal, middle-of-the-road, unpretentious psychiatrists than in the hands of any number of so-called radical therapists, whose line, glowing with all the proper libertarian lingo, was just right yet who seemed without that ineffable caring quality that was evidently attainable within bourgeois professionalism, even if by only a minority.

Perhaps it was true, as Yeats wrote, that "the best lack all conviction while the worst are full of passionate intensity."

And what of myself? I never knew whether I should be taken seriously or dismissed with amiable laughter. Here I was, in the midst of the world, doing the work as well as any of them, and moreover doing it with conviction, with a real feeling for psychoanalysis, which seemed despite all that had happened—all the carping, the fiddling, the sheer fatuity of both detraction and praise—to be something of indisputable value, even grandeur. Indeed, the last two talks and my meeting with R had only reinforced my belief that psychoanalysis was the worst of psychologies except for those others constructed from time to time. Better an uneasy synthesis of bourgeois humanism and science than fat-headed humanism or icy mechanism in isolation. Of that I was sure—but of how little else! This was the realization that plagued me, to have gone so far and yet to have so many fundamental questions yet unanswered. Why keep up the masquerade in the face of so many questions? And why the restlessness, since the work was so good and worthwhile? I supposed it flowed from some deep warp in my being, a crazy allegiance to—and perpetual attack upon—the father who, wrong-headed as he was, set for me a kind of mad example of opposition. And though I was glad that my own analysis had not ironed out this quirk (i.e., "identification"), I never knew whether my own opposition would not turn out to be equally wrong-

27

headed. Yet I would not yield, would neither step out of the world nor go along with it.

And for all that I have thought myself absurd at times, I was glad for this type of madness, because I found the world fascinating, especially from the perspective of one foot in, one foot out. Such a mass of contradictions, of splendor and tawdriness! So I gladly went on in absurdity, remembering Blake, who knew that "if a fool persist in his folly he would become wise."

I had by now reached the center of the park. I passed a group of students lying indolently in the deep shade of a grove of trees. They were evidently on a school picnic. The scene evoked Giorgione and the distance from the hotel was refreshing to my spirit. I continued musing. Of one thing I felt sure, though I could not exactly say why: there was something essentially wrong with everything I had heard today, and this had nothing to do with the manifest logic of the propositions put forth. All could be made to seem intrinsically correct, while each canceled everything else out, so that the observer of the spectacle came away with nothing, a nullity, a smoking heap of mutually destroyed notions in the place of a theory. No, that which was wrong was embedded in the spectacle itself—and theory, I recalled, had its root in the Greek *theoros*, to watch a spectacle. As I now saw it, this meant that the truth of something inhered in its concrete situatedness. One could not measure the value of ideas in isolation or even in an exterior reference to the objects posited by those propounding the ideas. This was the assumption of all the speakers, and it led to the mess I had just experienced. Instead, one had to include, in a way I could not yet formulate, the social existence of the speakers, i.e., their class, their place in the world, their interest in it, and their consciousness of this place and interest. Something called *praxis* would have to be invoked. And the least common denominator of all the speakers was their presence at that convention and their evident willingness to accept and be part of its conventions. From this standpoint it could be said that no matter how swift the mind or how elegant the exposition of the speaker, no *real truth* could come out of that convention or, by implication, the entire professional organism of which the convention was the flower, so long as one took that profession and its convention seriously; so long as one went along with the hierarchy, the codes, and the language; so long as one could stand in one of those nauseating halls and not say, at least inwardly, how preposterous it all was.

But what was "real truth"? Certainly there were truths expressed that day, as well as a kind of adherence to the principles of scientific discourse. Even the horrible humanist and the terrifying scientist had valid points to make. By what grounds could I, strolling in this park, head bent in thought, posit a truth that was broader or more "real"? I could come up with only one line of reasoning. Since "truth seeking" was practiced by some (myself, the speakers, R, and so on) on leave from all other persons whose efforts had to be augmented so that the truth seekers could pull their sight back from mere immediacy and focus it on what was generally and eternally valid, then the truth that would be more real would be made not just for the truth seeker in isolation but for all the people whose activity contributed to the process of truth seeking, that is, all humanity. In other words, valid knowledge always had to be *generalizable* (a chair belongs to a class of objects *all* members of which have to support weight, and so forth); now I saw that for knowledge to be of a greater level of truth, so to speak, it would also have to be *universalizable*, that is, for all humanity. And "for" was no lifeless preposition but the signifier of an attitude of active appropriation, of a striving to come to terms with history as it manifested itself in every human endeavor. I realized as well that since humanity was unfree and wracked by class divisions in which the oppressed labor of the many supported the privileged idea mongering of the few, the greater truth has to include in its terms a thrust for the emancipation of that labor so as to permit universality to take place. And to do this the truth seeker has to include in his or her activity a critical component, an element that reflects on one's position in the world and upon the unfreedom of the labor that supports it. We barely grasp the outlines of this continent of labor, so accustomed are intellectuals to thinking their ideas a higher, special form of existence without connection to everything else that, in fact, labors to uphold it, from the secretary who would type these words to the prodigious mass of labor around the globe. How much, for example, was the pure white thought of the western intelligentsia a negative of the darkness of those races from whose labor the West has wrung its surplus value? Such a consciousness was missing from the fine phrase turnings I heard today; and this absence gave the ideas of my profession the quality of an endless, ruthless affixing of names, names, names in the interest of achieving power and for all that it seemed lacking from their discourse: domination.

I recalled what the young Marx had written to Ruge and took

strength from it: "If the construction of the future and putting things to right for all time is not our business, it is all the more clear what our present task is: I mean the uncompromising criticism of everything that exists, uncompromising in the sense that it does not fear its own results and just as little fears conflicts with the powers that be."[1] But where to turn next? That I did not know. My hidebound profession, armored in jargon and stumbling over its credentials, was so ripe for caricature as to present too little of a challenge. And yet bourgeois rationality had already staked out so much ground, had taken account of everything except its own social presuppositions. (I remembered how, in this convention of eighty-three symposia, each consisting of three to five contributions, the supposedly liberal authorities had vetoed a rather tame forum titled "Radical Approaches to Psychiatry".) And while these presuppositions could serve as a basis for criticizing existing practice, I had a more difficult time envisioning how their contributions could be used as grounds for developing a future one. There was no point in ranting about how "after socialism, everything would be better." Aside from the remoteness of such a possibility, socialism had shown itself remarkably obtuse concerning problems of the inner life, so much so that I had often wondered whether its own theory and praxis were fundamentally flawed in this respect. But that was a matter for another time. For now, I was inclined to puzzle out the problem of psychology beyond the "criticism of everything that exists." And all I could see were the ideas about "concrete situatedness" and "unfree labor," ideas that remained distressingly vague, not to say confining.

"Concrete situatedness, concrete labor, situated labor, immediacy, dialectics. . . . Slogans all," I thought ruefully, lapsing into my habitual mood of "uncompromising criticism" and reflecting on how thought that strove for truth but was out of power could lapse into empty jargon of its own. The "concrete situatedness" was myself, now; or myself, later, writing; or the reader reading . . . that was all. And what was here now? Only a park between a lake and a row of massive buildings that enshrined the commerce of this particular city, commerce to which colleagues were contributing with their convening and from which I in the park had withdrawn for the time being. This was the activity now, thinking, pulled back from the world, my very thoughts existing by virtue of their negative relation to reality. But was that the reality back there, the stuffed shirts, the jargon, and the red-gold carpet? Or was reality out there on the lake, the water covered with a little haze that absorbed it into the infinity of the sky? Or was reality in-between the park itself and me, strolling within it? And if so, where was the negative? Who could tell? Why must there be someone to tell, anyway? What arrogance to think an answer was required, that reality and the mind had at least a potential correspondence: the same old delusion of science. Would not wisdom be that position which had outgrown such megalomania? If so, why not simply return to the hotel and make a few good contacts? Why fret at all, considering that I had it, as they said, made?

No, that was out of the question, less for political, moral, or intellectual reasons than because I found it disgusting. Funny how it comes down to taste, which is about as concrete as one can get. Meanwhile, my thoughts were spinning like tires on ice. I looked up, weary of cogitation. The afternoon was late; and the sun, coming in low and flat, broke through the trees in discrete quanta of light, which fractured and recombined objects within my ken. About fifty yards in front I saw a young couple. The boy picked up the girl and twirled her about, making her skirt fly up. Their mingled laughter filtered across the space that separated them from me, seeming to pick up resonance from the dappled light it had to traverse. I felt something akin to ecstasy as I observed this scene. And I was aware that I no longer observed as from a distance but felt a commingling with these unknown people, sensed that their joy and abandon—or so I imagined—were my own as well. I did not know these people, could not locate them except in their immediacy, yet it seemed that that very immediacy gave the scene before me more reality than all the pontificating I could ever hear or read. That is unfair, the analytic mind snapped back. What had happened was a momentary release from the practical cares of the day (even as I thought this I looked involuntarily at my watch, found myself thinking of an appointment that evening for which I would probably be late unless I changed my ways): unhinged from the reality principle, the pleasure principle took sway. What had most likely occurred, judging from the ecstasy, was that a primal scene fantasy had become unmoored from the unconscious and had temporarily dominated my conscious thought. Even now, I sourly observed, repression, mantled in the gray cloak of rationality, was setting in once more.

A sudden wave of revulsion swept over me, a fury at that which separated my experience, my work, and my life itself into seemingly eternal dualities: pleasure principle/reality principle; subject/object;

mind/body; society/nature; reason/desire; male/female. True, the mark of virtue was to differentiate, not to merge together. But to differentiate need not mean to segment, to tear apart and fragment, forcing the soul, like Ahab, to chase its own shadow through all one's days, forcing an arid reason to thirstily gaze upon desire, or aimless desire to greedily devour existence. Differences had to manifest themselves within a totality, an overarching union, a whole that becomes differentiated as the blastula of an embryo differentiates itself into organ systems while becoming an organism. Segmenting dualism, in sum, had to be transformed into historical dialectics, and that which seemed eternal and lifeless, given its place in time.

It is not enough to preach about immediacy and concreteness when what is involved is a field of sensuousness within which subject and object take form, and reality principle and pleasure principle exist as differentiations. This was the sense of my experience at that moment, a totalization comprised of the park, myself, the light, the sound, and the others, an event in space-time out of which subject-object forms had differentiated themselves. And what had taken place at the convention were equally sensuous events, as would be the attempt, weeks later, to write about them, a process just as fraught with struggle and totalized toward a goal. The sensuous, I now realized, was the location of history. And it was active. Once again the young Marx came to mind:

> The chief defect of all previous materialism . . . is that the object, actuality, sensuousness, is conceived only in the form of the object or perception, but not as sensuous human activity, praxis, not subjectively. Hence in opposition to materialism the active side was developed by idealism— but only abstractly, since idealism naturally does not know actual, sensuous activity as such. Feuerbach wants sensuous objects actually different from thought objects: but he does not comprehend human activity itself as objective.[2]

Engels termed this insight "the brilliant germ of a new world view." With one stroke Marx had leapt across a gap in Western thought as old as the pre-Socratics, that between subjective and objective. *Praxis* was experienced subjectively—in sensuousness—yet involved dispositions of the material world—in activity. It is the slice of human existence in which interior and exterior are joined, the point at which self-transformation and object-transformation mutually determine one another. And it centered on the body, the home of Freud's vision. Sensuous human activity, or *praxis*, is the cell of history. Integrated into the body of society, it becomes *labor* as well, from which value is to be extracted. It now struck me that what we study under the name of "psychology," and about which I had witnessed so many squabbles that day, is a kind of value extracted from a particular kind of labor. This labor includes as an essential component a praxis that forces people out of the ground of their participation in society, makes them, in other words, into discrete individuals, standing there, shivering and alone—and then studies their shivers and their solitude, giving names like "self," "personality," and "mental apparatus" to the outcome. I recognized that psychology does not study nature so much as things created by naming, but also—and this was perhaps a more crucial point and certainly a more vexing one—that the naming was no merely idle mental exercise but itself a very potent, highly rewarded form of labor. Lukacs had called those entities segregated out by bourgeois class activity "second nature," meaning by this that they took on a kind of naturality owing to their rooting in the material forces of history.[3] I realized that the psyche studied by psychology is, for all its false synthetic quality, a very definite entity. Being real, it can be studied "scientifically" and altered by praxes called psychotherapies. Its reality, however, its weight and structure, are given by historical activity—labor of various sorts—and not by the laws of physical nature. To take the example of psychiatry, the patient and the doctor are jointly involved in "sensuous human activity"—labor, the product of which is the patient's "behavior." Behavior, the object of psychological science, is not a property of some abstract entity called the mind, considered to reside within the patient. Rather, it is an outcome of the activity between a person and the world, in this instance, the patient and doctor, the former manifesting "something" and the latter giving this something a name, making it psychological, and securing it thereby within a powerful structure of social relations. The effort to locate the object of psychology within a person's so-called mind must be seen as a particularly strategic attempt to obscure participation in history. Psychology, psychiatry, psychoanalysis, the entire business, have consistently ignored this truth; and the very avoidance is also a kind of labor, highly rewarded and contributory to the given structure of the world. One would have to be a little touched, wandering in a park between the city and the water, to appreciate this.

I realized further that the task of reconstruction is an elaborate one. "Second nature" has to be given its due; and the manifestations of psychology, though seen in their historical aspect, require study according to the forms by which they present themselves. It is no good, for example, to declare that "mental illness" is merely a myth or a social convention for dealing with deviance, so long as everyone experiences others or themselves as mentally ill. Though this might merely be the internalization of a false label, what is internalized is also incorporated and becomes part of the existing mental fabric—an automatic category of thought by no means to be wished away. Mental illness might be a myth, but myth itself is a powerful reality.

At the same time, one needs an "anthropology," a notion of human potentiality, what men and women could be, given the overcoming of historical domination. "Human nature" is entirely too retrogressive and biological a term to convey what I was groping for, but it does suggest something I had in mind. It is necessary to stand by something that, if not natural in the sense of a physical object, is at least "transhistorical," across history and through it, entering history and shaped by history yet preserving some element that is beyond history and transcendent. Otherwise, what would be the point of overcoming historical domination? For what sake would we do so, if everything were entirely determined by history? That is one of the glories of Freud, who, with his notion of "instinct," posited a sphere of Eros (and later of Thanatos) that the given, historical world could shape but not reach. True, Freud too often took this notion in a backward direction, but its very presence lent his psychology a depth that was absent from his more facile, "culturalist" successors.

Yes, there must be a "human essence," a "species-being," an "anthropology," and it must be shaped by the conviction that humans are history-creating animals, that they have within them a kind of nature that overcomes itself, nature that refuses nature. To flesh this creature out a bit I realized I would have to learn to describe it, would have to begin with the mass of concrete situatedness out of which emerged the second nature of psychology, would have to account for that psychology in its own terms and then in terms of the dialectic I was struggling to evolve. I decided at that moment to try to construct certain individuals, drawing in part upon real people I had known (and who would be represented in composite form to protect their identities) and in part—for reasons I could not quite fathom—out of my own imagination. And as I struggled to construct these individuals I would also try to construct a theory that accounted for an individuality that was both false and true.

It was growing dark. I could see an exit leading out of the park. I decided to cancel my evening's appointment and to take the next plane home.

34

Part Two

CASE STUDIES IN HISTORY AND DESIRE

4

LOVE AND MONEY

It is said that Freud once declined to write a letter of recommendation for someone he had analyzed on the grounds that he did not know the person.

Let me begin with Curtis—more exactly, with Curtis and myself, he reclining, I seated two feet behind him and listening. At times I say something, never enough for him. Even when he seems satisfied with what is going on, the next day he is back, wanting more. What does he want? We do not know . . . that is what the analysis is about.

Curtis could be anybody. The quality of restless, unnamable, unappeasable craving is common to the experience of anybody who opens up to psychoanalytic discourse. I know this from my own analysis. But Curtis is not anybody. He is a definite, situated person; and his unnamable craving is unnamable in a definite way. He does not want what he has or is; but what he has had or has been shapes what he wants.

Curtis is very much part of the world. His situation is that of an executive in a large investment bank, for which he labors prodigiously. One reason Curtis seeks help is that he is driven at work. He cannot stop . . . no, does not want to stop. The work gives him pride, dignity and money, and the expectation of more to come. He needs to perform sixteen, eighteen hours a day. The more he does the better he does, the higher he goes, the more power he has, the more junior executives he orders about, the more secretaries wait upon him . . . and the less happy he becomes. He considers his work a kind of disease or intoxication. His wife left him because of it; and no other woman has been able to tolerate his fanaticism. He can barely stand himself or the loneliness that has become his lot. That is why, alone amongst his fellow executives, Curtis tries to change. He suffers, one might say, from a burden of surplus subjectivity, which he brings into analysis. In all other respects we must assume that Curtis is close to the norm for his class.

But like Freud, I do not know this analysand either. Or rather, I know only what he tells me and what I infer from it. One of the first things Curtis said gave me an inkling of the barrier to understanding him: "I try to tell you what my life is like. But it doesn't make any sense to me. The difference between what I do—there on the job or as I go through the day—and what I am experiencing could drive me crazy if I thought too much about it. The two worlds are completely different."

From his words in analysis I construct a notion of what Curtis is experiencing, and from that, something of the history of his inner life. His outer life can be stitched together only from scraps of what I know about the world and some guesswork about what he tells me. Otherwise I, his analyst, who shares with Curtis what is deepest and most personal to him, know nothing of what his actual material life is like. A puzzle, inasmuch as it is there, in the outer, object-life, that Curtis earns the money to pay me, that is, to keep me going materially.

The puzzle is essential, for if I took the trouble to learn more about Curtis's outer life—if, for example, I became enmeshed with his work in a real way—then I could never learn what I have about his inner life. What we learn about the inside is achieved with the utmost difficulty. Any notion of what practical consequences might be involved would be stifling. There is a definite kind of uncertainty principle at work here. To know a person inwardly, one must be truly engaged with him/her, but engaged in a very special, "unreal" way. Public life, which is where we work and become involved with people, is radically cut off by one degree from private, intimate life, where we can be with people in a trusting way, and by yet another degree from the inner life, the life of subjectivity. Because the analyst works at this second-degree remove, he/she is doubly turned away from the patient's public life.

This may be necessary for the practice of psychoanalysis, but is it an eternal human arrangement or a manifestation of our society, with its history? Need public life be severed from private? Need outer and inner worlds go their own way? This is equivalent to asking whether psychoanalysis need exist. If public and private were not so removed from each other, what would be the point of analysis? This is not a matter that the mental-health professional likes to ponder.

Meanwhile, in the fractured, predatory world into which psychoanalysis fits, something of interest may regularly be learned. Like Citizen Kane uttering "Rosebud" on his deathbed, we all have our secret, highly determined quest.

Money cannot bring happiness, because happiness is the fulfillment of infantile wishes and money is not the object of infantile wishes.
—SIGMUND FREUD

When he was a little boy, Curtis was taken by his father to see the railroad yards. Together they leaned against the iron railing of the causeway. Beneath them lay a great amphitheater of steel, wood, and stone. Trains scuttled back and forth like giant crustaceans, now mating, now pulling apart. Father and son stood there for what seemed a time without beginning, middle, or end, then returned to their small apartment, where dinner was waiting. There was his mother, fluttering around and chattering as usual. He remembers—and this was the single most vivid detail of the whole incident—how very dirty his hands had gotten. When he went to wash, great waves of black soapy water flowed down the drain. He stood there rapt, without thought, watching the water slosh back and forth, making little rivulets of pale-gray fluid next to the somewhat darker drops where the soot had condensed a little, until he was roused from his trance by the voice of his mother, calling him to the dinner table.

Those were the years before his father became prosperous. Hard work and being in the right place at the right time enabled him to sell his little hardware store in the center of town and, with the aid of his father-in-law, to purchase a somewhat larger establishment in a new suburban shopping center. This was the period after the war, when the demand for appliances seemed endless. One success led to another, and soon Curtis's father owned three stores, between which he shuttled each day. He rarely returned before nine-thirty at night to the big white house with two Grecian columns alongside the front door. By then a certain coldness had developed between the boy and his father; and since Curtis himself was usually engrossed in his studies during the evenings, he was scarcely aware of missing the presence of that harried, preoccupied figure who had provided for his entry into the world. Indeed, it was only the recapture of the railroad-yard memory during his analysis that convinced Curtis that beneath his own aloofness burned an intense longing for his father, a yearning that only caused him grief and from which he vainly attempted to free himself.

For years this longing had been quelled by mental pain and social indifference. When Curtis was seventeen his father took ill. One Sunday evening the boy noticed a cup fall from his father's hands. Three weeks later he was in the hospital, first for tests, then for an exploratory operation, after which he was given six months to live. The doctors told the family not to share their knowledge with the dying man; and so the first of the father's last days were passed in trivial chitchat. Soon, however, there was no need for secrecy. The malignancy invaded the brain, reducing a man once proud of his intellect to a blithering, unrecognizing thing. For some perverse reason the disease, having inflicted maximum suffering on the family, decided not to finish the father off too quickly. He lingered twice six months and more, first in a hospital, then in a "home." The once-affluent family was financially destroyed by medical expenses and by the looting of the dead man's firm by an unscrupulous partner. Curtis returned home from college (which he was soon to quit for financial reasons) for the funeral. He was numb and shrank from his mother's teary embrace. Overriding the guilt he felt for not wanting more contact with her was his irritation that her fingers, as ever, were digging so deeply into his shoulder. Wincing, he turned and contemplated his father in the casket. He saw not the cachectic figure of the last year, but an embalmed shadow that recalled to him the last feel, fourteen years before, of the man's rough-shaven cheek against his own. Suddenly Curtis was overcome. A wail—more, a howl—came out of him, and he would have fallen had not his uncle supported his sagging frame. The family was shocked. They had never seen such behavior from the austere and ascetic youth.

And they were not to see such behavior again. By the time of the reception, Curtis had sealed himself off again; and in the fourteen years that elapsed between this event and the start of his analysis, no further cry passed from him. He withdrew further from his family, and especially from his mother, who sank into bitter widowhood. For a while Curtis wandered, "went a little crazy." He left school, supported himself with odd jobs, drifted to California and then to Europe. The period, two years in all, was shrouded in drugs. This Curtis remembers: one stifling day, in Amsterdam, when he felt he had sunk about as far as he could. The next step, he was sure, would be suicide. He recalls lying for hours on his back in a dingy hotel room, tormented by flies and staring at a ceiling fan. From next door, some idiot—a Pole, he thought—was yelping a folk tune, cheerfully, endlessly. Afraid that he might go next door and commit mayhem or that he would go mad where he was, Curtis roused himself and went downstairs. The lobby was empty except for the clerk and a figure slouched in a chair. The man was lying so oddly that Curtis thought he must be dead. Sweating with panic, he approached, then saw who it was: an old bum he had noted on occasion staggering down the street. The man was sleeping peacefully. Curtis gazed at the ravaged, slack face. Suddenly he felt radiantly happy, ecstatic. A warmth flooded him and passed, so he imagined, from his fingertips to the universe beyond. In that one moment Curtis felt that he had died and been reborn. And now he *knew* what he had to do. He left the hotel, made his way home, and enrolled once again in college, taking out loans as he went. He did so well that a fellowship to a prestigious business school followed. From there it was on to the bank, which was always on the lookout for hard-driving talent. Once Curtis was installed, his steady rise seemed inevitable.

In the meantime, Sandra came and went. Curtis fell for her because she was sympathetic and had what he called "a great body." Also, there might have been something in the fact that she was Polish, unlettered, and a secretary, i.e., anathema to his mother. "Better that your father is dead than he should live to see his son married to one of *them*," she said and fairly spat with derision. For reasons Curtis could not fathom, this exchange, though it saddened him, also strengthened his resolve. The thought of giving in to his mother made him shudder. He was able to breathe freely only when he refused to obey her.

Still, he doubted whether he would have married Sandra had she not conceived. Sandra was a good enough Catholic to refuse to have an abortion and a good enough estimator of chances in life to know that Curtis was about as high as she could hope for. She wept, pleaded, and invoked divine judgment; he stormed, then sulked, then yielded, which is what he wanted to do all along. He yielded to Sandra as he never could allow himself to do to his mother—yielded, too, in order to establish a reminder of the time he had yielded once, in justification of never yielding again.

Sandra's wishes for prosperity and respectability proved weaker than her need for affection. As Curtis retreated into work, she became shrewish, driving him further away. Their sexual relationship, never strong, stopped completely. Affairs followed, as did the breakdown of civility. She began spending more time with her mother, whom Curtis detested for her coarse Old World ways. One day Sandra simply did not return. The divorce was savagely contested and left Curtis as financially desperate as he was when his father died. But, as Sandra and the divorce lawyers argued, he was in a position that afforded great opportunities for enrichment. And soon enough, he had recouped his losses and was able to meet all his payments with considerable funds left over for himself. Yet he still kept driving onward, beyond the bounds of his needs.

What made Curtis work so hard that night after night he would return red-eyed and drawn to the oversized apartment by the park, where he lived alone? He had purchased the apartment because it was a good investment and seemed commensurate with his station in the world. But although two years had passed, the apartment had none of the warmth, order, and harmony that one associates with a real home. A woman came in once a week to put some regularity into things, and a procession of girlfriends trooped through as well, but no one really left any imprint on the place. It was as if no one ever really lived there. The front room, the one with the park view, was still unfurnished, occupied mostly by several book cartons that had yet to be unpacked. Curtis intended to do this; meanwhile, he consoled himself with the promise that once he was no longer so busy, he would finish off the room. Besides, he rarely had time to entertain; and as for his small son, who stayed with him on weekends, he (a) would not appreciate good furniture and (b) would be likely to damage it. Better, therefore, to wait until the boy was a bit older. Maybe then, Curtis reasoned, he would take it a little easier.

The world had little reason to complain about Curtis. He had just been promoted to an executive position at the bank; and the senior partners, who were still in a sense his superiors, regarded him as an heir apparent, the very model of a bright young man in upward motion. A bridge had been built, spanning the distance between Curtis and the elders. All he needed to do was to walk across as he was doing and in due time he would be there with the highest executives. In the meantime, he had achieved the privilege of addressing them by their first name, was serving dynamically on the various committees by means of which the bank's central office was governed, and to all the world looked like a youthful model of an executive vice-president. Day and night he pored over figures and angled for the choice deals that would further enrich the bank.

An uncommon degree of intellectual perspicacity and personal daring was required for the job, and Curtis had both qualities in great measure. To instantly weigh the complex effects of rates of exchange, tax possibilities, investment risks—such as the potential for revolution in a foreign market—and a host of other technical factors demanded a clear understanding of the subtleties involved, as the numbers both had a truth of their own and were the ever-shifting abstraction of innumerable human tendencies. Moreover, those tendencies were personified by whoever was across the negotiating table from Curtis: another man or group of men (and only men)—colleague, antagonist, advisor, perhaps all three. One had to weigh him as well, constantly gauging the odds, calculating that hundredth of a percentage point around which millions of dollars turned, establishing trust, and, yes, dominating this other man, because that was how successful deals were made: men in scarcely distinguishable brown or gray suits weighing glances, unconsciously registering tiny shifts in tone of voice, building confidence and fear, then striking at the exact moment. Curtis derived a positive thrill from such transactions, which compensated him for much and was undoubtedly far more important to him than actual money; and he was very good at what he did.

The real income Curtis earned by his heroic endeavors on behalf of the bank mattered rather little to him as a medium of exchange. He had to buy the expensive regimental clothes and pay the exorbitant rents required to maintain his station in life, but he took no pleasure in his possessions; and despite his steadily expanding wealth, he considered himself no richer than he had been during his student days. Indeed, he lived frugally, not to hoard money but out of indifference to commodities. Credit cards eased his way through the world, limiting his contact with cash, and at the end of the month he merely presented his faithful secretary with a list of his bills and his checkbook: sixty minutes and a few signatures later, he was all set for another thirty days.

But inwardly Curtis never was set. Though he was unable to enjoy commodities or even to much use them, he was fiendishly interested in money for its own sake, i.e., as part of himself. Its accumulation warmed him and its expenditure chilled him. Nor did this occur metaphorically, so to speak, but was accompanied by direct bodily sensations. In sessions when Curtis talked of money, its passage through his hands or the relations at work through which it was made, sensations in his groin, or neck, or rectum,—stabbing pains or moments of flushing—would occur. Sometimes he felt as if a warm fluid were incontinently running down his legs, at other times as though his insides would rise through his gorge and choke him. To say that

Curtis was fiendishly interested in money is not an idle comment. As the analysis proceeded, we learned that, for him, to be declining in wealth was to open the portals of his body, especially his anus, to demons. These were variously described, usually as powerful men who resembled people in real life; at times they had a purely fantastic aspect. They would come for him, nail him to a rack, pull his insides out to extract the precious stuff. Curtis never yielded to the fantasies and would have been hard pressed to describe them in precisely such terms all the time. But the fantasies were felt and lived; they pressed their way into his consciousness with greater or lesser valence depending on his real fortunes; and as they pushed their way forward they caused words of description to be heaped up around them, the way a worm burrowing near the surface will reveal its path by creating little mounds of displaced earth.

Curtis did not believe in the reality of these fantasies, as a psychotic would. On the other hand, he lived them out and so in some sense was more self-estranged than the psychotic who breaks with reality and institutes his own beliefs in its stead. Curtis rather broke with himself and contributed actively to the construction of reality. As a maker of reality, his activity could be called sublimated. but it was carried out on the condition of self-splitting. The split-off part of the self adopted a double existence: loathed and repudiated like an insect crawling out from under a flat rock, and at the same moment a hated slave driver lashing Curtis onward. The point to be made is that the demon that afflicted Curtis was also what drove him at work: it was, in fact, a major condition of his success and so entered the fabric of the reality he created without for a moment being avowed.

Consider: When Ralph, an executive slightly junior to Curtis, was promoted from the investments committee on which they had been working together in order to move to the more prestigious executive committee under the direction of the bank president, Curtis was beside himself. He could not say what angered him more, the increased work load that now befell him or the sense of betrayal. In any case, he fumed inconsolably. "They fucked me," Curtis wailed, "and I just lay there and took it in the ass." And he said this, to himself and to me, in many ways and on many occasions.

Such an outpouring of feeling cannot be the result of convention nor even the simple product of anger. Why harp on it so? Why not just let the righteous anger out and get on with the job? Curtis had no difficulty being angry, but his sense of outrage was unappeasable.

44

After the fifth repetition of the theme, one became suspicious and, after the fiftieth, convinced that the fate he lamented was also the fate he *desired*—that Curtis had a wish, however disgraceful to him, to be assaulted anally by a powerful man who had defeated him, and that this wish was no less active in him than the contrary, to be himself the powerful man who penetrates the victim. What, after all, would bring back so manifestly unpleasant an idea unless there was an underlying force pressing toward its realization? It could be said that Curtis was unable to have one side realized without seeking the other: each defeat spurred him on to fresh triumph, and each triumph led him to seek defeat—either directly, in the form of humiliation suffered at the hands of another man, or, more subtly, by a fate he inflicted on himself, a savage lash of self-hatred, a cruelty that repeated the assault and goaded him to new accomplishments in a single gesture.

One is schooled by the canon of Freudian interpretation to recognize the image, or the *imago*, of the dead father as the real origin of Curtis's demon. The death, according to this reasoning, prevented Curtis from resolving the network of infantile conflicts surrounding his relation to his father. Instead, it threw the whole affair into the darkness of irreparable and hopeless loss. We could interpret Curtis's bodily sensations, therefore, as being somatic reenactments of the fantasy of being penetrated that he experienced in Amsterdam, anally or orally, by his father's phallus, or, in some way, either ecstatic or deadly, of being united with him; and we could also interpret the demon fantasies along the same lines, bearing in mind Freud's discovery, which has been confirmed endless times in clinical experience, that money is the symbolic equivalent of feces or body contents in general. By the logic of the unconscious, then, money, feces, and Father's phallus are condensed into one demonic entity, which Curtis is either to submit to or to seize. Finally, we could understand the "daisy-chain" fantasy of homosexual links by means of which Curtis fashions his work life as being yet another elaboration of the theme, this time one that clearly reveals his need to become the father who penetrates and dominates. And we could see all the variegated and motley themes as the desperate solutions of a small boy who wanted his father, who hated his father, who needed his father, and who felt betrayed by his father.

A reasoned psychoanalytic account would also expand on Curtis's inner life to include traces of that redoubtable mother from whom he fled at the funeral and whose wishes for him he seemed bound to defy. One could see a bit of Hamlet in Curtis at the funeral as he cringed at the embrace of the figure toward whom his father's death had unconsciously cleared the way. And one can recognize a counter-Oedipal reaction in his decision to marry someone who embodied the precise opposite of his mother's wishes. One might even regard his repeated failures in love as being not simply slaps at his mother but also reminders that he remains ready for her alone.

And yes, there are deeper, so-called pre-Oedipal issues where Mother is concerned. Recall the most vivid detail of his early railroad-yard memory of closeness to father: the soapy black water that flowed down the sink. This image incorporates two themes: the fluids that sexually bound him to father, and those that bound him yet more deeply to his mother. Several days after this memory emerged Curtis dreamed that he was following a trail of slimy liquid till it came to a pool that disappeared into a black hole in the floor. As he came closer to the hole he saw a black widow spider guarding the hole. He realized that it was too late to stop his march into the mandibles of the spider, and only a sweat-drenched awakening saved him from the fate he had prepared for himself.

The goal of his analysis is to allow Curtis to sink down into the pool and to emerge strengthened. There is no exact metaphor to describe the psychoanalytic process, but a serviceable one is that of the analyst as the support system for the patient's dive: a provider of a line and a boat to jump from and return to. More exactly, the analysis provides a setting in which Curtis can return to those split-off pieces of the self and reappropriate them. More exactly yet, and in the terminology of psychoanalysis itself, the patient reexperiences his infantile conflicts in the neutral psychoanalytic setting; he relives what he could not master as a child and, with the aid of a mature, adult ego, deals rationally with what has previously been improperly disposed of by repression and various neurotic defenses. In the course of his treatment, Curtis is to see his father and mother in his relations to me (the so-called transference) and, again with the aid of his mature, adult ego, is to repudiate, i.e., outgrow, the infantile side of himself.

The time has come to part ways with received discourse, not, however, in the spirit of the procession which left behind the root discoveries of the unconscious and infantile sexuality when it parted with psychoanalysis. Working with Curtis and others, or simply experiencing life in the world, leaves me as convinced as ever of Freud's breakthrough. But the spirit in which these discoveries were carried through was ambivalent, and the spirit with which psychoanalysis has since pursued them has been mainly a backward one. Psychoanalysis has been imprisoned by the very world its assumptions undermined. And it has turned into a good prisoner, a "trustie," working to rationalize the jail it inhabits. It is time to return to the root and renegotiate the way out.

Back to Curtis: Is the account just given of his demon a true one, or does it also reveal the imprisonment of psychoanalysis? It is a true one insofar as it reveals his impossible longing. But is the demon in fact his father or his mother, or some combination or part of them? Obviously not: the demon is Curtis himself; it is himself he seeks. No doubt the real father gave his shape to the search. But reality does not simply shape the contents of the self, i.e., its objects. Reality also shapes the self itself; it makes Curtis into a separated self with split-off parts that must find itself. The Curtis who seeks himself has a kind of isolated experience that is a specific part of the social reality in which he lives.

Psychoanalysis—and psychology in general—takes this process for granted. It assumes that the self is formed by us as a natural phenomenon, the way we form teeth; and it concentrates its energies on describing the shape of the self so formed. Thus, it focuses on Curtis's repressed wishes for his father. However great a discovery it was that allowed us to map the side of the self that was alienated, the crucial fact remains for Curtis that he lives in the kind of world that makes him into an alienated person. It was not the father that did this; and it is not an inevitable, i.e., "natural," process that it be so. Curtis would not suffer neurotically, work like a fiend, repress his lovingness, twist his bodily experience into knots, and be constantly depressed were he not in a situation that makes him essentially estranged from others, essentially at odds with them, essentially alone. In other words, neurotic alienation from self cannot be understood apart from alienation from others. And this alienation from others, which we deem essential, is not essential in a philosophic or existential way. Alienation is not inherent in the human condition, but it is essential as an aspect of *history*, of the real history of Curtis's kind. That which is historically essential is what is required to survive under given historical circumstances and to reproduce them. History is the great chain of human reproduction.

And this is what psychoanalysis (and here we may lump psychology with psychiatry) *essentially* ignores: essentially because psychoanalysis, too, is part of history, a real practice that is rewarded by society to help society reproduce itself. History is reproduced when people, unconscious of it, act blindly. To become conscious of history is to be able to change it. Psychoanalysis, being materially rooted in the interests of the dominant class, will not become conscious of history. Therefore, the hope of expanded consciousness it holds out is a puppet show constructed on the constricted stage of the individual psyche.

Concretely, I seriously wonder to what extent Curtis can change through psychoanalysis. Freud, who opted for the myth of the bourgeois father and so constructed an ambivalent theory, realized that the practice he discovered was fundamentally limited: replacing "hysterical misery with ordinary unhappiness"[1] was all one could hope for. This forthright statement is in any case to be preferred to the self-serving babble of the therapeutic zealots who followed him. But it does not go far enough, grounded as it is in an assumption that encumbered Freud and has hobbled psychoanalysis ever since. This assumption is not an easy one to shake, since it is at the center of all psychologic thought, namely, the notion that there is *something* to be called a *mind* (Freud called it a mental apparatus) that functions separately from the body, on the one hand, and society, on the other, and therefore has laws of its own. Freud separated mind from nature and from society (though it is a measure of his greatness and distinction from others that he provided some blueprints for bridges back); therefore, he found it possible to disentangle "hysterical misery," which was an intrapsychic affair based upon infantile sexual attachments to parents (such as Curtis's toward his father), from "ordinary unhappiness," which was seen to arise from another order of necessity: either blind nature or a history that was largely automatic because it was subordinated to human instinct. Psychoanalysis accepts the given fact that public and private, inside and outside, are severed from each other; in so doing, it gains a powerful vantage point for the scrutiny of the mental "inside." But it does not regard this fact in a historical light, that is, does not see the separation of inside and outside as a historical problem. If it did see things as such, psychoanalysis would be able to see inside and outside as constitutive of each other as they were alienated from each other. In other words, the fact that our social reality contains people who experience themselves as isolated, and frequently neurotic, selves is itself part of social reality. This social reality, then, is defined by the existence in it of social beings who do not recognize their fully social nature but are estranged from it, and therefore from themselves and each other. That is how it works, but it is a working that psychology does not seem interested in recognizing.

This recognition is what I have been trying to achieve. In so doing I understand from another angle why psychoanalysis would prefer the split to remain absolute. In order to see inside and outside as constitutive of each other complicates an already formidable therapeutic task. Everyone knows, though few like to admit it, that therapy flourishes on hope and illusion, and is not foursquarely happy with the relentless spirit of inquiry. It makes one wince as a thereapist to see that Curtis's problem can in no way be delimited to parents—good, bad, or in-between—but involves the constitution of his madness in everyday, present activity. The demon resides at the bank, too, as it is the real world of work and current associations that perpetually structures the infantile complexes initially established in the family. The bank, which here is but a symbol of work and the public sphere in general, produces the matrix of estrangement between self and others that is the necessary concomitant of Curtis's neurotic estrangement from his self. Curtis's quest for lost parts of himself is reinforced at the bank and is merely rewarded to the extent that it is necessary for the bank's functioning. True, the quest is repudiated, and no one recognizes it. That it is repudiated is essential, for the bank churns out rationality in its columns of figures. Hence, anyone like Curtis whose demon makes him unhappy enough to seek specialized help is considered "neurotic" and among the great marginal class of the "mentally ill." But the others who are more genuinely sublimated than he so that their demon functions automatically and silently are gainers in one sense and losers in another. What they gain is obvious: lack of pain. But they lose the other side of pain: the possibilities for greater awareness, the heightened maddening contact with that great realm of human experience that has become isolated in our society. And meanwhile their own madness, seamlessly absorbed as it is into their estranged functioning, is called normalcy. The reason contained in normalcy is too stunted, then, to see itself and what it does. Neurotics see farther, but what they see is twisted out of shape and comes back to torment them.

I wonder, too, how analysis can help anybody as badly bruised as Curtis. The pain is real, not just a by-product of repressed subjective wishes. I sense that the real mother, herself caught in the degradation of women, reproduced that degradation in a meanness of spirit that was passed on to her children. And the real father, caught in God-knows-what quest of his own, was in fact not there. I mean "not there" in a way that made his dying absolute. None can defeat death; but if a life is well and fully lived, its ending becomes a rounding off. The dead pass into the lives of those who remain. Like leaves falling from a tree in autumn, their passage is part of a cycle that includes the promise of renewal. But for Curtis and his father, and for all those whose days elapse in estrangement, mortality is final. Each separation through life becomes a wound that may be concealed but never healed; and the last parting can be nothing else but the greatest wound of all because it forecloses whatever lingering hopes exist for reconciliation. Hence Curtis's wail—throttled because it, too, had to place to go. How can this anguish be more than palliated in an analysis? I cannot be his father; one does not pay one's father for his time. How can therapy honestly represent more than stoicism in the face of reality? There is in Curtis—and perhaps in us all, if conditions can be provided to let it out—a nameless longing. It bubbles spontaneously out of him like steam from a geyser. For Curtis this longing is indelibly tinged with a sense of badness born out of real bitterness. I know he can do better than he has with this pain; but I think also that to rid him of it would be an act tantamount to depriving him of his reality: a kind of lobotomy.

Then there is the bitter irony, so confounding to me, that Curtis chose to allow his demon to move him even farther along than his father in the system that manifestly crippled their entire existence, and the predatory nature of which brought him so close to ruin. My despair on this score makes me wonder whether I can ever be the therapist he needs, for he seems, like a great majority, to have made a kind of vile peace with the monster and, indeed, to be busily helping it grow.

Is this simply my own demon at work? Am I not too judgmental here? What is so remarkable about the proposition that psychoanalysis is part of the scheme of social reproduction and that it does not step outside the society in which its practitioners and clients live?

Why should it, any more than schools, not be so? It might be fairly argued that therapy is a noble compromise that simply accepts the world in all its imperfections in order to help people, and that this is a more salutory way to spend one's time on earth than vainly barking at the moon of social injustice. Curtis, after all, can be helped. Why need he be saved as well? When has the world been free of folly and oppression? If therapy has to set such massive issues aside in order to be of help to individuals, then is merely chipping into the apparatus of social reproduction too much a price to pay, especially as the apparatus will go cheerfully on its way no matter what psychotherapy does?

And while we are in the mood for ruthless self-criticism, we should recall as well that all the societal generalizations in the world tell us nothing about this one concrete individual, Curtis. In the individual, tendencies and probabilities that belong to history are crystallized into a specific imaginative resolution. The human imagination takes hold of the given world, then rejects it and replaces it with an inner world of its own making. The validity of psychoanalysis as a discourse is based upon this split, even if the split itself must be accounted for on other than psychoanalytical grounds. So with Curtis, as with each person, we do homage to the reality of the reality-refusing imagination by not inserting him too neatly into any categories. Therapeutically and politically, this is ground for hope, even if the hope be at any given time an abstract one.

I recognize this, as well as that my demon is a hound whose instinct is to sniff out wrongs. So be it. But it is also a matter of taste. I do not like the way things work. It galls me that psychoanalysis should succumb to capitalism. Moreover, to opt for helping people on purely pragmatic grounds, without honestly confronting the obdurate social roots of their suffering, seems to me a rationalization for bourgeois complacency and cowardice. I take my stand with Debs: so long as one human being is in chains, no one else is free. And because there is no positive answer to any of these dilemmas, and much to whet the curiosity in their further exploration, it seems to me that there is nothing better to do than to take a closer look at the beast.

5

CONCERNING TOTALITY

Modern psychology, and psychoanalysis in particular, was born in that moment when men realized that they had lost control over their social existence; and having been so engendered, it both kept them further from this realization and played into their loss of control and estrangement. Carl Schorske has written of the political matrix out of which Freud's *Interpretation of Dreams* was conceived.[1] He shows acutely how Freud's illumination of the mental depths was won through a depoliticization in which the figure of the father was inserted for that of the mundane authority over whom Freud, the alienated Jewish bourgeois professional, had no power. And psycho-analysts from then until now have continued to draw such a figure. With our discussion of Curtis we have begun to unwind this process: not to lose the father or Curtis's desire for him, but to reinsert the authority, and the mundane dimension in general, in its proper place.

But what is this place? Curtis's subjectivity will not lead us to it. Recall that he, being a person of his time, experiences the inner and outer worlds as radically and inexorably severed from each other. Another way of perceiving this is to observe that Curtis experiences the self as an isolated particle; he is the true "individual," not of the human species in general, but of the social order he works to repro-duce: capitalism. Because he is cut off from others, his subjectivity moves back toward that phase when it was, in fact, relatively more as-sociated with others, i.e., childhood. Although this helps us under-stand how the painful longing for a father that suffuses his being is grounded in more than a biological instinct, it does not help us define the place in Curtis's total picture occupied by social reality.

Subjectivity in itself, and the whole labyrinth of psychology, will not produce this "total picture"; yet psychology, as part of the picture, helps shape it and is determined by it in turn. To resolve this dilemma we need to adopt an approach that is broader than psychology yet encompasses psychology; and we need to understand how people are related to this larger ground. Let us adopt the word *totality* to designate the larger ground, and let us use the term *praxis* to describe how individual people relate to the totality. By *praxis* we mean what people do in a conscious, purposeful, socially organized way to transform the conditions of their existence. Praxis is more than what is defined as "work." However, inasmuch as work is that sphere of human activity defined by necessity, it will provide the most direct path between the individual and the totality. Accordingly, if we are to understand what the notion of totality means on the basis of what already has been presented, we will do best to consider, not Curtis's fantasy world (which is, however, part of the totality) but his workaday world, which is what he does actively in the way of reproducing it.

Some portion of Curtis's work comes under the scrutiny of the analysis, as we have seen, notably, the human relations of the workplace: the rivalries, intrigues, power plays, and Curtis's own emotional investment in his career. However vital these matters may be, they remain peripheral to what his work is actually about, which is the production of things, i.e., commodities, and the quantitative relations that surround those things, or money. And the making of commodities, which is what capitalist production is all about, is simply not registered psychologically except as a faint and fading afterimage. Therefore, what we learn about Curtis in the analysis is isolated from what Curtis does with respect to perpetuating the capitalist totality. I do not mean to imply that the *idea* of money is absent psychologically. Far from it. As we have seen, Curtis is passionately—indeed, morbidly—fascinated with money, and in this he is merely representative of the typical individual in our society.[2] However, the idea is the fantasy-elaboration of a negative relationship. The money that characterizes capitalism—and that Curtis labors to "make"—is nothing but pure exchangeability: quantity itself without any occluding quality. The sensuous character of money is ultimately a burden to capitalism, which insists on an ever-widening abstraction of the world. The exquisitely engraved dollar bill is a sop to the human need for sensuous value and a hedge against counterfeiting. Soon it is gone, eventually to be replaced by the rearrangement of molecules on computer tape, better able to signify pure number. And Curtis, who yearns for the childhood experience of immersing his hands in soapy dirty water, spends much of his adult work life staring at computer print-outs.

The desensualized world of capitalist production is so arid and cold at heart as to be incapable of relating to human life. Since however, the system is also a human arrangement involving domination at the workplace and seduction at the point of commodity consumption, the capitalist totality must contain within itself a system of mediations that links the human end with the abstract principle of exchange. These mediations must permit exchange, i.e., capital accumulation, to proceed optimally; and at the same time it must relate to real human needs. The fundamental contradiction entailed here can only be feebly resolved through the expedient most commonly tried, namely, to shape human needs (as in advertising, education, et cetera) to conform to the exchange principle. People are malleable but not infinitely so, and they will ultimately resist the heartlessness of capitalist relations. On the other hand, they have until now not resisted so much as to overturn them. Therefore, the capitalist totality has come to contain an amazing profusion of contradictory elements, all bearing the trademark "Made by Capital."

It may now be possible to understand a little more clearly the nature of the totality that supercedes psychology. Consider Curtis's workplace, the bank. The bank is an element of the totality linked to the whole through other elements within it. These elements may be as different as individual persons and architectural structures; yet they are internally related to each other through the active influence of the contradictory needs of capital. Through these mediations, the intrapsychic relations that turn up under the conditions of psychoanalysis become organically linked to other matters that have no psychological referent whatever, or only an ambiguous one. Here Curtis's search for a missing paternal phallus joins with the nonpsychological facts that males of only a certain kind are at the center of power, and that his nighttime dream of a black widow spider guarding a sewer hole is related to the racist history that sees to it that there are only black women who clean his apartment and office, and whom he sees only at night when, working late on behalf of the bank, he peers from behind the mass of documents on his desk. The maternal secretary is part of the ensemble, as is the sleek, orthogonal, and completely administered architecture of the bank. The total control of his environment, from its precisely regulated temperature and humidity to the careful juxtaposition of blank monochromatic walls with torrid zones of Picasso and Miró, merge to form a reality of omnipresence, an unseen but all-seeing nonpsychological mind, a presence that builds into itself the human factor, even allows space between the half-partitions for corporate dalliance and play. This nonpsychological mind is known only negatively. Curtis's consciousness is, in fact, narrowed down by the smooth glass-and-steel surface of the bank's triumph. Outside the walls lives what is left over from its ruthless advance; and this, the realm of marginality, of fantasy and the perverse, is what assumes residence in Curtis's mind.

In every social order a differentiation necessarily arises between subjective and objective, between self and others. Only in capitalism, however, has the differentiation become a splitting and a dominant feature of the totality. We shall have many occasions during the course of this work to explore the splits in capitalist existence, particularly as they affect personal life. There is one characteristic split, however, that overrides all others, not because of any metaphysical quality it possesses but because the powers that rule society ensure that it is imposed above all other considerations. It is at the point of production—specifically, the work process we know as wage labor—that capitalism attains its identity as a system of pure production, i.e., production for its own sake and the aggrandizement of one class over the others.

Capitalism, which made the world a market, attempts to universalize the sphere of the economic by separating human activity from its outcome. This is the peculiar form of its domination, manifest in an ambivalent process that both accentuates and dehumanizes the human element at the same time. As Marx observed:

> *For capital the worker does not constitute a condition of production, but only labor. If this can be performed by machinery, or even by water or air, so much the better. And what capital appropriates is not the laborer but his labor—and not directly but by means of exchange.*[3]

In sharp distinction to other modes of production, capitalism entails an essential move to the subjective. Under capitalism, the worker is no longer tied *in toto* to the master, as was the slave, or to the land, as was the serf. She/he is to be set free individually and is given the potential to develop individuality . . . so long as some part of vital activity is split from the self, sold to the capitalist as labor-power, and turned into surplus value. In sum, human power is transformed, via the wage, into number, i.e., money. Thus work, the sustaining principle of necessity and the foundation of society, is no longer equivalent to the whole person's activity; it becomes the province of part of the self, a part that must be made enumerable for purposes of exchange—and the self has to be split in order to allow this exchange to take place. Curtis's bank represents the apotheosis of the process, since it trades in the ultimate distillate of capitalist production, the purified end product of money. Therefore, his example may be paradigmatic and, in any case, is removed by degree but not by kind from the average individual under capitalism.

Abstraction and splitting are the essential features of capitalist culture as it becomes marked with the identity of production. A personal side and a thing side, made by human activity but each apparently having a life of its own, seem to wander separately through the totality. The ruthless motion toward abstraction creates in the Cartesian split a disembodied human consciousness and a material, mechanical body, the repository of nature. Mind is cut off from nature, and nature becomes the endless scuttling of things.[4] The thing-nature world obeys the mechanistic laws of normal science, whereas the human world is subject to abstract ideal principles of mind. Time itself, far from being an a priori category, becomes severed from the rhythms of life and is seen as an impersonal quantity proceeding linearly and mechanically. Mechanical, and now digital, clock time is then reimposed upon human activity in the workplace.[5] Time becomes a way of binding people, and it itself is bound: metered and in seemingly arbitrary units, equated firmly to money, and imposed upon people as the apparently abstract condition of real human domination.

Analysts see the negative underside of these elements of capitalist culture in the stillness of their offices. Often patients panic if they are a few minutes late, feeling the analyst will be in a rage at them for their reckless defiance. They may be no less agitated to be early, which is regarded as a humiliating submission on their part. Such patients will go to extreme lengths to be exactly on time, i.e., to arrive thirty seconds before the beginning of the session or as long as it takes to get their breath. There is nothing impersonal about time in psychoanalysis. The session is fixed exactly in time, true; but this only ensures that the maximum tension, born out of longing and power, can be brought to bear. A similar relation holds for money, time's alter ego in capitalism. Some patients pay on the spot, others exactly two weeks later; some bring in checks stained with coffee, others enclose the precious thing in an envelope as though it would contaminate or be contaminated by the transfer of hands; still others, with averted eyes, drop it in the analyst's hand, as if to eliminate any direct material transmission. None, to my knowledge, treat money as a purely abstract medium of exchange. As far as the capitalist society goes in the direction of abstraction, so do its individuals go to negate that direction. The anal complex evinced by Curtis and so many others is a remnant of infantile life. It's power, however, is basically incomprehensible until we realize that the equation excrement=money is a specific historical formation: a negation or protest on the part of the body against the inhuman abstract power invested in the money-symbol. Excrement, then, as the most sensuously real production of the human body, links the infantile life of power with money, the sign of adult power and the most desensuously real production of the human mind. For each is an end product, the one of alimentation, the other of production.

Capitalism, to be sure, does not introduce splitting into social existence, just as it does not introduce domination. From the beginnings of class society people lived a twofold existence: they shared in the same society yet were strangers to each other, separated by the barrier of class. Such a barrier cannot exist only on the outside; it must be internalized. And once the self is separated from others, it becomes aware of itself as an individual entity cut off from the world in general, from nature and its own body as well as from other people. The consciousness of self as a distinct entity with internal organization and conflict enters Western thought only with Plato, where it is transparently tied to the great philosopher's attempt to rationalize the tottering class structure of imperial Athens.[6] The classes appear internally within Plato's notion of self, where their conflicts are transcribed into the mental struggles between reason and impulse that have since infested Western consciousness.

From this standpoint (and from that of other, even more ancient differentiations, such as that between female and male), capitalism cannot be said to have added anything entirely new. However, the particular splitting it introduces between one part of the worker and another adds a new order of estrangement and creates the conditions for the emergence of the modern psyche—and, with it, the territory for modern psychology, psychiatry, and psychoanalysis.

Production and consumption under capitalism are split from each other, and both entail a radical and historically original splitting of the individual person. The very condition of individuality in bourgeois civilization is this self-same splitting. From one angle the splitting is a sign of capitalism's strength, the power needed to drive so deeply into the heart of the individual. But from another perspective the same process is a mark of capital's fundamental irrationality and weakness. Though it pretends to drive toward universalization, the basic class domination of capitalism is continually reproduced in the individual heart, just as that of Athenian society was in the Platonic self. It would be simplistic and misleading to hold that history is ever exactly reproduced in any given person. This would deny that history has in reality effected the splitting away of the individual from productive, public life. Class, by definition, is not a psychological relation and cannot be identical to any personal property. The point to bear in mind is not that a nice map of class can be drawn over personal life, but that *wherever* an individual is within the class structure, she/he will necessarily be exposed to profound splits in personal existence. The splits will become etched subjectively, and the subjective splitting will resonate with the splits of the objective world. Capitalism feeds on these splits and is progressively weakened by its diet. Just as capitalist bureaucracy vainly attempts to harmonize large-scale contradictions, so does the split self of capitalism continually attempt rationalization and just as continually break down into neurosis. As the self decomposes, capitalist production and consumption feed like toadstools upon the product and so reproduce themselves.

By such means arises a culture peculiar to capitalist society: a language, a mode of thought, a structuring of time and space. And out of that culture, mediated through the family, arise people with a "capitalist psychology" who reproduce capitalist society through their class participation. In other words, the person does not arise from the point of production. Rather, the split engendered at the point of production refluxes into society, where it sets into motion a certain mode of personal existence and family life. Out of this conjunction arises the real individual. I do not wish to give the impression of a kind of "feedback loop" in which individual, family, culture, and work shuttle back and forth. The elements are not sharply discriminated from one another but are mutually constitutive. Nor is there any kind of a neat fit between individual, family, culture, and work under capitalism. Precisely the opposite is true. Capitalism works by not working. It works as it breaks down. Specifically, the individual who works within capitalism and makes it tick is not a functional robot but an inwardly torn creature, a "neurotic." His unconscious demon goads him to a more sterling performance, while, saddled with perverse wishes, he turns desire outward in a desperate search for commodities, which are never appreciated but thrown aside. Because the split is inward and nonidentical to the pathways taken by society as a whole, his performance and consumption never bring quiescence. Instead, he turns restlessly to new projects, new products, new objects . . . and helps keep the system turning.

Just as the individual who lives within the capitalist system becomes caught up in inevitable conflict, so is that system as a whole subject to a permanent state of crisis. This is a measure of its fundamental irrationality, which can only be rationalized, or papered over, through a fantastic development of the forces of production. However, rationalization itself is bound to fail inasmuch as it rests upon the twin pillars of the domination of nature and imperialism, both of which will necessarily crumble and bring disasters to bear upon the master system.

The foregoing analysis raises a number of interesting political questions. Can it be said, for example, that the primary point of revolutionary attack against capital must be directed at production, at the organization of labor, as classical Marxism has postulated? To a profound extent this must be true. Think what a difference would be made in this country were there a political body with muscle and teeth that represented the working people, who create wealth and have it alienated away from them. Think, too, of the immense resources that capitalist power has expended to check just such a development. Capital knows that if that sleeping giant could be aroused, the capitalist system would be finished. However, the fact that labor has not arisen cannot simply be a function of capital's efforts to suppress it. There must be a factor of compliance as well; and we are inclined to wonder whether those parts of the totality that have become split off into the "personal" sphere are implicated.

Marxism traditionally has tended to rest its case on its mastery over the point of production—what may be called political economy—and to regard the personal sphere as a derivative or even residual category. Yet, for all that it has accomplished, Marxism has no ground for complacency. It has never been able to account for the fact that the industrial proletariat, whom its theory predicted as the vanguard revolutionary force, has so regularly opted for conservatism. Nor has it been able to free itself from the capitalist habits of making a fetish of production or of engaging in the domination of nature.[7] Finally, Marxism has never been able to solve the problem of liberation versus authoritarianism, although it has remained the single force able to authentically promise the former. One thing is certain: control of the means of production is not a sufficient condition for liberation and can just as likely introduce another round of tyranny.

For all these reasons, then, we should not regard Marxism as sacrosanct. Indeed, the same question should be put to it as to psychoanalysis: Has it not neglected the totality in favor of one split-off element, in this case, political economy? It is the totality that is the object of radical action and understanding; and the totality here is no abstraction but society in all its reality, not only the way commodities are made, but the way love and children are made as well, and the way language is spoken, thoughts are thought—indeed, the ways reason and madness are constituted.[8] Might it be possible to sharpen radical social insight through a real grasp of that split-off dimension that coalesces, among other places, into Curtis's demon? And may not the goal of a humanistic Marxism, a Marxism of freedom and not of domination, be served through an appropriation of this sphere which, for all that it is repudiated, contains spontaneity and desire, the germs of transcendence?

But we cannot begin to answer these questions unless there is a reconstructed psychology.

6

DESIRE AND THE TRANSHISTORICAL

THE HISTORICAL AND THE TRANSHISTORICAL

Let us take stock. We have shown that a person, Curtis, cannot be adequately understood by psychological means because his psychological relationships are necessarily drawn short of his full participation in reality. Curtis is part of a society, capitalism, that is unique among all societies as it includes among its elements an intense curiosity about the individual. Psychology is but the formal science of this curiosity, and psychoanalysis one of its variants. But the individual is formed contradictorily in capitalism. Human power is estranged from the self, while its contours are shaped by alienated productive forces. No psychological discourse as such can capture this relationship because psychology, the science of real positive individuals, is built on the premise that the individual is self-contained. But this is not the case. Hence, psychology and psychoanalysis are part of bourgeois ideology; i.e., they profess to show the bourgeois world as timeless and perfect, whereas in fact it is historical and dominated by a concept of time bound by an equation with money and unfree labor.

Yet people in their unfree, incomplete individuality do exist. The subject matter of psychology is no myth but the product of a real, if estranged, life. Psychology needs to be reconstructed, not jettisoned. It needs to be reformulated to take into account what it leaves out; it needs to grasp the relation of the individual to the totality, capitalism; it needs to become what bourgeois psychology represses in the moment of its formation: historical. Psychology needs to recapture time not merely in its bound, capitalist form, but in time's fullness.

This is why we turn our attention to psychoanalysis, the one variant of psychology that opens onto history and begins to regard the person as a totality. Freud had many flaws, some of which we shall consider below. But it was his indisputable genius to grasp the sense of human beings as totalities, as historically developing wholes formed of disparate elements in a state of negation but with an over-reaching identity. Freud's greatness lay in his grasp of the negativity in humans, the fact that there is a nonhuman component to us that testifies to the historical incompleteness of the world. His weakness lay in repressing this insight at crucial points. And the blight of psychoanalysis has been to build on what was weakest in Freud and thereby to turn itself back into a positive bourgeois discipline suitable for accreditation by the state, patronage by wealthy patients, and remuneration by insurance companies. The project of reconstruction must begin with this insight, with what we may call the historical.

We have observed that human qualities are definable dialectically, as a system of negations; and we are interested in recapturing the sense of the historical totality within psychoanalysis. Putting these considerations together, we may say that we wish to develop the sense of the *historical* and its negation as conjoined qualities of the human. We shall call this negation the *transhistorical*. Therefore, we are interested in defining what is human along historical/transhistorical lines.

It may be said that these two notions are roughly like axes in a description of what is human. However, we should not succumb to any positivist imagery in describing these qualities, to any metaphor grounded in a tradition that has repressed the historical. Rather, the historical and the transhistorical are at once aspects of what is human, so we may describe the human in their terms; they are also constitutive of what is human, so that what is human emerges out of the tension between the historical and the transhistorical.

Consider Curtis's neurosis. We have emphasized how it cannot be understood without reference to his participation in history. His terror about money, which is tied to the fantasy that demons will come to tear out his insides were he to begin losing wealth, must be seen within a historical framework as the negated product of the real history of money in capitalism and, more specifically, of his relation at the bank to males both more and less powerful than he. Furthermore, Curtis's real family is a historical one. It is history that determines that the father should have been trapped by something of the same desperate alienating process in which Curtis himself becomes caught;

i.e., it is history that plays a decisive role in alienating the father from the son, as it will alienate Curtis from his son. And it is history that, by defining femininity in a certain way, played a decisive role in embittering Curtis's mother and makes him see her as a desperate shrew from whom he must flee. We can take this line of analysis as far as we like: wherever we turn, even to what is made of the body itself, we will find history's stamp and will see history being made. Therefore, the historical has a twofold aspect: it is the trace in people of their participation in history, and it is that which people do that makes history. History, to return to Marx's notion, is built out of human labor, or praxis—conscious, object-making, social activity. The historical, then, is whatever enters into that activity and, conversely, what is shaped in us by the fact of that activity.

But the historical does not exhaust human possibilities, nor can it account in itself for the relationships of psychology. For example, in Curtis's demon fantasy, the means of "losing money" is via opening his anus so that money-shit can come out and Father can come in. It is not history that provided Curtis with an anus or innervated it so extensively that bodily based fantasies about significant people would be played out in its terms. The body is not clay to be molded by history any more than workers are clay to be molded by capital: it makes an active input, a demand upon history, that occurs across all historical situations. It is neither above history nor below it, but somehow pressed into history and transformed by it—in other words, transhistorical.

But the body is not all that stands with one foot outside history. Curtis's family, as historically determined as it was, also had such an aspect, one, in fact, that must have preceded history. Before there was history there must have been a family-type arrangement, necessary to reproduce a species whose young were born helpless and unstructured, and remained dependent for a long time. There is no survival without such an arrangement, and no history, either, since the prolonged dependency of the human is necessary for the development of imagination, without which history is inconceivable. On the other hand, it has been history that made a family-like arrangement into a family; i.e., only when the imagination became historical and surrounded itself with language, the means of production, and a way of organizing the world that was human, only then did this arrangement acquire the name "family," as well as a particular name for a particular family, as the family of primitives is particularized for their life and the family of the bourgeois world for its life.

The historical/transhistorical situation includes the process of naming, of giving particular words to things and thereby transforming them, as the anus and the family are made into particular types of named things in the bourgeois world. Their transhistorical quality is not abolished thereby, nor is it passively absorbed into history. Though transformed it retains its character of being outside history. This permits the transhistorical to move in two directions: to tend to revert to prehistory if history is reversed or set aside, as in such extreme or catastrophic situations as starvation, shipwreck, confinement in concentration camps, et cetera; and to become further transformed as history develops into its next phase. If history did not contain what was to some extent outside itself, it would be complete and human time would stop. But history never fully overcomes the transhistorical, just as the transhistorical never exists without being historicized. If the transhistorical stopped making its demands upon history, that would be tantamount to dropping out of history: in human terms, to sickening or aging beyond productive life and finally dying. And because death is the final breaking away of the transhistorical beyond history, history has always included in its construction the giving of meaning to death, the naming of this one ultimate human thing. History, then, is not merely an active, muscular worker transforming the transhistorical, as Marxists emphasize. It is just as much a frightened child protesting against the transhistorical and attempting to conjure it away.

Some theses about the historical/transhistorical conjunction:

• The transhistorical may be roughly defined as "nature," but this involves ordering nature in human terms and not as nature "out there." Only a historical creature has ever bothered to ask about nature, and the asking has always been part of the nature asked about. We do not study nature at a distance but only as we participate —historically—in it.

• It follows that no one thing can ever purely and simply be designated part of "human nature." The "body" is not transhistorical in itself. To posit such a thing means we have already named it, i.e., drawn it into history. This notion has major implications for psychoanalytic theory, the diagnosis of mental disorders, and medical science in general.

• Just so, no one thing can be called historical as such, since what is historical is dynamically changing and arises out of working on and actively naming what is outside itself.

• From a historical standpoint, the past always has transhistorical qualities because it is what is transformed by historical activity. This means that "nature" and "the past" are to some extent synonymous. In particular, "human nature," i.e., "instinct," always has the quality of trying to restore the past, as Freud appreciated.[1] Therefore, "nature" tends to appeal to conservative interests. However, the transhistorical, as being outside history, also can define radical goals for the future. The utopian impulse, of which Marxism is the most important current embodiment, is based upon the forward projection of a past, i.e., "natural," state of bliss and a critique of existing civilization on this basis. One need not be ashamed of doing so on the grounds that this is "unscientific," unless one regards science in its bourgeois form, and bourgeois history alike, as complete and perfect.

• The historical and transhistorical should not be mystified into independent entities with value, i.e., one being good, the other bad; one being the location of freedom, the other of necessity; one being the source of liberation, the other of domination, and so on. Whatever explanatory power they have inheres in their relationship to each other and is intended to cast light on the perennial dilemma of the relations between society and nature. The notions historical and transhistorical permit us, no more and no less, to say useful things about these matters. We may therefore call something—for example, infantile dependency—transhistorical when we mean to say that no matter how acted upon by history—and it is always acted upon by and included in history—dependency is, in a sense, always there, like a piece of "nature." In other words, it cannot be explained on historical grounds alone; history does not precede infantile dependency but itself depends to some extent upon the "natural" existence of a creature like the human, who is born so incomplete that she/he needs history in order to develop. Indeed, if pressed to the wall to define "human nature," I would have to say that it is that part of nature that transforms itself; i.e., it is in human nature to make history.

• By the same token, we may call other things—for example, political economy—historical, when, for all that they draw upon transhistorical elements, they amount to the distinct creation of a historical epoch, and when, by implication, they may therefore also pass away.

• Since no particular entity can be called transhistorical or historical in itself, it follows that one should not sharply oppose these qualities to each other. One can do so, but this is a particular ideological choice that mystifies the human situation. We shold not succumb, therefore, to a *dualism* in which nature and civilization are opposed to each other. This was Freud's position and the source of what is backward in psychoanalysis. The dialectical position is *monistic*: we are part of nature but split from it so that it dwells, transformed, within us, while our own works are projected into and transform it.[2]

• Consciousness occurs as a function of history, i.e., out of the historical/transhistorical conjunction. Freud intuited this when he concluded that consciousness consists in giving a "word-presentation" to a "thing-presentation" in the psyche.[3] The unconscious consists of "thing-presentations," i.e., that which looks into the transhistorical, whereas consciousness is the historical act of emergence from this. For Marx, praxis is conscious activity. Freud shows us how praxis and consciousness are built from an unconscious mental primordium in which the traces of the transhistorical, seen now as nature and the human, infantile past, are represented.

• Consciousness is not therefore a unitary phenomenon; rather, it depends upon the particular character of the historical/transhistorical conjunction. Some praxes are near-blind. Specifically, consciousness depends upon one's relation to history, i.e., class activity, as well as to the transhistorical, roughly speaking, nature. And these must depend upon each other.

DESIRE

Man as an objective sentient being is a suffering *being, and since he feels his suffering, a* passionate *being. Passion is man's faculties striving to attain their object.*
—KARL MARX, *Economic and Philosophic Manuscripts*

The question is: How does this conjunction look in the real human situation? Until we describe it, the historical and transhistorical must remain excessively abstract. Let us leave Curtis for now and turn to someone else.

I am in my office with a patient we will call Jane. Jane is a lawyer in her thirties, well functioning in general, who sought help for a singularly vexing problem: periodic eating binges in which she gorges herself to the point of collapse. As a result, she has become moderately obese. It is not the weight that really bothers her, however, but the fact of the eating itself—more exactly, her state of "mind" during the binge. Jane gets transported by a relentless, savage, remorseless,

66

and consuming urge to eat. "It's as though I am not myself," she says, "but I know that it's part of me also. I feel possessed." Quite often the attacks begin when she is feeling good about herself, particularly when she is optimistic about her work, at which she can be very good. At these moments the good self-feeling is accompanied by a kind of sly companion of another kind, also seemingly good, which in effect says to her: "Hm . . . things are going so well, why don't I just have a piece of candy? It can't hurt." Before she knows what has happened, she has gobbled up the entire box and is uncontrollably on to bigger things, for example, butter, of which she once consumed a whole pound in a single sitting.

A part of Jane that is not Jane; in other words, Jane as "other" to herself, Jane as self-estranged. We should all be familiar with this kind of experience, though we probably do not experience it as Jane does. Also, I am sure that very few experience it even *approximately* as Jane does, and that no one goes through it *exactly* as Jane does, for it is characteristic of personal experience that it not be duplicated or exchanged. In contrast to Jane, we are not usually other to ourselves in such a sharply discriminated way. Our otherness more commonly lopes along like a jackal beside us, occasionally insinuating itself, occasionally forcing us to chase it off, usually politely sharing our repast. But Jane's other is explosive, sharply delimited, imperious, ravaging. This is her woe, but something of an aid to our understanding. I chose to describe Jane's particular version of self-estrangement for a number of reasons. One is its discreteness, the way it pops out at us and shows us its shape before receding. Another is its contagion, what it does to one. By giving me a chance to understand the problem a little more sharply, it allows me to explain an aspect of the practice of psychoanalysis and why it is peculiarly fitted for picking up such things.

Once after a session with Jane—it was at the end of the day—as I was walking home I too found myself seized by a kind of mad feeling, an otherness. I am not given to appetite disturbances, but I felt at that moment that if I could only pounce on something, chew it up and swallow it, there might be relief from what was assaulting me. There was no goodness in the feeling, though significantly it had come after what I felt to be a satisfying session with my patient. Rather, *my* otherness was a kind of blind, unreasoning frenzy, a distillate of pure hate. At that moment I hated the world and felt it to be a massive intruder into my space, an intruder against whom I must lash out. Had anyone jostled me then I would have knocked him down. When I arrived home I had to deliberately absent myself from those around me in order not to inflict myself upon them.

After I had calmed down, I reasoned that the session with Jane must have induced in me the same kind of attack from which she herself suffered. Just as her impulse arose after a moment of self-congratulation, so did mine. In each case Jane was being pleasing, first to herself, then to me; and for both of us the outbreak had erupted on the occasion of our saying to ourselves "good job." The woman must have tricked me, I thought to myself. But what had happened?

Jane had been most ingratiating that day, I recalled. She had a little-girl way about her that I found particularly appealing. Had her manner been directly erotic I would have had much less trouble dealing with it, but she chose instead to be a rather helpless, almost abject child, both needy and admiring of me. What most impressed her was my integrity as a physician. In contrast to a previous therapist—a man she recalled with considerable bitterness—I was someone she could really trust. Now for the first time she felt some hope that her symptom could be cured.

At that moment I felt, ever so slightly, some tuggings. The trouble was, they were headed in opposite directions. From one side, I wanted to—no, *did*—believe her: Was I not as good as she said, and certainly better than the boor who had so mangled her case? But at the same moment I felt that she was swindling me. She knew—or at least knew that I believed—that her symptom, such as it was, was rooted in some very nasty and complicated feelings and that it could not be coaxed out of existence unless she ceased to be herself. The result was a slight twinge of emotion, and then back to the analytic work. In retrospect, I had been dull the rest of the session. I had floated along with some tepid comments about how unrealistic she was, and otherwise left Jane to her own devices. Meanwhile, I reassured myself that therapy took time and depended mostly upon the patient's efforts.

What had been set aside was what Jane was doing to me. I had been playing at the analytic role or, rather, hiding behind it. Instead of confronting her with what was happening, I had let each of us rest with self-serving platitudes: she as the good girl, I as the good analyst. The price was my rage, which was the transmission of Jane's pathogen to me. But this only becomes intelligible if we recognize that psychoanalysis is capable of stirring up such emotional storms out of an apparently cloudless sky. To do so, a digression is in order.

The essential feature of the analytic situation is its moment of emptiness. It is a caesura in the ordinary flow of existence, a kind of space or, rather, an occurrence in which the customary becomes momentarily transparent. At that moment, something deeper is manifested, as when we can see the bottom of the sea while the surface waves are stilled. Freud called the process regression, meaning that forms of thought belonging to an earlier phase of life and of a more syncretic type of organization are evoked by analysis. This is a good term to use so long as we do not fall prey to the tendency to dismiss such thinking as childishly inferior to the syntactical, logical thought of ordinary adult discourse. That we do so is testimony to the fear with which we consider the "primitive" in us, a fear manifest in all that Freud termed "resistance" to analysis. Whatever is grossly called analytic technique consists of the fostering of such moments of regression. I had had such a moment with Jane, signaled to me by my "twinge" of emotion; and I had let it go by, no doubt because of the immanence in me of a feeling akin to that which afflicted me later.

The prototype of the analytic experience is not hard to identify. There can be no doubt that analysis is, in essence, an artful reconstruction of very early transactions with the mother.[4] The difference, of course, is that analysis takes place in the presence of adult discourse, what analysts call, in a clumsy way, the observing ego. Analysis as a therapy is nothing other than the engagement of these two phases of existence. This is its sole claim to distinction; and while it does not necessarily make analysis the best kind of therapy, it does afford it a matchless vantage point for studying the dimly lit foundations of the psyche.

We need a clearer notion of just what transpires at this point. To this real occurrence of which the analytic situation forms the distillate, let us give the name *desire*. Desire is transhistorical; that is, it exists within and is transformed by every historical situation. But it is, so to say, distilled in psychoanalytic work. Let me go further: psychoanalysis, in the most fundamental way, is the *discourse of desire*. Freud's core discovery was the analytic method itself as a means for trapping desire, the way a cloud chamber traps and traces subatomic particles. And the theory of psychoanalysis is the mapping of desire as it takes on various manifestations; psychoanalysis is, so to speak, its metadiscourse.

Of this, more later. For now, what is the phenomenon desire?

Understanding it exactly means forswearing the ordinary criteria of exactitude, for while desire can be named, it contains that which cannot be named. To put it succinctly: desire consists of striving toward an object that cannot yet be named in the languages of history. Desire refers to the earliest states of mind; to the fundamental unstructuredness of our infantile mind; to the prolonged dependency, which is a transhistorical concomitant of this unstructuredness; and to the imagination, which arises on this basis to give birth to history. Contemporary research has shown that the newborn child's psyche is no blank screen.[5] The neonate responds to the human voice, tracks objects visually, and engages in protoexpressive facial movements that form the raw material of dialogue. She/he is prestructured at birth to respond to and join the human community; this confirms Marx's thesis that the "self is the ensemble of social relations." But what Marx did not include—and what Freud made into a cornerstone of his discourse—is the fact that social relations undergo marked transformations throughout life, and that all modes are included at all times, though in varying states of negation and repression. Though desire *refers* to the earliest states, it is included in all later states until death puts the quietus to it.

Although the newborn child is prestructured, relative to later stages she/he is unstructured. The baby is preadapted to respond to the human world and from the first days shows an interest in that world. At first there is no "I," no subject, no self, who represents to the infant his/her particularity vis-à-vis the world. We have no reason to assume otherwise that the infant at first experiences neither self nor world, subject nor object, only a kind of continuum. The story of mental life is the differentiation of that continuum into subject and object qualities, a process of extreme complexity, as complex as the differentiation of the human zygote into an embryo. There is never any simple split between subject and object, but rather an infolding of object into subject occurring along with an exfoliation of subject into object: introjection and projection, in the language of psychoanalysis. And these processes occur back and forth, ebbing and flowing into each other throughout life.

It would be distracting to detail this complexity here. However, one facet needs to be emphasized. Although there is an ebbing and flowing between subject and object worlds in a lifelong way, at a certain phase early in life a kind of stabilization occurs wherein the subject achieves an identity; that is, the "I" sets in as an identifying inner agent: "This is me." The process is no sharply demarcated one (and has, in our society at any rate, a marked overhauling in late adolescence); and it need not eventuate in any particular kind of "I," certainly not necessarily in the alienated individuality of bourgeois society. Nonetheless, there is a transhistorical subjectification that occurs in the human species, a structuring necessary because of the original unstructuredness of the infant, which, if it continued, would be incompatible with life. And although the process of subject formation entails loss and risk, we do not think of it as a backward step. Anyone who watches the infant's progressive sense of triumph as she/he masters the world (including the body) and stakes out a sense of individuality knows that nature has seen to it that the growth of the self is richly rewarded.

But this transhistorical condition is always met with historical conditions. And here enters that aspect of history known as naming, as giving words of a particular kind to things. Here it is that language overtakes the developing person and fixes him/her with society's order of things. The "I" becomes a Kwakiutl, a Vandal, or an American; and if the latter, an American of a particular gender, class, or race, for it is these things that require structuring. Language—and history itself—in this sense involves a kind of binding, not the extreme variant of capitalist time binding, which is imposed upon people so that capital may accumulate, but a delimitation, a staking out of social reality from the provinces of the infantile imagination.

The triumph of history is never complete, however; the very process of binding with language creates an unbound preserve behind language within which archaic modes of being are preserved in negativity, i.e., repressed. Freud's major insight concerning repression regarded its self-negating character. Repression seals off that which is considered unacceptable; but in so doing, it invests with energy that which is blocked. Just so, the binding, which is always a historical process in that it occurs in a social setting, creates behind itself a realm of the repudiated and the impossible. This is the realm of the imagination, of the not-given-by-historical-reality. Into it are gathered those elements that are transhistorical insofar as they are set aside by history; and the demands made by this realm upon the established historical world are what we understand by "desire."

From the standpoint of the growing individual, then, desire may be conceptualized as object seeking that takes place between prelanguaged and languaged states, before and behind the "I." It is the striving for an object that exists as a mental differentiation but cannot yet be named, an object that is imaginary and retains thinglike qualities. The hidden qualities of the self that we project outward in the act of desiring are what we call the self's Other. When these are felt all at once, without dampening mediations, the person may be said to be undergoing an experience of Otherness. Desire and the Other are transhistorical elements of infantile life. However, the objects to which they relate are made and named according to history; and as the person grows and enters history, desire undergoes development and becomes the immediate representative in human experience of a given historical/transhistorical conjunction. The objects it seeks are shaped by historical exigencies but their imaginary, unnameable quality points toward the undifferentiated continuum of primary human experience, i.e., to nature. Desire is transhistorical insofar as the imagination, the infantile body, and infantile dependency are transhistorical. Because these have to be given up if the human is to survive, and because they are too precious to be given up, a special preserve is transhistorically set aside for them, the demands of which in reality we call desire. Desire is equally as necessary as a certain degree of repression. There is no intrinsic need, however, for desire to become problematic unless the society in which it arises is self-estranged and estranged from nature. To anticipate our story a bit, in the history of the capitalist world, the extreme degree of binding imposed by the culture necessary for the accumulation of capital has alienated desire itself, has twisted it about, and made it spectral and monstrous. And when desire became enough of a historical problem, psychoanalysis was created to deal with it.

Psychoanalysis sharpens the implication of desire in more mature modes of relationships. The analyst's method is one of narrowing action and blocking ordinary avenues of speech while retaining speech as the means for elaborating a very intense bond. Under such conditions language *decomposes* and in the notion of the simplest things becomes problematic. The analyst becomes the vessel into which the desire of the patient is poured; and analytic work consists of discovering the shape of this object and having the patient recognize it as her/his Other.

We may now see more clearly what happened between Jane and me, and how Jane's desire became located in me. The transducer is the analytic situation itself. In my role as analyst, I must be subjectively open to the currents of desire emanating from Jane, all the while preserving lucidity. Meanwhile, Jane tries to make me into the object of her need through the mode of speech. As she tries to name me, I try to understand, through my own feeling or empathy, what those names mean to her, and try also to convey this knowledge back to her. In the present situation, what I could not let myself realize until it broke on me was the rage that was brewing in Jane over the recapturing of her desire for an absolute union with me, and my frustration of this wish. She kept this feeling out of consciousness through the artful expedient of being the good girl and flattering me, thereby arousing in *me* a yearning for union which I could not fulfill without violating my integrity as an analyst. By appealing to that integrity she was both flattering me and holding me at bay through my self-imposed restraint, since it was as the "good," i.e., ascetic, analyst that I was winning Jane's praise. The seeming clumsiness of Jane's attempt to build me up was a subtle instrument of retaliation, for it stirred up my desire for oneness while turning me into Odysseus at the mast. Only after the session, when the sense of separateness became real, could I become unchained and let myself rage. It was her revenge at me *qua* analyst; and it worked, because by permitting myself a self-indulgent moment of bathing in Jane's praise, I had set aside the austerity of the analyst's role. To all appearances I was maintaining business as usual. However, the analyst cannot remain at the level of appearance. Analysis disdains the obvious and the temporally bound in favor of disengaged subjectivity. But it takes that subjectivity very seriously with respect to both its objective causes and effects. And it is, as you can see, a most demanding practice.

I chose this example to illustrate another point about desire. It does not simply entail subjectivity, which is the outcome so far as traditional psychoanalytic understanding goes. Desire is also a matter of intersubjectivity; it is transmitted between individuals and can be experienced collectively. That Jane and I did not experience it collectively at the time was due to an analytic failure: her desire remained repressed and mine exploded internally as soon as the session ended. This in turn was related to the maintenance of a false role barrier between us. By letting her make me into the "great doctor," I was keeping myself separate from Jane as the "helpless adoring patient." We were, in short, engaged in a kind of *class distinction* in which our social activity was structured along lines of domination, benevolent as this might have seemed on the surface. No doubt there were also elements present of the archetypical dominion between the male doctor and his "helpless" female patient. Thus, communication occurred, but no sharing. That desire is intersubjective follows from the fundamentally social nature of people. Therefore, no subjectivity can occur without intersubjectivity. In analysis, this particular intersubjectivity, which crystallizes into the transference, is rightly conceived of as the means toward enabling a person to re-experience desire through sharing, and so to re-appropriate aspects of the self long lost in otherness.

Notice that in my "attack"—and in Jane's "mental illness"—we hypothesize desire but do not observe it directly. What we see instead is much more akin to hatred, pure in my case, diverted verbally in Jane's. Hatred is, we might say, a particular negation of desire. This is a very important part of our story, for desire, lacking a definable object, is not to be gratified. Moreover, it enters under the highly vulnerable conditions of infancy. A delicate balance ensues. Although desire can never be absolutely fulfilled, there is a point of relative gratification that is experienced as a state of goodness, and below this, one of relative ungratification, experienced as badness. Under the conditions of goodness, the restlessness accruing as a result of the lack of desire's realization is transferred onto the child's exploratory activity. The objects that the child constructs in the course of his/her activity are themselves invested with desire. Here desire takes on the shape of Eros, or love, and unifies the self with object in ever-widening totalities. In the state of badness, on the other hand, lack of gratification is experienced as a danger to the self. Objects are then shunned or attacked, while consciousness is suffused with hatred of one degree or another.

This schema does not begin to do justice to the complexities of actual development. In the real case, love and hate develop simultaneously; and as they develop, they tend to repel one another so that the self becomes subject to a degree of splitting. Love, by opening the self to new objects, makes it vulnerable; hatred, on the other hand, insofar as it turns to hostility, tends to destroy not only the loved object but the loving self. In the course of this, hatred will be redirected outward toward objects in the world; and to the extent that it overbalances love and cannot be mitigated by it, it will manifest itself as one or another of the fantastic variety of human malevolence. Thus, the thing we destroy—whether it be the landscape or the love of another person—is always some part of ourselves, ejected so that the rest may live, and found again in the victim of our hostility.

Because desire is infinite while the desiring person is finite and

74

subject to loss, decay, and death, the conjunction of love and hate is an existential dilemma. However, different social conditions will allow for an infinite series of outcomes, many of which fall under the rubric of "psychopathology." To return to Jane, she has a boyfriend, Mike, with whom she more or less lives. Mike himself is divorced and has two children, Simone and Paul, who visit every other weekend. Mike has his problems, too, some of which are manifest where Simone and Paul are concerned. Jane feels that he oscillates irrationally between indulging the children and being distant toward them. This vexes her, and she finds herself being alternately sympathetic when he rejects them and resentful when he is spoiling them. Being a forceful woman, she has convinced Mike to do something about the situation; and being a reasonable man, he has obtained some counseling, with the result that his behavior toward the children has become much more sensible, while they themselves have turned into relative angels. All well and good . . . except where Jane is concerned. For now, just when all reasonable resentment has become superfluous, she began to report the following: Simone, the elder, is easy to take, being a bookish, considerate sort. But Paul, though engaging, is a lot more forward. He has a bumptious way of bursting into the kitchen and taking his food. Some people might have found this cute; for Jane, however, it had a catastrophic effect, all the more so because her previous rationale for disliking the children had been eliminated. While she generally liked Paul, Jane could not help feeling a kind of blind, insensate hatred when she saw him eat. The feeling was repugnant to her, and she strove mightily to quash it. But though Jane was clever and scrupulous enough to keep the notion out of other people's awareness, she could not clear her own consciousness of the impulse to savagely deny the child his food. And one vital reason for the obduracy of this idea was its rootedness in *sensuous immediacy*. The idea to violently deprive Paul of his food was no abstract thought. Rather, it was occasioned by seeing and, more exquisitely yet, by *hearing* him eat. Jane found herself tuned to the sounds of his mastication and swallowing. She not only could not help hearing the noises; she actually listened for them. And why not? Desire, however thwarted, is located in a milieu of sensory presence that the human organism cannot let go and forever seeks. Is this "human nature"? Perhaps, but the term has become worthless through ideological abuse. Therefore, we call it transhistorical, always a given element in a human situation, always historically elaborated and named. In any case, a person will always be drawn to the concrete and sensuous, no matter how far down the path of historical abstraction she/he has gone. This is only another way of saying that the sensuous immediacy of desire is omnipresent no matter how much abstract linear thought is piled on top of it. And it means that people can be very definitely more alive when crazy and full of folly than when nicely sane. I am not trying here to romanticize folly by calling it a higher truth but only stating a fact: that people are irresistibly drawn to unreason, and the more so in that they find it repugnant. Philosophers since Plato and until Nietzsche have held otherwise and claimed the life of rational contemplation to be the highest good. One need not dispute this goal in principle to recognize that the great bulk of mankind has never had any use for it.

Desire, whether "pathological", i.e., hate-filled, or not, has its specific personal history. The origins of Jane's "pathology" may be better understood if we consider another episode drawn from the analysis. For a long time at the beginning of her therapy Jane would go into a rage when the phone in my office rang. She would bitterly accuse me of dereliction and on a number of occasions threatened to break off the analysis if I failed to remove the offending instrument. This behavior was remarkable in contrast to her general complaisance and doubly so in light of the fact that I never picked up the phone but had an answering machine, which would automatically answer the call after the first ring. Despite this, it took a good deal of work to convince Jane that her fury was part of her problem and not something that needed to be changed in the objective world. In fact, she never was convinced; rather, a kind of truculent lull set in over the issue, a truce without passion, but without insight either. It took several years and endless work before the matter once again surfaced. Then it came as a kind of imaginary visualization. One day the phone rang again and Jane fell silent. I asked her what her thoughts were at the moment and she replied, "Oh, nothing much. I imagined that you had picked up the phone and were listening, and then I had a flash image of my mother picking up my baby brother to nurse him." "You call that nothing?" I replied. "Because you would like to eliminate it from your consciousness now as much as you wanted to eliminate him then." Even now Jane, the good girl, remonstrated that the recollection was insignificant, for, you see, she had entirely forgotten her outrage over the same matter at the beginning of the analysis.

We need not trace Jane's disturbance beyond these broad outlines:

that her wish to get rid of her brother became one to specifically poison him, and that this wish converged with the need to be the good girl into a symptom whereby in effect she poisons herself through her symptomatic gratification. Our concern now is not to explore particular psychological dynamics but to show that desire is sensuous, absolute, and unrelenting, and that its manifestations in hatred are themselves savagely repressed (as in Jane's forgetting her phone outrage). The point deserves emphasis, since it underscores something very special about us: the conjunction of perfect madness and perfect reason in the same individual, each aspect oblivious of the other and each determined by the other. Madness does not proliferate unless reason has staked out positive ground and so created negativity outside it, whereas reason thrives by repudiating irrationality. It is necessary to add that for this dialectic to flower, a certain kind of historical milieu is required, one that in Jane's case fosters a high degree of individual acquisitiveness, on the one hand, while on the other, forces on the same individual an abstract rationality that is severed from the real bodily roots of acquisition. Jane was from birth made to feel that virtue accrues mainly from excelling over others in tests of intellectual achievement and, later, in the courtroom. Her unreason was allowed to fester partly as a fulfillment of her hostility, partly as a protest against her work. Whatever the details of Jane's case, however, the pattern she showed is characteristic for unreason in general. Self-estrangement always includes self-deception. Thus it is that the paramount condition of human "badness" is not viciousness so much as folly, a kind of unremitting dream, a search for what was never there and a denial of what is. Needless to add, such folly can simulate viciousness quite neatly.

We should not think of Jane as some kind of freak; nor is it the case that her disturbance is simply localizable in capitalism. It may be helpful here to recall some words of St. Augustine, who writes in his *Confessions*:

> . . . *if babies are innocent, it is not for lack of will to do harm, but for lack of strength. I have myself seen jealousy in a baby and know what it means. He was not old enough to talk, but whenever he saw his foster-brother at the breast, he would grow pale with envy. This much is common knowledge. Mothers and nurses say that they can work such things out of the system by one means or another, but surely it cannot be called innocence, when the milk flows in such abundance from its source, to object to a rival desperately in need and depending for his life on this*

77

one form of nourishment? Such faults are not small or unimportant, but we are tender-hearted and bear with them because we know that the child will grow out of them. It is clear that they are not mere peccadilloes, because the same faults are intolerable in older persons.[6]

Common knowledge, indeed: transhistorical though infinitely historicized. "People are like that," we say and leave the matter rest whether we are Marxist or bourgeois. Whether we attack the existing order in the hopes of a better world or defend it as the *summmum bonum*, we are embarrassed to think that people can be like that, and relieved by Augustine's assertion that "the child will grow out of" these faults. To be sure this wish is contradicted by all the facts of everyday life and history, the experience of which shows again and again that whatever "higher" functions may have been tacked on, a consuming infantility ever dominates the affairs of humanity. But this painful truth only spurs us to prove the opposite. This may help explain why Freud, who showed just how the child does not outgrow these peccadilloes, has proven to be a perenially vexing thinker—vexing to revolutionaries with his insistence on the power of unreason and vexing to conservatives with his demonstration of a radically opposed inner self that will not be appeased by official arrangements.

However, Freud proved willing to repress his own radical tendencies. Having established the omnipresence of desire and explored its semantics, Freud proceeded to bleach the stain he had made on bourgeois existence with a recycled theory of Platonic essence. He found the primary cause for desire in nature and, therefore, outside history. As a result, Freud succumbed to dualism. Desire was the product of two radically separated instinctual formations, sexuality and aggression, or, on a higher level, Eros and Thanatos. Each was an "immortal piece of nature." The dialectical position, by contrast, is basically monistic: a single basic force—for Hegel, the idea; for Marx, labor; for Wilhelm Reich, the orgone—is invoked, and phenomena are seen as internal to the self-development of that force. In the dialectically monistic notion, reality is viewed as the outcome of opposed forces that remain internally related, i.e., part of each other. Therefore, the worker suffers the domination of capital, which is ultimately the transformation of his own alienated labor-power. In that part of Freud's psychoanalytic system, which remained close to mental phenomena (for example, in his essays "The Unconscious" or "Negation"), he elaborated just such a dialectically monistic point of view. The repressed, alienated parts of the self are, after all, nothing

other than the subject's own desire come back to haunt her/him. But
when Freud moved to the larger stage of explanation, a kind of fatal
dualism overtook him. Despite the implications of his own discoveries, the founder of psychoanalysis grounded his metatheory in
oppositions that were not internally related—for example, in civilization versus instinct, an unconquerable piece of nature that social
forces could at best contain,[7] while within nature, instinct itself dissolved into the eternally opposed antagonists of Eros and Thanatos,
sexuality and aggression.[8] The invocation of unconquerable nature in
the shape of the instinct toward aggression was not without some
ideological merit, for it at least freed Freud's doctrine from the banal
reassurances of liberal reformism and made it impossible to evade the
realities of human beastliness. But these virtues were part of Freud's
deep ambivalence toward his own society. On the one hand, Freud
had succeeded as had no one else in unmasking society's brutal
hypocrisies and the hidden erotic dreams that were the testament to
bourgeois culture's inability to provide real happiness. Yet his loyalty
to this same culture and its patriarchy was such that Freud saw the
need for exoneration. The problem became not why bourgeois patriarchy was so foul a mode of social organization, but rather one of
making excuses for its susceptibility to forces such as instinct, which
were, like the weather, beyond its control. Therefore, no society could
do more than contain "natural" human aggression and turn it into
guilt. And so Freud resorted to the same tedious explanation as the
very Church he had elsewhere so magnificently excoriated:[9] repression is necessary because of natural human badness, i.e., original sin.
The same may be said of Freud as he said of Dostoevsky, that he
arrived at the same conclusion as did weaker minds with less effort.[10]

I know of no better way to account for the falling off of Freud's
culturalist writings, which are, for all their grandeur and plentitude of
insight, among the most monumental misconceptions ever to issue
from a great thinker. These are the mutterings of a late bourgeois
looking fearfully at the rabble—women, lower classes, darker races
—who have come to represent the life his class has repudiated. This
life, or desire, turned into hatred, was about to become Nazi murderousness. The actual horrors of history make it imperative for any
system of substance to take into radical account the problematics of
human evil. But these nightmares became too readily conflated with
another reality, that of violence, which can be a mode of overcoming
real historical repression. Freud's error was in placing both violence

and evil under the instinctual rubric of aggression. Being natural, an instinct is beyond moral distinction. Therefore, aggressiveness as such was to be opposed *en bloc* by civilization as the representation of the other great instinctual force, Eros. Civilization achieves this distinction by a crudely linear syllogism: Eros serves to unite individual units into larger collectivities; civilization moves in such a way as to "bind" people into ever larger units (as, for example, by imperialist conquest); ergo, civilization does the work of Eros and is to be entrusted (as, for example, by the use of police) to contain aggression, to "bind" it for its "higher" purpose.

The poverty of Freud's conception is striking. It founders, as does all dualism, on the problem of differentiation. At some point, every dualistic system is going to come up against a distinction it fails to differentiate, except by teasing a subtle unit into crudely opposed categories that violate reality. In Freud's case, despite the notion of "unnecessary repression," most prevalent in his earlier works, his system gives us no way of differentiating between violences or, indeed, civilizations. Each is a manifestation of immortally opposed tendencies; hence, they are locked into an eternal historical duality that serves power. Violence is basically aggression, whether it is the violence of slaves revolting on a plantation, Nazis burning down the Warsaw Ghetto, or the inhabitants of that ghetto fighting back. It all comes down to a nature that must be controlled under the terms of Freud's dualism. Similarly, civilizations, whether Allende's Chile or Pinochet's, must be regarded, according to Freud's system, as equivalent outcomes of a mysteriously undying Eros.

It may be seen how helpless are Freud's sociological categories for doing more than buttressing bourgeois conservatism and fear of spontaneity. But Freud never actually saw the dualism in which he lost himself: he constructed it. What he saw—and constructed into psychoanalysis—under the lens of his method was desire itself. This is what floats up out of the silence of the analyst's office like mist from a pond. And desire, being the movement of life as it becomes mental and names the objects for its existence, is a part of nature viewed monistically. It is nature as it becomes historical. Desire occurs at the moment of self-appropriation. It always stands outside history insofar as it contains nameless striving; yet desire is also always part of history insofar as it is carried out in a world of real, already named objects. "Men make history," wrote Marx, "but they do not make it just as they please."[11] The circumstances are already there; in their immobility, what Sartre termed the "practico-inert,"[12] all of past praxis lies sedimented, petrified, "the past that weighs like a nightmare on the brain of the living." Desire is an eruption into historical inertia, something from the outside that momentarily permits the renaming of objects from the standpoint of self-appropriation. In this moment, objects are constituted. Without desire, the world consists only of *things*, inert masses. Thus, desire is as necessary for history as it is repudiated by it. Desire makes of inert things "things-for-us," that is, objects. Desire is therefore at the same time a craving to merge the self with an object and a constitution of both self and object.

Although desire is necessary for the constitution of objects, it is not sufficient to provide more than the subjective end of the process. Freud grasped this distinction in his differentiation between the pleasure principle and the reality principle.[13] The pleasure principle is sufficiently accounted for by desire: it is the establishment, according to Freud, of a thought-identity between a need and an experience of satisfaction. The most elementary example would be the hungry infant's hallucination of the breast, or, to be more exact, of her/his reconstitution of the experience of nursing. But the pleasure principle remains on the subjective plane. To actually meet the need, real food is required; and to eat this food, more than desire is necessary. In other words, the real world, too, must be altered. However, the acting upon reality will also be at the behest of desire, since the person never gives up on the pleasure principle but rather turns reality to work toward its ends. The operation contained under this rubric Freud called acting under the terms of the reality principle. However, he failed to consider that reality is also historically made, through praxis.

Let us consider Jane once more. Her "pathology" is an outcome of desire or, to be more exact, desire as hatred, which is constituted as a rupture from the socially given configuration of the object-world. When overcome by "it," she sets herself the task of mastery by eating objects, that is, cookies, ice cream, butter, and so forth. But this breaks down and, as it does, leads to a widening circle of chaos, which is checked only by physical exhaustion. In the course of her attack, objects are tried in succession, destroyed, and found wanting. But note what Jane has also done. In a good-sized attack, she will go through a major portion of her refrigerator. This may be bad for Jane, but it is good for business. Under the impression of her desire, Jane, experiencing herself as vacuous, seeks objects relatively indifferently and consumes them. If the attack can be just continued a wee bit so that she does not kill herself, and it can be spread out continuously and, most important, predictably, Jane will become the model consumer. Another way of putting it is that Jane's "pathological" object is temptingly close to the ideal form of the commodity itself: "an object outside us, a thing that by its properties satisfies human wants of some sort or another."[14] For the purposes of advanced capital, however, it is increasingly imperative that the commodity lead not to satiety but to restless reconsumption. And it is best if it is destroyed in the consuming act, that is, if its use-value be fairly well obliterated. Monopoly capital, perpetually assaulted by contradictions stemming from overproduction, wants nothing more than a society of Janes: not so dysfunctional that they cannot work or too sick to consume steadily, yet never satisfied either. The sugar with which capitalist industry loads its products is, to be sure, an obvious ruse to induce a chronic state of unsatisfaction. However, it would never matter in the slightest unless it were offered to a sensibility that is bound to remain unsatisfied, one that will move on to new objects, to more commodities under the guise of food.

At this point a major contradiction looms. Desire must become relatively pure for consumer society to stabilize itself; and a restless yearning incapable of real gratification is the means to this end. This desire, as we have seen for Jane, is pointed toward the infantile world of sensuous concreteness. At the same time, the commodity itself is a pure object, something infinitely capable of exchange and entirely abstractable. The pure object, though it may be administered, quantified, and endlessly rationalized, is increasingly incapable of satisfying the concrete and sensuous needs of desire. Desire is mobilized in late capitalism, therefore, at the price of its self-perpetuating alienation. And for the society as a whole, an increasingly drastic split takes place between subjective life and objective movement. This split is reflected in political economy itself.

The secret of capitalist society is the domination of living, sensuous labor and its conversion into the commodity of abstract labor-power, salable on the market for wages. This entails the splitting off of desire from human activity and a repression substantially beyond that necessary for survival. However, desire operates behind the screen set up by history. And political economy, which concerns itself with the abstract transformations of value arising out of human labor, knows nothing of this. It reasons by quantity and linear point-to-point discourse. It is the discourse of the object and the masters, and desire is the hidden secret of history. Capitalist society, in its never-ending struggle for survival, continually represses desire, and in so doing becomes ever more cold and objective, on the one hand, and subjective and fantastic, on the other. Thus it is that psychology and the individual will appear more and more irrelevant to the functioning of nations, while at the same time they will loom ever larger in the immediate conduct of life.

The economy tries remorselessly to exclude desire at the workplace, more generally, in the sphere of production as a whole. However, since the workplace is a human arrangement before it is a politico-economic one, desire makes itself felt there as well. The actual capitalist workplace may be described as a scene of the contest between the imperatives of production and those of desire. The outcome, engineered by the powers in charge, is the administration of desire. We already noted this when we observed that Curtis's office is designed, for example, to include carefully selected artworks, or that it includes controlled space for dalliance, and even a program whereby the more vigorous workers may get T-shirts with the bank's name emblazoned on the front, so they can go running in the park. We shall return to the question of the administration of desire. Meanwhile, we must note that even this administration fails to capture it entirely. This is, after all, what Curtis's analysis is all about—desire that is there in him, that drives him at work, yet remains outside the tentacles of administration. Indeed, his analysis must, in fact, be kept a secret at the workplace.

The capitalist workplace, then, has as its identity, if not its whole reality, an exclusion of desire. Business and pleasure do not mix, as they say. Only when the crises of late capitalism make consumerism an imperative is desire, highly administered, officially allowed access to the economic process, though even here, as we have observed for Jane, desire must be disjunctive with the commodity it seeks to consume; that is, the wish for the object never contains the commodity as such but always drives the buyer on to new things. The sphere of political economy as a whole, then, may be seen as a gigantic and self-contradictory negation of desire.

Where does this leave Marxism, which is supposed to be a negation, i.e., a critique and a revolutionary transformation, of the world created by capitalist political economy? Should not Marxism recapture the moment of desire instead of reproducing the cold tenets of political economy? Indeed it should, and the road lies open.

Political economy, though it has become the discourse of power, is not the singular determinant of history. It itself is a product of history and enters back into history. But history encompasses more than political economy; and Marxism, as the historical discourse par excellence, must do the same. In other words, Marxism should direct itself to history as a whole, not merely to the politico-economic organ of history. History is the movement of society, which is a totality. Political economy is but an element of the totality, i.e., capitalist society. A totality cannot be reduced to any one of its elements; rather, it is determined by all of them in their differentiation. When capitalist society sired political economy, it set loose desire as an unwanted, delinquent child. This is desire's particular historicization under capitalism, its fate. Both political economy and desire are differentiations in the history of capitalist society, split apart, as we shall explore, in the material severing of home and workplace, and subject to endless further development. Following the moment of differentiation, the elements take on a dual existence: they go their own way inasmuch as they have been differentiated from each other (hence the curiosity about the individual); and they also retain a common identity inasmuch as they belong to the totality that determines them and whose history they in turn shape. It is not enough, therefore, to dismiss "psychological factors" with the observation that economic laws of motion are indifferent to them. The point is that political economy is constituted to be indifferent to desire. That is just what makes it so galling. The very heartlessness of the economic system is historically decisive precisely because our history is made by passionate creatures whose yearning is thwarted by the impersonal world wrought by the class antagonism of capital. History is not the record of political economy, though it requires political economy. History is the struggle against political economy, or the succumbing to it. It is the human and therefore passionate account of combat and acquiescence, of victory, defeat, loyalty, passivity, cunning, and folly in the face of disembodied human institutions. To grasp history theoretically and to develop a politics of liberation, it is necessary to develop a theoretical comprehension of desire, which is that excursion of human existence wherein all that is passionate is subsumed. Not desire in the abstracted and encapsulated form by which official psychoanalysis recognizes it, but desire as it is torn loose from material power and as it hurls itself against the abstracted system of power described by the terms of political economy.

Political economy is the location of the abstract and the home of what has been made rational. It is, for us, the historical source of the reality principle, i.e., of necessity. It defines not only the economic process of production, consumption, and capital accumulation but all the structuring of everyday life necessary for capital accumulation to proceed. It should be recalled that we are a capitalist society not simply because the capitalist mode of production dominates economic activity but equally because the class of capitalists, the bourgeoisie, has taken state power and holds it firmly in its grip. To the extent, then, that the state penetrates everyday life—and this process inexorably accelerates under the conditions of monopoly capital—so will everyday life become increasingly determined by the logic of political economy. In other words, personal life becomes increasingly administered. This does not mean the abolition of desire but rather—as with the historical movement of political economy in general—its splitting and repression, i.e., its differentiation under the conditions of alienation. In late capitalism, desire festers, and this is why the mental-health trades loom so large in contemporary existence. Under the conditions of capitalism in general, and late capitalism in particular, desire becomes the location of the concrete and the irrational. It is hell to the heaven of political economy.

And since persons are totalities whose lives reproduce the society of which they are an element, it should be possible to understand this history as it intersects with an individual life.

7

RICH GIRL

I am not what I am.
—Iago, in *Othello*

For a long time Sarah could not work. She would lie about dully, alternately staring at the green paisley wallpaper or the television, and eating sunflower seeds, carefully cracking the shells between her molars and then expertly shifting the debris to the front of her mouth, where her tongue and incisors, acting in concert, winnowed the nut and ejected the fragments of shell. Sometimes she would not get out of bed until the pile of shells had grown so large that it could no longer be ordered in a neat mound and would spill uncomfortably under the bedclothes. She would rise scratching, stumble about the apartment until the means of cleaning up the shells were gathered, and then sink down again, either onto the bed or the toilet, where she could sit for an hour at a time, poring over *The New Yorker* and waiting for something to happen.

On better days she would rouse herself to go to dance class. There she could forget her troubles. Sarah regretted not having stayed with ballet, as her parents and childhood teachers had so often urged. Even now, with so little practice and being out of condition, her tall, slender body retained its grace and suppleness. No matter how infrequently Sarah went, she was the pick of the class. She reveled in the envy of the others and delighted in the praise of the instructors. In response to their encouragement, she even considered dancing professionally. After all, there was still time, and the way she was floundering, what was there to lose? Sarah would muse this way, actually growing excited, until she recalled the precipice she had stood upon long ago. She was thirteen and radiant in her new lavender outfit. There was Mme. Deschamps at the piano, looking eagerly at her, and there behind her, rank upon rank of eyes, their gaze (adoring, she could feel it) merging with the school footlights. The music swelled and she swelled with it, swelled with a joy that turned into frenzy, and then panic, paralysis, a silence of movement and tears of mortification. Her mother was most understanding, and even her father showed no disapproval, but it would be ten years before Sarah would again step onto a dance floor.

Upon reflection Sarah decided that there was a lot to lose just then. There had always been a lot to lose; and now, as she headed toward her thirtieth year, there seemed to be more and more. True, her limbs flexed as of old; but the long hours Sarah spent staring at the mirror confirmed with all the violence of the eye that the invisible elastic cords that had knit her body wondrously together for so many years were snapping one by one. Entropy was overtaking Sarah. She could see the sagging beginning to set in; tiny wrinkle by tiny wrinkle, a droop there where once a fine tense arc had held sway. Her train to balletic glory had left years ago; what she faced now was watching the younger, confident women step aboard while she awaited the inevitability of physical injury. Sarah felt like the proverbial athlete dying young, one, moreover, whose real triumph was strictly in the imagination. She had had so much. Only her mother really knew; and her mother was the only person in the world from whom Sarah would turn away at that final, triumphant adoration her imagination was preparing for her.

Sarah's mother had once been a champion swimmer. Even now, in late middle age, time, abetted by the skill of plastic surgeons and the carefully screened rays of southern suns, had been kind to her. Sarah despised her mother's coarse cultivation of youthful beauty no less than she loathed her own helpless imitation of the older woman's values. Yet, the disgust she felt for her mother when the latter periodically sailed through the door like an armada was never without an admixture of envy. This great whale of a woman, with belted muscles running across her upper back (the product of decades of smashing tennis balls no less than the backstroke) and narrow Tartar eyes, this foolish, fond, empty, powerful woman never failed to excite awe in her daughter. And for all of the amused contempt with which she treated her mother, the truest feeling Sarah held for her was terror, which was why months passed without a visit.

"Sally! Look at this mess! What have you done with the allowance we sent you? I told you to get a cleaning woman with it. Even though

THE AGE OF DESIRE

you're too depressed to work right now, dear, the least you can do is to maintain appearances. It's the best therapy, after all. Dr. Rhapsode was saying so himself just the other day. Why don't you answer me, dear?"

"I would prefer not to."

"Prefer not to? What kind of talk is that?"

"You wouldn't understand. It's from a novella, *Bartleby*, about a man who wouldn't work. Sometimes I feel that way . . . about everything!"

"Sarah, darling, you read too much. Your father was saying so himself just the other night. 'She's too sensitive, that's all'; that's just what he said. He thinks, too, that you're going to make it. We believe in you, Sally, just remember that. No matter what the world does to you, just remember that you'll always be Number One with Daddy and me. Of course, we love Martha, too. But you were the first, and somehow, I know you hate it when I talk this way, but give your old mother the satisfaction just once, you know we hardly ever see each other, though goodness knows, it's not *my* fault. Where was I? Oh, yes, somehow, Sarah, you were special right from the start, the way you looked at us from the crib. Forgive me, dear, I'm getting maudlin again. By the way, you know how I hate to ask you these things dear, you're so touchy about them, but how is that new doctor coming along? You know, the one with the funny name?"

Sarah was the firstborn of her generation. Both sets of grandparents had come over from Eastern Europe to escape pogroms and the tsar's conscription, and to make their fortune in the West. Many who undertook this exodus failed or returned to the Old World; but her grandparents held on and held together. On her mother's side, Sarah's grandfather started with a pushcart, then gradually accumulated sufficient funds to buy a small clothing store. He never became wealthy; but he did well enough to end his days in Florida and to watch his only child rise in the world, first through her athletic prowess, then by a marriage whose material fortunes he was pleased to have helped launch with a little capital. Sarah's paternal grandfather stitched the clothes from whose sale the modest dowry arose, and remained an ardent anarcho-syndicalist to the end of his long days, an end likewise passed in a Florida retirement community, where he argued fiercely with ancient Communist adversaries by the side of the pool. Sarah's father was the youngest of three children and the

88

only one who ever amounted to anything. His success as a salesman alienated him somewhat from his brothers; and after his marriage and first auto dealership, he managed to have less and less to do with them. The old man lived with his successful son for a while around the time of Sarah's birth. But when Sarah's father acquired the Mercedes dealership, long-smoldering tensions erupted between the two. Claiming he would not live off the profits of Nazi capital, grandfather took his ever-docile wife with him and moved South, where the union pension fund provided him with a dignified end. All this took place before Sarah was three. Of her paternal grandparents nothing remained but a dim recollection of shouting. Nor does Sarah know what anarcho-syndicalism is, despite seventeen years of an education more elaborate than that offered real princesses.

Sarah could pick her head up at two weeks of age. She sat at three months, walked at nine, said her first words at eleven. She began swimming lessons at six months of age and had her first exercise class at a year and a half. By three she was picking words out of a dictionary and had begun violin lessons for toddlers. Tested before entering kindergarten, she scored off the scale in all categories, and so was moved immediately into an enriched program at school. The principal told her mother that the tests were designed to select the winners right from the start. It was the post–Sputnik era, America was going unabashedly toward a meritocracy, and Sarah was to have heaped on her all the resources the most potent economic organization in the history of the world could bring to bear on the cultivation of an individual.

By age five Sarah had begun to suffer from the piercing headaches that would afflict her for the next decade and then disappear as mysteriously as they arrived. All test results were normal or inconclusive. Her case kept a lot of suburban doctors busy for a long time, and its ramifications extended for miles into metropolitan medical centers as well. Sarah's father used to say, half-boastingly, that he had to sell a Mercedes 300 each week just to keep the doctors going.

After a few years of this, it was decided that the case was psychosomatic, and Sarah was packed off to a child analyst, Dr. Freestone. By then it was apparent that something was definitely troubling the child and that the headaches were, in the words of the school counselor, a "cry for help." On Sarah's first visit, Dr. Freestone found a sulky, whiny girl clinging to a mother who anxiously watched every move for signs of disorder. While the doctor tried to play with Sarah, her mother kept up a steady patter of supposedly helpful descriptive comments, alternately calling attention to the child's brilliance and warning her against breaking the toys. Once when Sarah paused in the middle of doll play her mother anxiously interjected, "Sally, I know that look in your eye. You're going to have a headache. Here, take one of your pills."

After several sessions, Dr. Freestone took the parents aside and gave them her opinion. "Sarah's headaches aren't only a cry for help," she said. "They are also a protest against everything that is being jammed into her head. I think I can help her, with your cooperation. But if we don't all work together, she'll not make any progress. And to co-operate means that you must learn to stop pressuring that child. Certainly she's gifted. But she's beginning to believe that nothing she does is for herself. She's under incredible pressure, which is just not healthy for a seven year old—or for anybody else. Now, it's been my experience that often when parents put so much pressure on a child, it's their way of dealing with their own problems. So, I'd like to ask you a little about yourselves; and if it's necessary, I'll refer you to a colleague of mine who will see you as a couple."

It proved necessary; and in summarizing the case to her colleague, Dr. Menschlik, the family therapist, this is what Dr. Freestone said:

> These people have not differentiated themselves from each other, and they're trying to hold the child in a symbiotic tie to keep their own dependency needs met. Without her they'd either tear each other apart or the marriage would dissolve. Sarah pays the price by being made into part of each of them. The mother is a markedly hysterical individual with strong phallic needs and tremendous repressed hostility. She's a typical combination of colossal egocentricity and vanity, on the one hand, and a mortifying self-abnegation, on the other. That's one of the sources of the hostility: the frustration of feeling so great yet living a life in which everything she does is for husband and daughter. Of course, the hostility goes deeper than that. I couldn't help feeling anxious just sitting with her; imagine how Sarah feels! Her mouth reminds me of a piranha. As you might imagine, the husband degrades her terribly. He has a tremendous castration fear, which he handles as would a typical male: counterphobic . . . macho . . . the supersalesman. Meanwhile, he keeps the wife down and avoids her, for fear (accurate, I suppose, if he's reading her unconscious) she'll bite his penis off; and he enormously overindulges the girl, both to show what a big man he is and to make his wife jealous. At the same time, she overprotects Sarah, wanting to make her into the penis she herself can't have, and by the same token, needing to guard her against her own jealous hostility. And the worst of it is that

the parents don't really talk to each other but through, around, or by each other. And inconsistent! The father is indulgent one minute, then harsh and punitive the next. In addition, he's away a great deal. I don't think he knows who he is, really. He told me his own father was strictly from the old school, had rigid values and all that, but that he himself wanted to be different, which is why he became a salesman, where the puritan ethic, so to speak, doesn't belong. And because he found himself successful at it, he drifted futher from his father's way, thereby feeling empty and impoverished. Then there was some kind of break between them. Needless to add, there's a lot of that punitive old man embedded in his superego, but of course it's not integrated with the ego, so he's inconsistent. And his wife's even more so. She's fluttery and like a little girl one minute, stern and demanding the next, and the third, turns into a howling banshee. It took some time to get extract from her the fact that she has a temper, so concerned is she to maintain appearances. Evidently, it's a dilly and must really terrorize the little girl, especially as the rages usually come out without any warning. Apparently, she never hits Sarah, but I doubt whether that would make any difference; it's the mental abuse that counts. And for all that the mother is constantly on the child, watching every breath and every movement, I get the feeling that she's never really there, that she never sees Sarah as Sarah, that she's really only looking at herself.

What else can I tell you? Oh yes, there's a baby sister, age two. I think Sarah's ferociously jealous of her, but the hate is pretty well buried; not much comes out of Sarah, in any case. As far as I can tell, the parents for the most part leave the baby alone, which is the best thing that could happen to her. I feel sorry for Sarah. She's so young and so brilliant, but seems aged and burdened already. I feel sorry for all of them. They're not bad people, for all the pathology I've ticked off, but trapped. You have your work cut out for you.

The sessions with Dr. Menschlik lasted six weeks. It was the father who withdrew, then dropped out. This is usually the pattern in family therapy, though Dr. Menschlik was not misled into seeing the matter as one-sided. He noticed from the beginning how Sarah's mother subtly set her husband up as the villain; how she made herself—or allowed him to make her—into the frustrated, put-down, all-faithful and all-suffering wife; and how this made him guilty, an emotion he never revealed except through a mounting evasiveness. Such was the result when Dr. Menschlik tried to get them to talk openly with and to each other. Evidently, they needed their distance and found authenticity an intolerable threat to the intactness of their marriage. Sarah's parents, for all their means, were of the common type who can neither live with nor without each other. Solitude was unbearable to them; and it was impossible to distinguish whether their world was constructed for the positive material benefits it afforded or as a buffer against facing reality alone.

Sarah's sessions lasted almost a year. Dr. Freestone made her feel a little safer; and after an initial period of resistance to going, it was hard to keep her away. Then she went away to summer camp, and the headaches disappeared. In September the parents suddenly found Dr. Freestone very expensive and decided not to resume the sessions. Sarah pined a little, then appeared to forget the entire experience. She was doing brilliantly in school and had made a few new friends. The headaches came back periodically until they finally withered away in adolescence. Meanwhile, better days seemed to have set in. Sarah's gifts were acknowledged in school; and the satisfaction this afforded her parents kept their intricate personal system in a state of balance. Even the incident at the ballet recital hardly seemed to matter, so accomplished was Sarah, so able to recoup gratification from other achievements. Mr. Dichter, the able and demanding literature teacher at the Lorelei School, was positively awestruck by her poetry and openly called her "the next Sylvia Plath." Communications Co-ordinator Elaine Dirndle, on the other hand, was even more taken with Sarah's capacities in the performing arts, and in the end, her influence held sway. Lorelei was one of those schools favored by the fortunes of prosperous alumni and had, among other riches, its own television studio. By her junior year, Sarah was writing, directing, and producing shows of exceptional promise. And applying to college was just like shopping at Saks Fifth Avenue with Daddy's credit card. She even had the extra pleasure of turning down scholarships.

True, she was aloof and had by then already shown a knack for becoming unhappily involved in brief, savage romances; yet, in all, one could not have found a young woman of eighteen more poised on the edge of a fair future than Sarah. This is why it was so baffling to her doting parents when she refused to get out of bed one Sunday morning and, in a dry, strangled voice that her mother could scarcely recognize, said that all her achievements—from the merit scholarship to the tennis trophy to the laudatory inscription chiseled into the school library plaque—gave her no sense of who she was and what she wanted, and that she was indeed the most unhappy person she knew. And could not her parents help?

Not since the ballet recital had Mr. and Mrs. M had such a shock.

But they were prudent people; and after satisfying themselves that they could not prove to Sarah the fallaciousness of her reasoning, they set about trying to help. A call to the local rabbi yielded the name of Dr. Brisket, a psychologist-counselor well enough known to reassure the Ms that he was capable of handling their daughter. "Just remember, dear," Mr. M told Sarah before the first visit, "that you have nothing to hide. In fact, he should be paying you for the privilege of listening to what you have to say." And with that benediction Sarah set off for therapy.

Sarah was first surprised and then irritated that Dr. Brisket spent so much time listening without ever acknowledging the cleverness or profundity of her insights into herself. Nonetheless, she was beginning to like the man when, in the middle of the sixth session he abruptly interrupted her train of thought with the observation that he could no longer be of help to her alone. Instead, she would have to be seen with her parents. "You see," Dr. Brisket later explained to the three of them, "this is a knot that will have to be untied at the level of the family." The situation had not changed fundamentally since the time of therapy with Dr. Freestone. Sarah was finding it psychologically impossible to differentiate herself from her parents; and they were equally reluctant to let her go, undoubtedly because of what they feared would be stirred up if they had to deal with each other directly instead of living off Sarah's accomplishments. As for these achievements, it was no wonder Sarah took so little pleasure in them. "Nothing Sarah does can be felt as her own," Dr. Brisket pointed out, "since it is all done for praise, and as this is the glue of the family's sickness, the greater her achievement, the less free she can feel."

Dr. Brisket could be very persuasive when he wanted to be; and because there was nothing in the world the Ms desired so much as the happiness of their daughter, before long he had the three coming together to the handsome office over his garage. At first they tried talking—the doctor, much more active now than when he saw Sarah alone, frequently interrupting with observations of the various tricks they were playing on each other, and how no one spoke directly to anyone else or made any real demands. This seemed to go quite well, but after a month, Dr. Brisket, ever sensitive to people's resistances, began to realize that it was going *too* well: the Ms, talented and well-intentioned, had figured out the rules of this game and were now succeeding in being good, dutiful, even creative patients without making the slightest real change in their relations, which had always been characterized by a veneer of perfect correctness. They had learned to survive Doctors Freestone and Menschlik, and they were going to learn to survive Dr. Brisket as well. "Too much intellectual bullshit here," snorted the doctor, and he set about to vary his tactics. First he enjoined them from reaching any conclusion or commenting with any insight about their mutual condition. Instead, he assigned them tasks that were to turn their old ways topsy-turvy. Sarah, for example, was made to stop writing poetry and to do the dishes, while Mrs. M had to take up painting, and her husband, who could scarcely recall the color of his wife's eyes, was told to spend an hour a day waiting on her hand and foot. There was some grumbling about the new regimen, which encouraged Dr. Brisket for a while, but the grumbling itself was so good-natured and the tasks carried out too dutifully for his taste. Once again the family seemed headed for a well-oiled and intelligent nonresolution of their problem.

"Stop the music!" Dr. Brisket cried out one day in the fifth month of treatment. "You people are so afraid of change that I could send you all to different planets and your relations would remain the same. I think we have to go much deeper." Stroking his goatee, he explained that unlike his colleagues, he was not satisfied with the therapeutic status quo. In his restless search for a therapy that would break through emotional barriers, he had come upon the teachings of a new, ethological school. According to this doctrine, man's behavior is rooted in deep-set, instinctual animal rhythms. Any therapy that did not touch this profound biological core was like a prescription of gargling for throat cancer. Brisket was not holding to the Freudian doctrine about instincts, which regarded sex and aggression as animal forces within an individual that limited his growth. No, the instincts were *social* and *life giving*: one had to get in touch with them in a setting with other people. Thus, family therapy was still the treatment of choice, but it had to be a deep, biological family treatment. Only by touching her rootedness with her parents could Sarah gain the strength needed for her full development into the wonderful person she was. But they had to go deeper than words or role playing; they had to go all the way back.

Accordingly, when the Ms appeared the following Tuesday, they changed into simple body suits before the session ("to break down the cues without stirring up too much excitement," explained the doctor). The consultation room was dimmed; and in place of the rather severe Danish chairs upon which they had been used to sitting they found mattresses and cushions. Now they were on the floor and, with the doctor hovering above them, formed a ring joined hand to shoulder. And instead of talking, they had to stare at each other. The gaze was the thing. It was eye and body contact, according to Dr. Brisket, that formed the earliest unity of the human bond, and this could be broken into right here and now. The new regimen went as follows: two of them would stare uninterruptedly for twenty minutes at each other, while the third endured his or her separation. Then they would switch roles, so that each family member experienced his or her bondedness as well as separateness in any given hour. All the while they had to breathe deeply and slowly, with particular attention to expiration. The doctor's job was to keep this going—no easy task, considering the massive anxieties stirred up by the novel procedure. But once the giggling stopped and the exasperation wore away, the Ms got down to business and things began to happen.

As Sarah later described it:

Sometime in the third session I began having this woozy feeling. There was a tingling in my fingertips and then my mother's face began to get mushy, you know, as if the features were no longer distinct from each other. I began to feel excited and then mushy myself, looking into her eyes, not knowing whether to cry or to be blissful. Then maybe my mom couldn't take it any more, what was happening, and she began to say something, in that grating, whining way she has, something like, "Why do you look at me like that, dear?" and it wasn't so much the question itself as the way she ended it by calling me "dear" that flipped me. I suddenly felt I could never get anything from her, that I couldn't stand being with her one single instant longer or something awful was going to happen. I started to get up and the doctor tried to stop me and my dad said, with his phony manner, like he was trying to sell me something, "Wait, Sally dear, we're just trying to help you." There it was, the "dear" again, and the fact that it was me who needed help and they were all there just as before, just as complacent and remote and full of shit as ever. The next thing I knew, I was being pulled off my mother. Her glasses had broken and the pocket on her blouse had been ripped, but she wasn't hurt otherwise. My mother's quite a bozo, but I don't know what would have happened to her if they hadn't stopped me. But they only stopped me from killing her physically; I was still besides myself and for the next half-hour went on and on denouncing them however I could for their bullshit values and ways, the box at the opera where they could pretend they were cultured; driving the Mercedes to the synagogue, where they pretended they were religious; and the

five-thousand-dollar burglar alarm at the house, where they pretended
they were safe and free. I really let them have it. It felt great, and after
I got it all out there was even a glow of warmth in me for the first time,
a wish that we could hug, bathe ourselves in tears, and make up. The
doctor was real pleased, too, and said we were finally getting down to
brass tacks. But I could see how hurt they were, even when we tried
hugging at the end of the session. The next week my father suddenly
managed to have a pressing business engagement the day of the appoint-
ment, and my mom and I could hardly go through the motions. Two
weeks later my folks pulled out. To tell the truth, I wasn't half sorry to
see them do it. Funny thing, I felt a little easier with them from that
time on until I left for college. But slowly, over the years, a kind of cold-
ness has set in; and now, except for my mother's occasional visits, I
hardly ever see them. I don't know why; there seems to be nothing there
for me except pain. They would like me to be close, but I can't handle it.

After a distinguished career as an art major in college, Sarah decided to try her luck in the great world of creative media. She worked
in television awhile, then at a family magazine that was inserted as a
supplement to the Sunday newspapers of middle-sized cities nation-
wide. When she grew discouraged at the thought that her work was
appearing anonymously in one or another Springfield, she left the
magazine to find something more expressive of her individuality. But
all she could locate was a job in an advertising agency. Sarah was
learning the unpleasant truth that this world is full of brilliant young
women like herself, and that the path to advancement is by and large
open only to those who are both rapacious of their fellows and sexually complaisant to the men in command. This discovery was a great
blow to Sarah, who until then had expectated that her gifts alone
would act as a lodestar, drawing recognition and reward her way. To
learn that she was not complete in herself was crushing. A certain
integrity prevented her from adapting to the ways of mundane success; at the same time, however, a kind of quiet despair set in, which
she experienced as a depletion of what had always seemed to her an
endless fount of creativity.

Sarah felt hemmed in. Her inward horizon was narrowing while
her outward prospects had shrunk to a narrow cubicle in an advertising agency. When she gazed out the window all Sarah could see
were other young women engaged in similar work in the glass box
across the street; and when she looked down at her desk, all she could
see was the fantasy image of fulfilled, exuberant young femininity she

was helping to engineer for a cigarette ad. There was a beautiful and exotic tropical tree in the lobby of the agency. One day it was gone, and Sarah noticed how the room had been architecturally crafted to contain a well for the placement of just such a tree, one that would maximally enhance its wild and lush character. The next day another gorgeous tree had been put in its place.

So she quit, and tried love. She had a trust fund from her father and doles under the table sufficient to keep her from invading it. After a series of desultory and/or excruciatingly painful relationships, Sarah met a professor of established family, a man much older than she and a world authority on Romance languages. Despite, or perhaps because, of the fact that he reminded her of Mr. Casaubon, the desiccated pedant of *Middlemarch*, Sarah decided to turn all her charms to the end of marrying him. By this time she wanted nothing so much as the security of a genteel life that would allow her to circulate amiably among the intelligentsia of a large university; and her experience with sexuality made the prospect of a celibate marriage as reassuring as bodily rapture had once been enticing. When, however, this illusion faded, too, and her marriage turned to dust, empty formality, and eventually cold separation, Sarah began taking to her bed again, as she had not since the age of eighteen. And it was this turn of events that brought her to me.

O Rose, thou art sick!
The invisible worm,
That flies in the night,
In the howling storm

Has found out thy bed
Of crimson joy;
And his dark secret love
Does thy life destroy.
—WILLIAM BLAKE, *Songs of Experience*

At a certain point quite early in life Sarah began experiencing bodily excitement as anxiety. Undoubtedly, this was an organismic event and was grounded in what Wilhelm Reich called *armoring*,[1] i.e., a kind of mechanization of the body's innate flowingness. But armoring is also a historical event that depends on a person's social function. Sarah's body could be quite supple under certain conditions, such as when she was on the dance floor. Here she was her own object; while subjectively she could identify herself with the others who were watching and admiring her. When, however, actual erotic arousal began, then her body would turn against itself. There would be a mental aspect of this organismic event that might be translatable into words, thus:

> I am no longer me but myself and an Other—and this Other I have become is a menacing, murderous creature. It will kill me if I do not kill it; but I cannot kill it because to do so would be to deprive me of a vital part of myself. I need this Other; I depend upon it; my life-energy is sequestered in it; it is my life itself. My only recourse then is to petrify myself into a dead, mechanical creature, so that my lover does not break into me and open us both to my murderous Otherness. But this means that my lover, or anyone who gets too close to me—this analyst, for example, on whom I am coming to depend—is a menace to me and has to be shunned. And so, in order to preserve myself against a deadly fragmentation, I must become deadly myself and turn into stone.

It took much work on our part to establish this and to trace out concretely what could be surmised on general principles: that the original model of the Other was, to be sure, Sarah's mother; and that the peculiarities that Dr. Freestone had noticed long ago had become enshrined in Sarah's inner experience. The conjunction of two qualities was to weigh especially heavily on the child: that the mother could not let Sarah alone; and that she was not there for Sarah but for an image of herself that she projected onto Sarah and confused with the reality of the child. Such a conjunction is itself based on some very definite historical arrangements as they devolve on the nuclear family. To these we will turn shortly. But for now we should concentrate only on the edge of this massive historical arrangement, which cuts immediately into Sarah's being.

Sarah was almost always physically with her mother. The latter had little else to do and, as we have observed, became panicky when separated from her daughter. The child therefore found herself in the presences—indeed, *omnipresence*—of a person who overwhelmed her, intruded upon her, yet did not recognize her. Had recognition occurred—and had some differentiation, if not separation, taken place as well, then Sarah could have developed a sense of herself that would have been reasonably coherent. A child will form a coherent mental image of a parent who is *there*, consistently yet neither to much nor too little. This image can then be incorporated by the child and will undergo a process of internalization. If matters go well, the child draws substance from the parent, modeling it into its own mental tissue (to be sure, under the influence of a mutually shared culture). It is a kind of alimentation: the parent becomes mental food, a raw material for the child, broken down internally and used as building blocks. If, however, there is "too much" of a parent, the process parallels the experience of swallowing more food than can be digested: some of it remains inside in its original form. And if the parental object inside is the represenation of an actual parent who does not recognize the child, then neither does the internal parent recognize the child. It becomes the kind of Other that could hound a Sarah throughout life, a malignant entity that may be stilled only through a permanent falsification of self-experience—i.e., a splitting into a Sarah who has to continue living out her mother's expectations for her; and a Sarah who, to preserve herself from the intruding mother, refuses to do so. This uneasy balance permanently impedes Sarah in conducting her life and thwarts the realization of her powers; it fails as well to do more than keep the murderous Other at bay. However, it is the best she can do.

Why is the Other murderous? Because desire, thwarted, readily turns to hate, and remains so if the conditions of self-alienation are established; and because Sarah's mother, it must be recognized, had murder in her heart for the child. We can be fairly sure that the mother knew nothing of this, for the love she also bore Sarah mantled the hatred and kept it out of consciousness. Her hatred was a curious amalgam: part carry-over from her own infancy, i.e., a pathogen that mothers transmit to each other across generations of patriarchy; part unconscious hostility born out of her jealousy of Sarah's exalted position and the frustration engendered by her own need for self-suppression; and part conscious irritation at Sarah's very real sullenness, spite, and provocation. The latter element, while "superficial" in one sense, was from a continual spring of poison that seeped downward to irrigate deeper layers of hatred. But the more swollen hatred became, the more it would have to be checked, not by love, which in Sarah's mother's case was a finite and nonrenewable resource, but with cloying attentiveness, omnipresence and fidelity to the rigmarole of child rearing, qualities that in Sarah's milieu were practically inexhaustible.

Checked hatred festers. Sarah and her mother lived locked together in the steamy cage of a modern suburban nuclear family. And where the mother's hatred accumulated to eventually thicken her joints and narrow her arteries, for the child, hatred became the immediate outcome of desire itself and in desire's place flowed into the foundations of the psyche.

In the course of Sarah's extensive indoctrination into Western civilization, she learned to develop the senses; learned, too, that the artist sees through, and not with, the eye, and that she/he maintains the sensuous naïveté of the child. This, however, was one lesson Sarah could never master, for she was never naïve. The defense against her mother induced a preternatural cynicism in the girl, which later would turn to disgust and render impossible the realization of her cultural and genetic gifts. The infant's mind transvalues things and can exaggerate every nuance; details, however insignificant, suppressed by the adult may be magnified many times their original dimensions by the child. The world of the infant is primary, "primitive" in the full, rich sense of the term. This is "infant joy" in Blake's *Songs of Innocence*; and it goes with innocence, which is not freedom from sin but the capacity to preserve the integrity of the primitive zone of experience. The child must be able to live her/his life, with its own categories of experience. It is for the parent to make that zone safe and not to violate it. Physical safety is entailed, but equally, acceptance and a kind of animate dialogue responsive to the infant's experience. The parent who spontaneously engages in "baby-talk" or mimics the infant is recognizing this need for innocence.

Sarah was never innocent in this sense, and correspondingly scarcely ever felt safe. Parental presence was not acceptance but intrusion, and the dialogue drew itself from the estranged world of behavioral expertise that supported the immensity of Sarah's upbringing. The immediacy of parent-child contact being too threatening, intermediaries from the class of mental managers who parasitically feed on the bourgeois family were called in. But all the king's horses and all the king's men couldn't put little Sarah together again, so long as she was concretely in the presence of the sources of her Otherness. Without innocence, the best-intentioned, most artful intermediary becomes another focus of estrangement. And so Sarah's consciousness, instead of playing freely in the field of primary experience, became prematurely watchful, shrewd, calculating. She was aided in this by a rich diet of television, for whose images the child showed a proclivity remarkable even in these times. The family had four sets—to forestall quarrels—and there was something ineffably soothing to Sarah in the contained and tightly administered images that regularly appeared on them. The television seemed to fill a gap, or hollow, in her intensely cultivated life. And her mind itself began to conform to its rhythms. In sum, Sarah was becoming bound into capitalist rationality. She watched, both outwardly and inwardly, looking for the eruption of her malignant Other; and, at the same time, she became closed and emotionally withered. A dense cloud of self-consciousness shadowed the girl, while the sensuous circumference of the self, its body, became a minefield that had to be fenced off from the world. So it is that a childhood spent without visible marks of trauma—a childhood, moreover, in which all the riches of a great civilization could be brought to bear on the cultivation of an individual—could eventuate in a subjectivity consumed with disgust, despair, and endless self-preoccupation.

In their restless striving to be *au courant*, Sarah's parents attended a workshop in sexual liberation given at the local community center. Here the latest behaviors designed to remove lingering puritanical stains on a healthy eroticism were instilled in the family. Sarah was provided with contraception at age thirteen; and her parents were careful to provide her and her boyfriends with plenty of leeway, as well as isolated, comfortable space, to engage in whatever experimentation their healthy young bodies could concoct. Yet, for all the manifest relaxation about sexuality, Sarah was never able to attain either gratification or intimacy. What the engineers of sexual liberation had omitted was the presence of a split-off set of fantasies that were in every sense libidinal yet were not to be immediately appeased by any real event. They arose from Sarah's earliest days and were among the most basic imaginative configurations of desire: the means by which desire pressed toward realization as it clothed itself in the human body. The fantasies were historical, no less than the family's pathetic attempt to seek an administered freedom; and the two histories intersected, the public one seizing the stage and driving the repudiated private fantasies deeper into a hidden precinct of desire. Thus, the sought-for lack of "hang-up" concerning the erotic was real, but its reality was partial and forced the alternate reality of desire into a deeper state of repression; i.e., it rendered it more twisted and fantastic, more suffused with hatred, indeed, part of the Other that haunted Sarah. Her grandparents, who would have been horribly mortified by the liberal atmosphere of Sarah's sexuality, had, for all their limits, an easier time of it. Eros, though heavily repressed, was not driven so deep, nor did Otherness penetrate so far into their existence.

For Sarah, the public aspect of eroticism was affected little by this split-off reality, which was too banal in any case for her to establish symbolic contact with it. Therefore, she could *do* anything she wanted; and, like others exposed to the open climate of sexuality in late capitalism, she found excitement aplenty. However, her future attempts to find love and genuine gratification, being states in which the totality of a person must become involved, were disastrously affected.

What was the configuration of this deeper stratum of desire? During her analytic sessions with seven-year-old Sarah, Dr. Freestone had learned that Sarah's headaches were indeed suggested and therefore inserted by the mother, as the latter's behavior during the initital visit had indicated. But she learned more than that: to the child, there was a fantasy concerning this insertion, that of a maternal phallus, which had become a specific, potent form taken by Sarah's Other. And from the standpoint of desire, she herself could become that phallus by incorporation. The headaches were therefore her drawing inward of the phallus, her suffering from it, her destruction of it, and her self-punishment for that destruction. The sensation of swelling during the recital at age fourteen was based on a similar fantasy —and the disastrous consequences, a similar punishment.

That this complex would play a destructive role in her later sexual life can readily be imagined. But what is essential to emphasize here is less the particular contours of any given phase of Sarah's sexuality than the quality common to all of them, and the outcome to which all her phases were led. As did many people from sophisticated urban settings, Sarah went through many sexualities, using at times either gender as object, now promiscuous, now celibate, now frankly experimental. The common feature of all her phases, namely, their lack of gratification, was predicated not on any quality of any sexual act itself but on an enduring inner state that she brought to all of them. There is no doubt that her inner state included what psychoanalysis has described as a castration complex, manifest here as a fantasy of destroying the phallus and at the same time becoming it. Nor can there be any question that such a complex would obstruct any loving relation, at least with men. However, the castration complex itself does not account for Sarah's particularly ungratifying experience with sexuality. A more diffuse state of affairs obtains as well and is crucial. There is also a major element of *undifferentiation* in Sarah's sexuality. No particular "organ sexuality," be it oral, anal, or phallic, can be invoked to account for this. For all stages of sexuality, all organizations, that is, of an erotic drive, require, as Freud discerned, some definite notion of the *object* of that drive.[2] The object is preserved in the algebra of sexuality; however much it is transformed, and though it may appear to have been destroyed, it always reappears somewhere in the equation. For Sarah, however, the object begins to lose its quality. The very prominence of the phallus in some of her fantasies is defensive—a heightened inscription to conceal an underlying dissolution. Her real problem is that the objects themselves dissolve and become reconstituted along the lines of Sarah's Other; in other words, they became estranged from her. The object quality in general tends to disappear in Sarah's experience; what stands forth instead is an overall subjectification manifest as self-preoccupation, a lack of spontaneity, an inability to freely give, or to affirm social projects. The self, consumed by attention to its Other, cannot be creative with others. This loss of the object-quality is not what we see in psychosis, which is characterized by a loss of the object-world. For the psychotic, objects are drawn into the self, which then shatters, destroying its contained objects along with itself. Sarah's self-experience, however, remains basically intact with respect to phenomenal reality: she knows what belongs to her zone of subjectivity and what is outside it; she knows, that is, the distinction between thought-reality and fact-reality. Objects, then, are drawn into Sarah's self-system but collect in the Other, where they remain intact; Sarah can therefore go her way in the world, working as political economy demands, bartering her charms in a marital contract, and generally moving quite acceptably in society, for all her misery and desolation. But as she does so, the objects of her desire are shrouded and rendered undifferentiated by their absorption into her monstrous Other, leaving her self sick, swollen beyond proportion, yet weak, the way dystrophic muscles grow large to compensate futilely for their essential weakness.

We have come around to considering a term that has been avoided so far in order that it be kept well clear of the fetishism certain schools of psychoanalysis have imposed on it[3]: *narcissism*. Sarah is, if we are to reduce it to one "diagnostic" word, narcissistic; or, to be more technical yet, Sarah suffers from "pathological narcissism." Our intention in delaying its disclosure so long is to indicate that Sarah suffers not "narcissism" but from a life led in late-capitalist society, one that chooses a certain kind of sickened narcissism to be its subjective signification.

Psychoanalytic students of pathological narcissism, struck by its undoubtedly increasing prevalence in clinical practice, have observed that it is a disorder that somehow fits into the order of things, specifically, that many who suffer from it may also function rather well in the world.[4] For example, during the time Sarah worked in the advertising industry, she in fact functioned quite well; and those aspects of her that we regard as narcissistic—her suspicious watchfulness, for example, or her capacity for distance, or especially her alienated contact with her desire as Other—were perfectly tooled for the production of advertisements. We cannot delve further into this matter until a later chapter has established some of the peculiar conditions that obtain in types of bureaucratic organizations where the narcissistic personality flourishes. But the basic point needs assertion now: that what is loosely called mental illness always fits into the order of things, and that different historical epochs will select different pathologies wherein their characteristic form of domination may be reproduced on intrapsychic soil. And pathological narcissism is a leading candidate for the archetypical emotional disorder of late capitalism.[5]

We may define "narcissism" variously, for it has different aspects. Two definitions spring to mind immediately: (1) the investment of desire in the self (including desire as hatred); and, (2) from a more structural standpoint, the process by which the self receives value from its Other. Viewed from another angle, then, we regard the self and its Other as differing points of configuration in a narcissistic organization: the self being the internal organization of subjectivity, tending always to have a predominant identity; the Other being the shadow side of the self, that which does not belong to the dominant self-organization yet has self-feeling projected into it. Being in the shadows, the form of self-feeling inherent in the Other has the quality of desire, resulting in the tension and negativity inherent in narcissism. It remains to be added that qualities of the Other may also be projected outside the self. Therefore, there are a myriad of particular forms by which narcissism may be manifest, from relations of the self to the outside, as in matters of vanity, pride, "egoism," self-adornment, and so forth, to those in which the self relates to part of itself as Other, for example, self-regard, ideals, goals, and, indeed, values themselves, including moral ones. In all these instances, some form of desire appears in a quality of self-experience; and in all such experiences, the self receives its value in a structured way.

Narcissism clearly has its transhistorical side. When Sarah stares at herself in the mirror, or when her mother invests so much pride and aspiration, we are witnessing something timeless: "Mirror, Mirror on the wall." And when one further considers the role of narcissism in human folly down through the ages, from Caesar to secretaries of state, it is impossible to avoid the conclusion that something very powerful but of an essentially recurrent nature is at play. What, then, is *historically specific* about the narcissism of Sarah? Or, to put it more generally, why does the question of pathological narcissism loom so large in late capitalism, and hence in contemporary psycho-analytic discourse? To examine this matter, we need to look more closely at what transpired in Sarah's analysis, for psychoanalysis, whatever its clinical merits, is an unparalleled instrument for illumi-nating the more shrouded regions of subjectivity.

A session with Sarah seems like a week in the Arctic. There is winter in her soul, and a cold dry wind blows from the couch to my chair. If, as analyst, I must empty myself out to become a vessel for the reception of Sarah's desire, then in working with her I experience myself as empty, too, save for that wind.

I am writing of transference, for the description of that metaphor is a necessary recourse. Transference is known intersubjectively, with the analyst in the role of Other to the patient's self. It is what emerges once one listens long enough to allow desire to break down the screen of ordinary language into more elementary particles; and these par-ticles serve to refract desire into the configuration specific to each individual. Sarah's transference is not contained in the particulars of any utterance, nor in any remembrances. It is rather, as Freud de-scribed, the past *repeated*, not holistically or exactly, but as evoked by the conditions of the present, i.e., the analytic relationship.[6] When Sarah looks straight through me at the beginning and end of a session; when her voice takes on the quality of a listless monotone, so different from its usual musicality; when my ostensibly helpful interventions meet with scorn and derision; when I feel myself so often alone in the room or talking to a masked dummy; when Sarah goes to sleep or falls silent for twenty minutes at a time; or when, in general, she talks *at* me, as though I were a thing, or at best a mirror to her, and not *to* me, the way one does to another person, then transference is happen-ing to us.

Transference is layered, and what we are observing here is only the

surface of Sarah's Other, that which is immediately behind the socially presented self. It is the first inner line of subjectivity and the
contour of Sarah's defensive organization, protecting her from the
more malign, murderous, deeper Other, which we have reconstructed
as a composite of mother's invading phallus and Sarah's own ravening
condition of emptiness. And to her eyes the cold hollowness is also a
defense for me, a means of keeping me away from the malignity inside
her lest I, too, upon whom she is coming to depend, succumb to it.

Contemporary narcissism has taken the form of an empty vessel,
shaped by the specific historical conditions of family and society into
which Sarah is thrown. This history has the curious property to be
forgotten and ignored by those who live it out. Just as the peculiarities
of Sarah's family are no accident, as we shall see in the next chapter,
so was it no accident that at no time during the extensive "management" of Sarah's case was the issue referred to a stage wider than that
of the family itself and the individuals within it. This was true of Dr.
Freestone, an exemplary individual who undoubtedly did the child
Sarah much good; as well as of Dr. Brisket, whose important insights
into organismic roots were rendered puerile by his inability to ground
the organism in society. It seems as if bourgeois psychology has been
constructed to help reproduce a family structure that appears freestanding, separate from history, and sufficient unto itself. As a result,
individuals are blamed for not fulfilling their personal duties when, in
fact, these duties are constructed so as to be internally inconsistent
and incapable of fulfillment. Contemporary psychoanalytic discourse
falls willy-nilly into the trap of blaming parents and, specifically, the
mother, for failures in socialization; indeed, it is quite possible to read
our account of Sarah in this way, for it, too, has had to be constructed
out of the existing materials of discourse.

Would it not be just as correct, however, and as limited, to say that
Sarah suffers from a neurosis of *consumption,* just as we might have
accounted for Curtis's troubles as a neurosis of *production*? Are not
her problems those of someone who is made into a passive object—
and here the image of vessel acquires an additional level of meaning
—distended and weakened by having all the so-called goods of
commodity society poured into it? And are not Curtis's problems
those that must befall someone who blindly participates in capitalist
production? Are they not signified by that mode of production?
Should Curtis's and Sarah's parents be blamed for producing authentic individuals of our time?

106

There is an additional feature of Sarah's analysis that deserves mention before we go on to consider her family in its wider perspective. One has to wait in analysis; such is a hallmark of the therapy. As I was told during my training, the analyst has all the time in the world, which is to say that she/he works with those who have command over time, and money. In any event, once such conditions of work are established, one becomes privileged to partake of an order of temporality radically distinct from the ordered clock-time of production. It may be that the narcissistic character affords a particularly good vantage for the experience. Often with Sarah, and in consequence of the fact that she structures herself along the lines of an empty vessel, I would become aware of another kind of time that, so to speak, seeped through the interstices of our experience together. Where public time is linear, rigidly segmented and bound according to the equation with money, i.e., where it is time under the servitude of capital—this alternate time appears *unbound*: moments drift by while one is entirely awake, without any awareness of their elapse. It is as if the hollowness of Sarah's subjectivity, into which she blows her cold wind of warning, could also contain a different clime, an aimless drifting of time, a time that meanders, lapses, starts up again, sometimes circles round about itself, and lazes right up to the end of the session, which arrives with a jolting start, as if to remind us of the world of hard necessity that encircles us. Is this a dialectical counterpoise of the cold wind, a negation and, more significantly, a liberatory moment of narcissism? Does narcissism contain a movement of resistance to capital, along with its obvious character of acquiescence? This must be so, inasmuch as capital has arrogated to itself so much sensuous human power behind the lifeless fetish of the money-form. Whatever, it seems to me that any real movement of liberation must appropriate some of this unbound temporality if it is not to recapitulate the existing mode of domination.

It was while working with Sarah that I first became aware that Freud's insight into the "timelessness" of the unconscious might have a referent in actual experience, and so in real history.

8

DESIRE AND THE FAMILY

If we stand back from psychology a moment, we will see that Sarah's neurosis occupies but one point in an immense network of historical exchange. To say that she has a "neurosis of consumption" means more than that she was raised in a milieu saturated with commodities; it indicates as well that human relations are dominated by the logic of commodities. Consumption is also production; and what gets produced are not just objects for sale, but people. In Sarah's case, some of this is obvious; after all, such parental concern can aptly be called an investment when it is so palpably determined by the need to have a daughter whose glitter can help light the parents' way through the bourgeois community.

But there is more to the matter. There is significance to the fact that the grandfather who broke with his son and became forgotten was the garment worker whose labor created commodities, while the shopkeeper who sold those commodities and realized some of the surplus value extracted out of that labor became lionized as the founder of the family's wealth. The planes of cleavage according to which historical relationships are played out also determine lines of psychological value. Therefore, it is important to note that the seed capital turned over to Sarah's father became multiplied many times over in the sale of automobiles, while the surplus extracted out of that process was what was plowed back into the nurturing of poor Sarah. These relations would in fact be trivial if kept at the level of money or commodity viewed as pure object. In reality, however, desire enters into the processes of political economy at every point, albeit in a hidden way. Money under capitalism does not occur without the binding of time; and time bound, when viewed from the standpoint of living people, is created historically with its dialectical negation, time unbound. It remains to clarify how this takes place. However, some notion may be suggested if we consider the relationship between the bound time of the workplace; the surplus time (contained in the money-form) accruing to the man who controls the making and selling of clothes or automobiles; the conversion of that money-time into the goods, services, and education of little Sarah (including, to be sure, her extensive medical-psychiatric care: a productive outcome of her neurosis); and finally, the emergence of the negative of this time in the limitlessness and objectlessness of Sarah's desire. The time bound at the workplace reappears in unbound form within the ana-lytic transference, where it seeks new forms of connection (and is, of course, bound again into the analyst's fee, such being the general economic movement of the mental-health industry, as we shall ex-plore later). We hypothesize a liberatory moment to unbound time but remember ruefully that it is a negative without practical orienta-tion, that it flaunts the bourgeois clock from behind the bars of its cage of neurosis, and that it is glimpsed only under the exceedingly artificial, hothouse conditions of analysis.

So, too, do the other elements of Sarah's condition take their place in this scheme of things. The women who flutter over Sarah and instill a self-contradictory identity into her are themselves parasitical upon the productive order monopolized by the father. The social weakness, i.e., productive irrelevance, of Sarah's mother make her a ridiculous figure from one angle. From another, however, her public weakness is an essential condition for the monstrous position she occupies psycho-logically. The enormity of her influence over Sarah is negatively related to the accumulated frustrations induced by her powerlessness in a male-dominated world. The mother, therefore, becomes the mediator through whose influence bound time is converted into the unbound form.

The Otherness that haunts Sarah as the mark of her self-estrangement bears a notable relation to the totality. As the trace in Sarah of her indigestible mother, it represents the conjugation of a failed *per-sonal* relationship with an inflamed desire. But it is also the trace of a broken promise and a failed *historical* relationship, that of the bour-geois family, as played out by the female side of the human race. Inner and outer estrangements do not exist without each other; nor, however, are they related in a direct way, any more than bound and unbound time are directly related. To examine their relationship requires a look at the history of which Sarah's case has been a recapitulation: that of the family under capitalism.

Capitalism did not create difficulties for the family. The entire chronicle of class society has been one of a continual struggle between family—which represents, in its multiplicity of forms, the totality of social organization in primitive cultures—and the state, which introduces a superordinate form of authority and social regulation. States have always grown through the colonization of the family, and at its expense. However, for all that the problems of the family do not originate under capitalism, a new order of contradiction does, and stamps itself upon the individuality of the modern age.

The history of the family can never be recounted with the clarity of, say, the history of an army general staff. While the reasons for this are to some extent obvious, they deserve a slight elaboration. It comes down to this: generals, kings, church councils, et cetera, are *instituted* creations of society and therefore enter the stage in a discrete, documentable form. They are made, so to speak, by people who have their eye on monuments and history books. But the family is an informal, spontaneous, and mass-based arrangement. While the family is in every sense a historical creature—and, in my opinion, is more crucial to study than the exploits of individual generals—it is also more rooted in the transhistorical than any other agency of society, and more the setting of desire. Up to this point at least, people have had no choice in the matter: our biological dependency, born of infantile helplessness, has made it necessary for every person who has ever lived to undergo a substantial portion of life in a family. And this "natural" arrangement, which no doubt stems from the gregarious habits of great apes, also became the original setting for economic and political organization. The state knocked the pins out from under the latter function but left the former one relatively undisturbed. Even though the class structure of statist society was one in which the means of production, notably land, was owned by one small portion of society, nonetheless production itself was mainly carried out locally. Though the circumstances were sufficiently intricate, varied widely from region to region and across nations, and underwent a slow but definite historical development, it is a fairly safe generalization to say that up until about two hundred years ago the great mass of people in the Western world did not experience any sharp distinction between domestic and productive life. This is not to say that production was strictly carried out at home or that the individual domestic hearth was the center of social existence. Far from it: as a general rule, the individual domestic hearth simply did not matter all that much. The lack of sharp distinction between domesticity and productivity meant just that, a blurring in which the particular qualities of each setting were not highly developed. There were no workplaces with clocks to punch and carefully painted pale green walls; and there were no suburbs cut off from production with those individually developed palaces for personal life we call homes. There was little privacy and little attention paid to children as such. The entire notion of individuality was far more weakly inscribed into culture. There were no self-help books, no parent-effectiveness manuals, and no taxpayer identification numbers for the central computers, either. Nor was there commuting to work, worker discipline, or a culture of the workplace. In the place of these highly developed fission products stood their forebear, the local community, an informally developed yet rock-hard fusion of mores, and the setting and superintendent alike of work, culture, sexuality, procreation, child rearing, and death.

It would be well not to sentimentalize about the ways of this "world we have lost." Allowing for the haziness of historical evidence (a difficulty that becomes progressively more serious as the more intimate and subjective side of things is approached), what we know of the life conducted in these settings is not likely to stir envy in the breasts of contemporary readers. I do not wish to give the impression that the masses of yesteryear were incapable of intimacy or devotion. However, it would seem that the traditional community of the West provided Thomas Hobbes with evidence for his false speculation concerning life in pre-civil society, namely, that it was "nasty, brutish, and short." Certainly the statistics on infant mortality and the fairly pervasive evidence of infant brutalization makes the flesh crawl.[1] Perhaps there were some Arcadian exceptions. If so, they must have been especially lucky as well as resourceful, for the cards were stacked against them. The traditional Western community could scarcely have approximated the dignity and freedom of primitive society, however problematic this might have been[2] for the simple reason that the West had groaned under the burden of class oppression since the conquests of Caesar. The shadow of the noble, the landlord, and the priest hung over traditional society, and within it, bitter scarcity and endemic disease permeated everyday life.

Enter capitalism, which, in order to make a market of the world, needed first of all to create a mass of wage laborers, propertyless and mobile. While we know that, by and large, this process required violent expropriation (owing in part to the rocklike conservatism of the local community), it does not take much imagination to grasp that the culture of capitalism, dangling the twin prizes of material plenty and personal mobility, could also serve as a powerful magnet (as it still does to peasantries around the world). In any case, capital's world-historical function has been to smash the traditional ways and to erect radically new conditions for personal life.

From this standpoint the essence of capitalism takes on a slightly different appearance. Where class society as such merely severed political functions from the archaic family, capitalism went one decisive step further: it removed the economic functions as well. The reason is simple if twofold: if work is done at home, then nobody is available to do the large-scale wage labor out of which capital is extracted; and if products are made there, why would anyone need to buy commodities on the market? Characteristically, capitalism severs a unity between activity (work) and its outcome (product), which had been functionally united in the local community; it assigns to one the sphere of wage production and to the other commodity consumption, and removes both elements from the personal control in which the original process had been embedded. If the hallmark of capitalism is the primacy of the economic dimension, we now recognize that an absolutely essential condition of this is that the economy be wrenched from its previous domestic location. If people traditionally experience no sharp distinction between domestic and productive life, under capitalism such a distinction became a ruling feature of their whole existence. It is no exaggeration to claim that this distinction is the single most historically important feature of the entire modern era so far as personal life goes.

The point bears further emphasis, for it underlies the peculiar features of both economic and personal life under the conditions of capitalism. The splitting between production and domestic life is not a simple partition. Rather, it is one of those historical sunderings that drastically affect the character of its products by having each incorporate the shadow of the other. It is helpful to invoke here Marx's notion of the fetishism of commodities:[3] commodities are not simple products of exchange but products endowed with a mysterious power that originates in the active labor abstracted out of production and alienated into capital. So with the economic sphere as a whole. This too is fetishized to the extent that seemingly impersonal economic activity is abstracted out of the rhythms and relationships of domestic life. The efficient factory, the rationalized office, in which every manifestation of what is informal, spontaneous, or emotional is ruthlessly suppressed, is in reality a seedbed of fantasy. The secretary daydreaming over her typewriter is only at the manifest tip of the process—which, it is important to note, must be kept under control to ensure productivity, and is shored up by an immense cultural industry whose products—for example, Muzak or pulp magazines (kept hidden in her desk)—invade the workplace. But as with other attempts at administered rationalization, the attempt to manage fantasy at the workplace only pushes the edges of fantasy farther back, makes it more diffuse, and casts upon production a mystique that goes far beyond its brute economic significance. Desire thwarted and made unrealizable in a sphere of vital activity lends that sphere a mysterious power, a power of checked yearning.

And what happened to the family proper under the conditions of capitalist estrangement? Here, too, a remarkable development ensued, which can only be grasped as the outcome of radically opposed tendencies. This can be plotted in the fairly abrupt shifts that took place toward the close of the eighteenth century (i.e., with the consolidation of industrial capitalism) in two elementary areas of personal life: sexuality and child rearing.

As Edward Shorter has documented in his *The Making of the Modern Family*,[4] on the basis of a large body of investigation concerning most countries of the Western world, an upsurge of sexual and romantic activity in general occurred during this period, reflective of increased personal mobility and the decline of the local community as a conservative force controlling personal life. The findings, though difficult to interpret, nonetheless point toward a "first sexual revolution" concurrent with the rise to hegemony of capitalism. Capital, by removing productive functions from local village and domestic life, served to delegitimize the ancient modes of control as nothing else could. The effect was similar to, if less extreme than, that of Yankee imperialism on native American populations. But in the metropolitan region the destruction was only partial and accompanied by a liberatory movement typical of capital in its earlier phase. Peasants leaving the land were headed for an obscure future in which most would be crushed and some would prosper, but in which all would be exposed to a relatively liberated climate of sexuality and the expression of personal feeling. The change was particularly decisive for workers and women: for workers, sexuality signified their rising potential as a class-for-itself and could be correlated, I should think, with the upsurge in revolutionary activity that characterized the close of the eighteenth century; while for women, the new personal freedom signaled the gathering senescence of the patriarchal yoke, which had oppressed them since the dawn of state-run societies. From this time forward, capital, by enhancing the potency of the individual, would set the individual against traditional family arrangements no less than the worker against the capitalist. Since these traditional arrangements had been centered about a patriarchal suppression of women, the new order would be in some measure defined by the release of female individuality, manifest in both workplace and home. We need not detail the extreme complexity of this process, played out over two centuries. However, an inner dynamic was laid down at the beginning. A woman whose activity could be sold for wages was no longer a creature to be exchanged, complete with dowry, so that the traditional family could maintain itself. Indeed, she could potentially see herself not as an object at all but as a subject who could decide her own destiny, including choice of mate. She was not yet a free woman but a freer one, a Jane Eyre, for example, someone whose productive capacity and sexuality began to matter.

The sexual upsurge, though not confined to workers, was first centered in them, and only recently has overtaken the bourgeoisie. The propertied classes, like all who have something to lose, for long remained relatively more inhibited in their sexual desires. For them the historical awakening took place at another decisive point: the care of children. As Philipe Ariès was first to document, and as many others have shown since, one of the more remarkable and fundamental shifts that has characterized the rise of the modern West has been a continually increasing degree of care given to children.[5] Through the mid-eighteenth century, young children were, if not an ignored burden, little more than a crude source of income for indifferent and otherwise unemployable wet nurses. Mortality and neglect went hand in hand in those years: it seems as if the category *child* did not exist as a distinct sphere of life and certainly not as a tender, vulnerable creature to be nurtured and protected. Again the revolution struck, this time breaking on those classes who had property to pass on to children and resources, including, decisively, *time*, to expend on their behalf. Here is where the unbound time created as a fission product of capitalist production passed into the hands and minds of its masters. A wave of sentiment struck child rearing and has yet to spend its energy. From *Emile* to *Parent Effectiveness Training*, the attention of the West has become centered on children. Freud, with his "discovery" of infantile sexuality, represents the attainment of a heightened degree of consciousness turned toward a historical process that preceded him in its origins and has swept beyond him toward its uncertain conclusion. Children expressed the new individuality of the West. Moreover, they were the adornment of classes who had extracted enough time from the labor of others to reinvest in the rearing of young. Later, as machinery (which developed *pari passu* with the accumulation of capital) freed up a certain degree of proletarian time (never as much as that made available to the bourgeoisie), the families of workers, too, became focused on child rearing. Meanwhile, the children produced under the new order were drawn into the rhythms of capital. When the need for living human labor was great (a need that peaked early in the nineteenth century), children—like women—were swept into the work force. And when this need subsided—the result of the machine-driven autonomy of production—children, again with women, were swept out of the work force and reserved for the socially necessary (for the circulation of capital, that is) task of commodity consumption.

For all the complexity of the process, its regional and temporal variations and as yet unexplored recesses, a fairly definite historical generalization may be extracted out of the impression made by capital on family life. This may be stated as follows: where in precapitalist times the community was the locus of a relatively undifferentiated productive and domestic life, capitalism created, as dialectical counterpoises to each other, the *workplace* as the location for productive life and the *nuclear family* as that for domestic existence.

The nuclear family, we have come to recognize, is no God-given arrangement. What is becoming clearer, however, is that neither is it a historical accident nor the creation of some free-floating sentiment, but the precise and conflict-ridden creation of the golden age of capitalist society. The nuclear family is not an older extended-family structure reduced to its core and stripped of productive functions. (In fact, within the traditional community, people generally lived in small households and not in a truly extended family.) Rather, it is the outcome of new human needs and capacities, and respondent to new forms of human distress, all characteristic of the age of capital. If it expresses the new need and capacity for intimacy and tenderness on a mass scale, it also expresses the new alienation and loneliness attendant upon the replacement of older mores with the relations of capitalism. Indeed, the intimacy of the nuclear family, which above all is an affectionate arrangement marked by radically enhanced attachments toward a decisively smaller number of immediate kin, must be seen in its multifaceted historical contradictoriness if it is to be understood at all. The family under capitalism is like the individual under capitalism: a creature split into greater strength and greater weakness than that which went before, and a stunted, shriveled creature compared to what it could become in a society where people can freely appropriate their own powers. The strength derives from the new power of individuality, mediated by sexual desire and the care of children. The weakness, which has lent desire an edge of impossible longing, is not simply the loss of the traditional community and its spontaneous culture; it is more essentially the freezing of human capacities under the conditions of capitalist production, a stunting that, combined with the loss of old ways and powers, thrusts an impossible burden upon the emotional support provided by the nuclear family.

We are not describing here simply the loss of power suffered at the workplace but something much more pervasive and densely mediated in everyday life. The workplace situation is real enough, and in a sense, paradigmatic of the whole, but it does not encompass capitalist alienation of public life. If it were the whole—if, in other words, the only thing that mattered was that the worker, sensing the alienation of his power at the workplace, came home to put an excessive burden on his wife—then we would have a serious situation, perhaps a maddening one, but we would not have something that stamped its mark not upon a whole civilization but only upon an unfortunate and historically strategic fraction of wage laborers. The problem manifests itself not at the workplace as such but in the interlocking social arrangements necessary so that the workplace can arise and be sustained. In sum, the problem is one of a *culture* necessary for the *economization of reality*: a set of practices essential so that the world becomes a market out of which commodities can be made and in which labor-power itself becomes a commodity, a world of linear clock-time and orthogonal space, a world in which nature is divorced from man and men from human nature, a world of objects split off from an empty subject and of a subject that sees itself split into an ethereal soul and a vacuous thing. It is possible to trace in the development of each of the crucial institutional spheres of society—in law, education, architecture and city-planning, religion, scientific practice itself, and, of course, medicine and psychiatry—a concrete historical struggle wherein the dominant form (dominant because of the dominance of capital) worked to reproduce the economization of reality. To do so here, however, would distract us from the overriding point: that these arrangements intersect and converge to create a social reality in which public existence in ruthlessly objectified, i.e., depersonalized. Into this vacuous personal space steps a creature with increased needs and capacities, born of the stimulating effects of capitalist production on personal life. No matter where this creature turns, the needs will not be gratified, the capacities will be underutilized. True, public life whether at the workplace or in school or elsewhere, may be in some respects absolutely enriched compared to the level of two hundred years ago (in numerous respects, for example, in its level of craft required in ordinary production, or in community participation, it may as well be said to be impoverished, but we may set these aside for now inasmuch as they strengthen the argument but obscure it as well), but it is nowhere enriched, except in purely accidental exceptions, to the level of demand created by the development of the personal sphere. This is because, to repeat, the iron requirement of capital for a depersonalized world is the other side of the growth of that personal sphere. The two movements are fission products from the same nucleus, flying apart yet reacting on each other to keep the splitting going. They are not only opposed but mutually constitutive as well.

Under capitalism, an enhanced individuality encounters a deadened public world. The supports of the traditional community are gone, leaving in their wake those afforded by two children of capitalism: the nuclear family, a micropersonal decomposition product of the older community; and the bourgeois state, a macro-impersonal regulatory order of society as a whole. The state, as we shall see, has a lot to do with the eventual outcome, but at this point in our arugment it may be set aside, for the evident reason of its sheer impersonality. The burden, then, of overcoming the general depersonalization of public life in the face of increased personal potentialities falls to the family, or better, falls *on* the family, squashing it and eventually causing it to rupture. Before this crisis—which now is everywhere before us—took place, however, the family lit up under the pressure to which it was subjected and suffused Western society in a glow of sentimentality: as the title of Christopher Lasch's recent book put it, the family became "haven in a heartless world."[6] Through the nineteenth century and well into the twentieth, family virtue and emotional support were trumpeted throughout an entire civilization as a fountain, indeed a cornucopia, of goodness and the capstone of the material progress made possible by capitalism and its faithful servant, technology.

Before continuing to explore the inevitable contradictions to which the family as a whole has been subjected, it is essential to briefly consider those experienced by the women within it, who were to become identified with the family's power as such. Recall that the revolution in personal life centered upon women. Through the notion of economic individuality, the great mass of women begin to break out of the prison of precapitalist society. But if it was the fate of this revolution to fly off in the two opposed directions of productivity and domesticity, it has been the peculiar destiny of women to become identified with *both* of these trends: with wage productivity as a means to social power, and with domesticity as the maturation of their traditionally defined role as a childbearer and rearer.

And women have been torn by this historical destiny or, to be more exact, by what capitalism made of each of these potentialities. We have already observed that the impersonality of the public sphere as a whole excessively burdens the nuclear family with emotional support functions. That this burden fell almost entirely upon women is common knowledge; but to the explanation that women were "chosen" for their nurturant role because of their historical role should be added a peculiarity of the capitalist mode of production. Wage labor, which admittedly forms one angle in the pathway out of feudal stagnation, turned out in reality to be not only oppressive in its own right but relatively unavailable as well. As Marx documents thoroughly in *Capital*, and as we know from bitter experience, the workings of the capitalist economy as a whole mandate a degree of structural unemployment among the working class. In concrete reality this means one thing: as the need for labor declines, women (and children) are the first forced out of the work force and back into the home. No doubt, the expendability of women resulted from pre-existing attitudes according to which they were considered the weaker in matters of the world; but there is no doubt as well that the forcing of women out of the work force in the nineteenth century was the particular mode shown by the history of the time to perpetuate the myth of female inferiority. In any case, the actual history of capitalism, as contrasted with its public promise, has been until very recently one of crushed hope for women. Jane Eyre became Emma Bovary. At the apogee of capitalist society, surrounded by gadgets, child-rearing manuals, and fashion catalogues, Sarah and her mother played out the grim game assigned to their gender: pure consumer and reproducer, stripped of extrinsic power, doubly alienated, and a mere caricature of her former productive self, not to speak of what she could become.

As a result of the historical conflicts locked into its structure, the nuclear family becomes from the outset an inexorably contradictory entity. On the surface a necessary bastion of love and security, inwardly it becomes the arena of intense and insoluble struggles. For the emotional demands forced upon the nuclear family in capitalist society cannot be met without sacrificing the very individuality of its members, in particular the mother. In other words, the family's task of emotional sustenance, the result of which is full individuation of its members, is *inherently self-contradictory*. Given the surface need of the family to ensure a feeling of security and to reinforce the ideology of capitalism, these contradictions are driven inward, where they eventuate in a mentality whose rational functions are dominated by the bound time of capitalist production and whose inner emotional life is the preserve of an unbound time that is the reflection of a particular type of childhood. Such a split is not the result of an immortal opposition within human nature between "ego" and "id." Rather, it is the outcome of a particular historical situation in which a mutually alienated family and workplace squeeze desire and human capacities a certain way. Indeed, the very usage of the terms "ego" and "id," and the fate to which they have been subjected by psychoanalysis and the mental-health industries in general, is itself part of that history.

Mental-health trades are ordained to rise in a society dominated by so basic a contradiction in personal life. Without detailing the pathways, it should be obvious by now that the opposition of bound and unbound time in the individual will saturate the social order with neurosis and other forms of mental crippling that mock capital's promises of personal well-being. And as capitalism moves to its contemporary stage, the crisis of the family and of personal life in general sees to it that the pursuit of mental health reaches truly industrial proportions.

The great army of mental-health workers who now practice in the United States—it has been reliably estimated that some time in the 1970s their number surpassed that of policemen[7]—owe their existence therefore to the inability of the nuclear family to perform the socializing tasks it has been handed by capitalist society. One should not take this to mean that the nuclear family is collapsing, as some rash accounts would have it. Such is far from the case, although crushing economic forces (wives now being forced back into the workplace while still having to take care of the home, for example) are steadily shearing the size of its household to the vanishing point. No matter, however, how steeply the divorce rate has risen, remarriage rates keep pace. And as the marriage rate itself remains high, we may safely assume that the family as a bastion of intimacy, the traditional "heart of a heartless world," is very much an alive ideal.

Still, it is not a soundly functioning one, as the divorce rate eloquently testifies, or as can be ascertained by checking the relationship of indifference between adolescents and parents. Although still a prime hope for intimacy and personal security, the family is pretty much decrepit so far as the transmission of values is concerned, while its intimacy becomes all too often either inadequate or, as in the case of Sarah, unbearable. The result is mental disturbance of one kind or another. Since the family, shorn of productive functions and swollen by commodity consumption, can no longer regulate itself, the disturbances it generates become fodder for the mental-health trades. The mental-health professions function then as bilge pumps for the leaky vessel that is the nuclear family. At the same time, they feed parasitically from its decay. The ultimate benefactor is the state, which steps in to train the new professions, to regulate them, and to reimburse them as well, and so acquires an invaluable agent with which to extend its control over society. There is nothing new about this doleful development except its extension to the inner life. The process as a whole has been familiar for a century now: the rise of *monopoly* capital and the ascendancy of its peculiar demon, the total administration of society. From a historical viewpoint, then, madness, neurosis, or self-alienation in general is neither more nor less than the ever-expanding negation of administration.

Capital accumulation necessarily drives toward economic concentration. In its course it relentlessly tears up previous modes of production and consumption—including its own—and so transforms personal life at its core. One of its essentially inhuman features is to progressively replace living labor—that of the worker—with dead labor—that of the machine. We are sufficiently familiar with the diminution of human toil, which this development makes possible, and with the increased material power now at our disposal as a result of it. We should be yet more familiar, however, with the enslavement of living workers by dead machines and with the elimination of workers altogether by technological unemployment, for these are the actual, as opposed to the possible, consequences of the automatization of production. And we should be equally cognizant that the *real* aspect of material abundance according to this same ruling class logic is a continually overproduced glut of commodities, the artificially stimulated consumption of which becomes an imperative to ward off collapse.[8]

These various structural features of capitalist society combine to create monopoly capitalism: titanic corporations and an equivalently bloated state apparatus on the societal level, and tightly managed technocratic work, frantic commodity consumption, and administered culture and leisure on the level of everyday life. In the face of these imperatives, previous institutions, including the nuclear family itself, warp and crack, and personal resistance is forced into new channels.

In one sense the nuclear family continues as before, although in an increasingly disastrous direction. The loss of productive function, which characterized its inception, is accelerated in an era when human production in general begins to drop out of the picture of political economy. Instead, the family becomes an island of consumption floating in a sea of commodities, and a ground for the development of new capitalist markets. We must be precise here. The family does not cease to be the location of toil. Indeed, it has been estimated that the contemporary suburban housewife, beset with driving the children to their nature classes or therapists, and surrounded by gadgets that need repairing, puts in as much time at her chores as did her unenlightened counterpart of a century ago. What is changed is the quality of this toil, which becomes less and less regulated by immediate rhythms and personally defined needs, and increasingly subjected to the intrusions of market rationality.

As consumption becomes the personal mandate, children move ever more to the center of the stage. The child loses her/his functionality in the household and becomes a pure consumer, epitomized in our story of Sarah. With this the child-mind in everyone becomes celebrated, as indeed it should be by the managers of society, who are clever enough to sense in the infantile mental organization a possible way out of the crisis instigated by the glut of commodities. However, the child as consumer is in an inherently antagonistic relationship to the parent as provider, so long as the desires of the one are yoked to infantile yearning, while the largesse of the other is bounded by the impoverished reality of capitalism. This antagonism, rooted in the deepest assumptions of capital, is responsible more than any other factor for the schism between generations that afflicts late capitalist society; and in a fundamental way it enters into the kind of emotional disturbance now prevalent.

Despite the onslaught directed against it, the nuclear family continues to be a fountainhead of personal life. The privatization characteristic of the entire capitalist mode of production is anchored there in personal subjectivity itself. The nuclear family provides intense and prolonged contact throughout infancy with one or two adult figures. The floodgates of desire are opened onto them; and since these parents are unable to fulfill the wishes so aroused, a permanent longing for the archaic parental imagos is etched into the structure of character. This unfulfillable desire has three fates in late-capitalist society: a part enters into neurosis and the other forms of self-alienation; another is diverted outward onto the mysterious world of the commodity, whose fetishization in the alienated act of production is consequently fused with deep infantile wishes; and the remainder is expended on the reproduction of the nuclear family itself, i.e., on the search for past gratification, possible or not, in current figures of intimacy, including children. To some extent, of course, this "works"—capitalist society would long since have faded away did it not—but in another real sense it can never work too well lest it cut too deeply into the consumption of commodities or, to be sure, turn out too many people who will not tolerate the existing arrangements.

Capital, therefore, finds it very congenial to cultivate the personal life, and the more so in its monopoly style. So long as matters do not get out of hand, every flourishing of the personal is at the very least a new market, not to mention a provider of legitimacy for the whole system. And self-alienated personal life is all to the good so far as decreased political resistance and increased proclivity for commodity consumption go. Again, a line of self-alienation must be drawn, above which is "normal capitalist restlessness" and below which is neurosis and frank psychosis. The mental-health professionals have been stationed to patrol this boundary no less than their brethren police exist to hold the line against objective criminality.

However, their ministrations are also the intrusions of the society they work to reproduce. As Lasch, and more recently, Jacques Donzelot have demonstrated, the mental-health professional, functioning self-consciously as an individual helping other individuals, and often against the very impersonality of society, is at the same time an instrument of that society or, to be more exact, its state, working to tame that individual and to place him/her under surveillance.[9] Whatever their particular functions, the general historical role of the mental-health trades is to change the family from an informal, spontaneous entity into an administered one. And this is a highly original position. No doubt society has always attempted to control the family, usually through the church. With the mental-health professional of capitalism, however, we have a difference of degree that is also one of kind, for now control becomes bureaucratized and consciously technocratic, and so places the state against desire itself. As a result of this new turn of events, the "neurotic personality of our time" begins typically to take on the shape of pathological narcissism.

Although the nuclear family never existed as such except in the sentimental imagination, and although, shadowed with patriarchal domination, it has been the foundry of endless numbers of stunted and miserable individuals, it may be said after all that the myth reflected something of reality, and that this type of family was something of a bastion through the earlier phases of its development. Whether or not this was due to the relative weakness of the state is besides the point; in its youth, the nuclear family had some integrity to it and was capable of the transmission of values. What this meant from the standpoint of the developing child was that she/he remained exposed to a coherent set of behaviors on the part of parents. In brief, people usually knew who they were and what they were supposed to do. Therefore, the adult was seen as the same person throughout the child's development: control played a definite role with respect to intimacy, and gratification was consistently and recognizably connected with prohibition. As dreadful, punitive, or even absent as the parent may have been, she/he was either there or not there, punishing or not punishing; i.e., the parent was *known* to the child. As such the Other to whom the self related was modeled after a recognizable human being. Moreover, the parents were related to each other in a definite way. In such an articulated and coherent human surround, the developing child could differentiate itself from the parents; a real parent was internalized; and the earliest self-systems, dominated by a primary narcissistic grandiosity, gradually came under the control of the more modulated influence of later stages.

Again, we should not sentimentalize about this arrangement. The nuclear family as such never insured against madness. Hatred as well as love could be instilled under its terms; and the character it formed could turn out a wretch or a murderer no less than a saint. Furthermore, it served as the template for sexist domination. More generally, the pattern of development we have been describing as characteristic for the early nuclear family is that of the Oedipal triangle itself; indeed, the predominance of such structures in Freud's milieu (or, to be more exact, their threatened dissolution) was undoubtedly what brought the complex so forcibly to his attention. The Oedipal relationship is essentially a triangulation: the father enters the mother-infant dyad as a third party, an Other to the Other primarily given by the mother. This differentiation within the Other is perhaps responsible for the sharply defined superego of Freud's structural theory[10]; in any case, it is predicated upon the sharply defined arrangement of the early bourgeois family.

In the invaded and fractured family of late capitalism, however, a twisting of narcissism is the result. For all its intensity, life under such conditions requires a new term for its description. It is, one might say, *desociated*. Sarah's parents were tightly bound to each other, no doubt, but in an incoherent way and without such rapport as could have been translated into a sense of integrity for the child. Sarah became subjected instead to a *series* of dyadic relationships that remained unintegrated at the level of the family. The primitive dyad with the mother looms over the rest, to be sure; what matters, however, is less the singularity of this relationship than the fact that it could be linked neither to the dyad with the father (or younger sister, who always remained a cipher to Sarah) nor, equivalently, with later dyadic relations, to the mother. As a result, differentiation was stunted; and the full force of the archaic mother-imago broke upon Sarah's emergent self, inundated it, and took up its residence as the malignant Other, charged with grandiose primary narcissism.

The Oedipal complex did not thereby disappear from Sarah's life. All phases persist in a historical system, as feudal arrangements persist in the midst of late capitalism. A person is a totality. Like the society to which she/he belongs, however, the person has an overarching identity that signifies all the elements of the totality. The signification of the individual is related to the identity of the society but lags behind it owing to the inertia of the transhistorical. Therefore, for some time in the history of capitalist society the dominant personal identity was Oedipal, a hearkening back to precapitalist days when paternalistic relations dominated both the family and the society at large or the state. Throughout early capitalism, the patriarchal nuclear family remained as a line to that past and kept turning out individuals whose signifying identity was Oedipal. The emergence of the narcissistic type indicates, however, that capital has succeeded in hollowing out the individual to the point where the remaining Oedipal relations lose their capacity to serve as a signifier of the person. At this point, which might be regarded as a ripening of the essential tendencies of capitalism, a link is established between the *commodity* itself, or its representatives, and that element of the individual most suitable in its abstract inhumanness to signify the commodity, the spectral Other of the narcissistic character organization. The narcissist relates to things and makes people into things in their intimate relationships. Recall here the content of Sarah's transference to me (page 105). This is exactly what capital does in the creation of commodities: it turns vital labor into abstract labor power and eventually into the petrified form of the commodity. The great menace of capitalism, the one to which the entire ecological movement is responsive, is that all of nature itself will come under the sway of the commodity and be violated. In the emergence of the narcissistic character as the central figure of late capitalism, we see this movement appear in the self and reflected in the contemporary predicament of the family. From one standpoint capital has reason to gloat, for it has in a sense finally subdued the individual to its will. But this very triumph only indicates the fundamental weakness of capitalism; the emergence of an inner tendency is also the occasion of decadence.

It is now apparent why the modern era is the age of psychology. In it the self is both inflated and crippled. In each of its spheres— production and domesticity—personal life is created in a problematic form. As wage labor produces shoddy commodities for an empty self to consume, so does the nuclear family produce enucleated selves for wage labor to consume and to further hollow out. Wage labor demands an individual self split from itself in the alienation of labor-power, while the nuclear family produces a self inwardly torn by neurosis yet needful of outward securing, which it obtains, in part, by virtue of the reassurances of psychology. The two splits reinforce one another and produce, by their mutual effect, a self characteristic of capitalist society: swollen, torn, and inwardly hollow.

From this angle we can say with greater precision why we can discuss the "neurotic personality of our time" without lapsing into empty hyperbole. Capitalism does not create neurosis, but it does decree that neurosis be a part of its totality. More concretely, capitalism creates awareness of neurosis, as it creates awareness of self generally. More concretely yet, capitalism creates a world in which people necessarily see themselves as individuals in search of an individuated happiness. Since the conflicts of the family are ingrained in these individuals and form the immediate fiber of their mentalities, the most immediately accessible surface of their unhappiness is often in fact neurosis; and since to interpret matters otherwise would be to question the whole society and its history—something that has been made largely unthinkable—increasing numbers of people who are unhappy yet freed from harsh material want interpret their total alienation as a matter of neurosis.

I expect that it may strike the reader as somewhat dubious to assert that the conditions of capitalist personal life in America inevitably drive toward neurosis. Capitalism, after all, has been around for quite some time, much longer in any case than today's hordes of mental-health workers, the existence of whom testifies to at least a significant preoccupation with inner self-estrangement. Even today, when people are so possessed with straightening out their inner lives, the majority would probably not describe themselves as neurotic but as "well-adjusted" personalities with functioning families to which they are deeply attached. And a century or more ago, it is certain even a greater proportion would have done so. Finally, the image of a country built by confident and aggressive pioneers such as have been mythicized in the Western romance does not fit with that of a race of potential neurotics.

In short, while it is undoubtedly *logically* true that a society built on alienation of human power will eventuate in widespread self-alienation, or neurosis, as well, this is not the same as concretely demonstrating the process, and it gives little clue of its timetable. By the same argument, though only a very dull mind (of which there seem to be many among our social scientists) would accept people's manifest statements about themselves as true-in-depth, to simply dismiss the lack of overt mass awareness of neurosis that has been evident until quite recently as "false consciousness" is not very persuasive in itself. There are definite reasons why widespread awareness of inner alienation, and a concurrent crisis of the nuclear family, surfaced only in the past few decades. However, it is also incumbent upon us to demonstrate that the real precursors of this inner lesion existed throughout the time span of industrial capitalism at least, else we should find no reason other than dogmatic faith not to yield to the argument that it is merely the "pace of modern life" or the "loss of old values" that has produced the current turmoil in personal life. In other words, we should show that the "old values" themselves spawned a way of life with the seeds of profound personal alienation in it, and that the answer to the crisis lies not in a return to the good old days but in a social revolution now that reappropriates human power.

I do not think we have enough direct or systematic evidence to show absolutely that capitalism itself has engendered these seeds. Nor could we, given the inaccessibility of such immediate data to the historical eye. In any case, those who wish to hold to the values of the "American way of life" will remain unpersuaded by mountains of facts. However, there are a number of clues that support the argument.

One persuasive line of evidence stems from the fact that nineteenth-century America was extraordinarily unable to face the existence of madness. We know this from the clearest evidence possible: the treatment of the insane. As far back as the first Progressive era in American life, that associated with Jacksonian Democracy of the 1830s and 1840s, grandiose schemes were unfurled to incarcerate psychotic people in institutions with a shockingly capitalist fervor for order and timeliness.[11] These buildings were among the first of that species of architecture that eventuated in the Pentagon and the World Trade Center: severe orthogonal lines, endless corridors, all clean, neat, and mechanical, just the antidote for psychosis. Here madness would be cured through immersion in the cold water of capitalist relations: strict punctuality (the day being divided into tiny fixed segments), lots of work, and edifying lectures. Such a dehumanized regimen did little to help psychotic people; and when historical developments, such as the Civil War, led to a reallocation of priorities, the mental hospitals sunk into a slough from which they were not to recover until the recent burst of interest in mental health. During the long night of psychiatric practice the sweeteners of progressivism were dissolved away by neglect, leaving behind the underlying dehumanization. Psychotic people are a fearsome threat to public order, *virtually unproductive* as *workers* (i.e., unable to generate surplus value) and *useless* as *consumers; ergo,* they need merely custodial care so far as capitalism is concerned. The result was the scission of the madman from the body social, which became unable to recognize itself in him. From a practical standpoint, this meant the conversion of all those fine early-nineteenth-century asylums into "loony bins," places where madmen were simply dumped, away in general from social activity (often out in the country, as, for example, in Long Island's Suffolk County, which only recently contained so many patients in its three large state hospitals that they had to be disenfranchised lest they outweigh the sparse local populace at election time), and where they suffered outright neglect or, as often transpired, the savage brutality of custodians. Much of this pattern still persists despite reforms of the twentieth century, and reminds us that what Dostoevsky said of prisons holds as well for mental hospitals, that these are among the best places to learn the truth about a society.

The superalienation of the insane under capitalism should be contrasted with other attempts to cope with the problem. As Foucault showed in his now classic study,[12] from the late Middle Ages through the early Enlightenment, madness was much misunderstood and often brutalized, but it was not subjected to radical exclusion from social existence. Indeed, it was often conflated with divine visitation or a special form of knowledge (as in the madness of Hamlet or Don Quixote). And the mad were practically lumped with other types of social misfits—the poor, the aged, the infirm and the criminals. It took capitalism, with its attempts to order and economize existence, to radically segment out psychotic experience. The first critical distinction between the mad and the sane misfit was that the former could not work productively. The segregation of madness under capitalism was therefore less a matter of advancing rationality and care (for it was not associated with any commensurably deeper knowledge or practical benefits to the disturbed) than of the imposition of an inexorable rationalization—the mystique of production—upon all phases of existence: a rationalization unstable at its core because of its basis in the alienation of human activity and, therefore, intolerant of the nonrational, the disordered, the insane. In other words, the history of unreason should be viewed as the history of reason, i.e., that of capitalist rationalization.

There is, to repeat, no direct or totally satisfactory way of determining whether the seeds of widespread neurosis lie latent in early capitalism beneath the confident and unreflective exterior of life. No psychoanalyst steps forward to bear witness to self-estrangement; indeed, the very absence of such discourse testifies to a repression of neurotic manifestation, or at least to the fact that such manifestations as existed were not experienced as especially problematic. But self-description is a fabulously poor indicator of the truth. The human capacity to deny what is real seems boundless across history; while America, obsessed with the need for confidence and expansion, has promoted it to a central feature of its culture. If we wish then to determine that the seeds of self-alienation had been sown, we should turn not to the positive evidence people offered of themselves but to the record provided by those artists who, out of their own estrangement, portrayed in depth the true image of their times. The spirit of capitalism forces genuine art to the margins of society, where it must remain if it is to be true to its essential nature. Under capitalism the artist begins to serve a *critical* function; and if his or her calling is to write imaginatively of real people, then she/he begins to portray their humanity critically, i.e., to call attention to what is suppressed or alienated in it, and to the despair behind the positive façade. By the early twentieth century this trend had become sharply defined in American letters. Earlier, in the high-water days of positive nineteenth-century culture, the theme had to be less overtly drawn. We still recognize it, however, in the writings of the particularly original and penetrating. Poe, for example, establishes his vision on the field of the imagination as such. His tales of horror are, from the historical viewpoint, significations that the inner life—desire itself—had become *unbound* in American experience. Not desire as love but as hatred: a malignant fantasy unbound, repudiated, yet recurrent. The great theme of Poe's work is the *return of the repressed*: the black cat, Madeline Usher, whoever, achieve their horrific function by becoming unmoored and revisiting an initially confident yet eternally damned subjectivity. Unlike fairy tale and myth, which build along similar lines, Poe encompasses more of the historical totality: he represents, again and again, a mad rationality being overcome by its own rejected phantoms, bearing witness to the historical unhinging of an alienated subjectivity, unreason intertwined with a haunted rationality. Poe's tales are ultimately parables of capitalist rationalization being overcome by its own negativity in repressed desire.

Poe's critique left the subject inundated by his own phantoms but otherwise intact. This cleared the ground for yet a deeper reflection into estrangement. Herman Melville began his literary career with *Typee*, which depicted a South Sea Edenic paradise that could be visited by Yankee sensibility but from which it could return. This proved popular in a way that presaged the modern tourist industry, since it represented nature *outside* the dominant identity. As Melville matured as an artist, the locus of nature shifted to within the body social and became increasingly problematic, and Melville became progressively less popular. With *Moby-Dick*, which was quite correctly perceived by author and public alike as a blasphemous work, his career foundered and sank. The reason for the oblivion that befell Melville lay not in any depiction of a timeless struggle between man and the universe but in his shocking insight into the enmeshing of capitalist aggrandizement with its own projections, played out here—as has become historically immediate only contemporaneously—against all of nature. He simply showed bourgeois society too much of itself.

Melville's oblivion did not dull his artistic sensibility. On the contrary, it was turned inward, toward the creation of an astonishing series of late works (written before the artist had turned forty and retreated into a long exile) that depicted estrangement as it affected everyday life. In *Pierre*, which put the quietus to his career, Melville dared present American family life not as the location of a privatized bliss, but as one where intimacy degenerates into incest. And in *The Confidence-Man*, the last of his works before self-imposed exile, Melville placed all of American society aboard a riverboat and revealed it to be a monstrous organism built on self-deception, a masquerade. In this incomparable work, Melville recognizes, a century before the them would surface into pop psychology and sociology, that the self under capitalism is inherently problematic, that the figure toward which narcissism turns loses the concreteness of a Pharaonic leader and becomes the pale shadow of the commodity form. Into the swarming yet vacuous and desociated world of the riverboat steps the Confidence-Man, the universal Other. Successor to the Trickster of primitive legend, the Confidence-Man succeeds in insinuating himself into the fabric of social discourse as no Trickster ever could, the kind of swindler not even American society could muster, except in the imagination of a Melville, until late-twentieth-century technology had perfected the mass cultural apparatus to place him in the White House. Playing upon the fractured narcissism indigenous to a society whose public and private spheres were severed from each other, the

Confidence-Man feeds on and confirms the hollowness of the self. He offers the people on the boat an identity, confidence, and trust, and so draws them further into self-disintegration. As he tells one of his victims, a merchant: "Who knows, my dear sir, but for a time you may have taken yourself for somebody else. Stranger things have happened."

In none of his works is Melville's grasp of the madness inherent in capitalist existence more exquisitely revealed than in his tale *Bartleby*. This work is often thought enigmatic because it depicts an act of refusal that seems profoundly irrational, all the more so as it is presented without any evident motive. The scrivener (or law-copier, a forerunner of the automatic duplicating machine), Bartleby quite suddenly refuses to work, by stages and without any manifest emotion (merely uttering the celebrated "I would prefer not to") until he stands transfixed in the Wall Street law offices of his employ and forces his employer, who is "strangely moved" by Bartleby—to move to other quarters, following which society incarcerates the madman and he dies of self-imposed starvation. To be sure, it takes only a minimally Marxist sensibility to perceive that Bartleby's refusal is profoundly rational with respect to the exploitation inherent in his employment, not to mention entirely prescient, since his act is a dialectical one that foreshadows an identity with the machine that is to replace him while it epitomizes as well a very human, albeit self-defeating, form of worker resistance. Yet so repressed is this sensibility that generations of interpreters, admiring the story and also "strangely moved" by it, fail to appreciate this obvious level of meaning.

On the other hand, it must be said that a purely economic interpretation does not clarify the emanations from *Bartleby*. There is something baffling about the tale—and our reaction to it—that may be part of the domination of labor but is not encompassed by the terminology of the economic. For one thing, much of what happens at the law office is painted in imagery drawn from family life. For example, Bartleby, who suddenly appears without antecedent description or ties, i.e., as though newborn, is depicted in his initial work relationship as feeding upon his documents, while the particular nature of the work—copying—is greatly like the kind of mimesis that goes on between infant and parent, and that plays so decisive a role in the development of the child. Here it seems as though Melville is saying that *this* child-worker, psychotic Bartleby, is failing to mature, failing to copy the ways of the world, and so refusing the nourishment that derives from work and reproduces social life itself.

But the crucial point that extends a purely economic interpretation comes when the employer—the narrator of the story and so the sensibility of the reader herself/himself—traverses the deserted streets of the business district one Sunday in order to get to his office on a mundane errand and encounters the scrivener in his chambers. He realizes with a shock that Bartleby has decided to *live* in the office—in terms of our discourse, to undo the historical scission between work and domesticity. It is this discovery that fills the narrator with the deepest emotion, as it must, for it touches the history of personal life under capitalism at its most contradictory point. Bartleby, victim of the most dehumanized office work, tries, in one mad yet inspired leap, to undo the history of capitalism, to bring desire and human concern, no more sharply drawn than in the care of infants, into the heartlessness of the workplace. It is for this he must die, just as his artist-progenitor Melville had to be shoved back for exposing too much of the truth. Bartleby, like the Confidence-Man, is a universal Other for late-capitalist society, the shadow of capitalist development cast over its emergent self.

Bartleby is a worker, and Bartleby is insane. In him the economic and the mental underclasses meet. Curtis, Jane, and Sarah, the three individuals we have chosen so far to present in some detail, are neither workers nor insane. This fact is fitting insofar as it dovetails with the reality of psychoanalytic practice, which, as everyone knows, is for those who control money and, perhaps more significantly, time. But psychoanalytic practice attends to a minuscule portion of the mental disturbance that afflicts and illuminates bourgeois society, and our understanding cannot be said to be complete until we have taken a look at the remainder of mental disturbance. It goes without saying that many psychotics are middle-class, and that the great majority of proletarians keep themselves mentally intact in the struggle for existence. Yet it has also long been known that the more morbid diagnoses tend to be made among the poor and Third World people.[13] Moreover, the state has a special interest in administering such problems. It may be particularly instructive, then, to reveal the frayed edge at which history and desire intersect by constructing a portrait in which all these qualities converge.

9

THE VIGILANTE

I would . . . describe men—even should that give them the semblance of monstrous creatures—as occupying in Time a place far more considerable than the so restricted one allotted them in space, a place, on the contrary, extending boundlessly since, giant-like, reaching far back into the years, they touch simultaneously epochs of their lives—with countless intervening days between—so widely separated from one another in Time.

—Marcel Proust, *Remembrance of Things Past*

Hector T. roams between the proletarian and subproletarian classes. Since a class is not an organization that one joins formally but a deployment of goal-directed social activity, or praxis, when we say that Hector changes classes we mean he is now and again apportioning his vital activity in different ways. As a proletarian, or worker, he sells his labor-power for wages on an open market; and as a subproletarian, or socially useless individual, he is forced to the margins of society, where he must live on handouts, or beyond the law. Hector would like to be a worker and has been one for about half his adult life, driving a truck, servicing cars, pumping gas, doing whatever comes his way. The fact that he drops below this level the other half of the time is due to an unfortunate concatenation of factors: that Hector belongs to a group—young urban Puerto Rican males—for whom unemployment is structured at about 25 percent; that Hector is partially disabled, having gotten most of one of the bones in his left shoulder shot away in Vietnam; and that he is intermittently mad and always very troubled. Accordingly, the handouts Hector receives are administered by the Veterans Administration and the public-hospital

133

system, which is where he turns whenever things get to be too much for him. This is where I first met him.

The woman was old and the boys were young, no more than sixteen. Two of them had pinned her against the cyclone fence, and the third was rifling through her bag when Hector came along and surprised them. Though young they were also big, and high on their exploit and their numbers. Hector, by contrast, was alone, no bigger than the smallest of the three, and unable to raise his left arm above the horizontal. Yet, as he put it, "There is no way I can stand back and watch someone getting picked on." In an instant he was upon them and in another instant he was beneath them, submerged by a mass of fists and boots. He does not remember much of what happened afterwards. His next clear recollection was of being in Pedro's bathroom, staring numbly at his battered reflection in the mirror. Then the feeling became the sick one that Hector knew from before, a sense of despair, of a world that would have no end and for whose duration he would have to suffer a lashing pain of mockery as though he were in the middle of a circle of people taunting him, the way it had been back in school when harmless children's games had degenerated into persecutions. Deliberately, his eyes still on the face in the mirror, Hector pulled out his belt, tied one end carefully about the pipe in the ceiling, looped the other about his neck, and stood on the edge of the bathtub. At that moment, Pedro, alarmed that his friend had not emerged from the bathroom, knocked on the door, which, being unfastened, opened under the pressure of his fist.

For Hector, time begins with the swoop of a blade—the momentary glint as it catches lamplight, his mother's scream, the backward lurch of her body against the table, the crash of dishes, the sudden red line appearing over her cheek, and his father's drunken stumbling out the door. He does not know whether he saw his father again until he was twelve, and then for only a few hours. Was there ever a return to pick up the few belongings? Hector cannot remember; he was only eighteen months old at the time and cannot recall the incident itself; he only knows it happened because of the angry scar on his mother's face, the various legends that grew up to explain the occurrence, and, most of all, the indubitable absence of his father.

There are no fathers in Hector's discourse, only packs of marauders, helpless victims—and himself, a lone vigilante. Usually things end badly for him, but he keeps on hoping. He went to Vietnam that way, not to escape the ghetto but to "Get the Cong" (who were "out to get us"), lying his way in at fifteen so as to be with his brother Angel, to protect Angel, really, since the latter was gentle and would not stand much of a chance, to Hector's way of reasoning, amidst that yellow, treacherous sea. Then there were the scrapes within the army: a punk from Chicago who taunted Angel and was paid back spectacularly by six of Hector's buddies behind the mess hall; the black from Richmond who did the same—they fixed him even if it cost a court martial. Even so, at first the army was not so bad at all, plenty of buddies, a few enemies, even the chance to perform in base shows as a juggler, a skill Hector had developed on the streets and pursued with great success in the service. Pictures of Hector doing his act appeared in the GI newspapers. He kept them as treasures afterwards; and the best sign I had during my time with him was when he warmed up enough to bring them in for me to see. They showed a man who was not the Hector I was getting to know; instead, a swarthy, callow face expressing a cheerful outwardness, as though the soul came right up to the eyes and rested there like a man at the door of his house greeting a visitor. It was not just nine years and a military haircut that separated this face from the harried one of that moment, with its darting gaze and slight but omnipresent twitch, the face of one who considers himself prey.

And Hector became prey when, the base shows over, he was sent into the field to take on the enemy of his State. Military combat, Max Weber writes, makes the soldier "experience a consecrated meaning of death which is characteristic only of death in war. . . . Death on the field of battle differs from . . . merely unavoidable dying in that in war, and in this massiveness only in war, the individual can *believe* that he knows he is dying '*for*' something" [italics Weber's].[1] Indeed, he *can* believe so, but he need not; and it was characteristic of the war in Indochina for its combatants to feel no such thing but only an inexorable dread that lapsed into meaninglessness and often enough flared into unspeakable horror. Pierre, wandering about the battlefield of Borodino in *War and Peace*, came again and again upon men hurling themselves insouciantly into oblivion or stolidly awaiting the likelihood that a cannonball would come from nowhere and tear them to bits. A similar observer circulating among the American troops in Vietnam would find little of this. Rather, he would see men—Hector and those like him—huddled together being driven mad or numbed with drugs, and periodically bursting into acts of extraordinary barbarity. This demoralization was the essential reason America lost the war, for it did not obtain among the enemy, who knew they were fighting for something that they could value and that brought them together. By contrast, the lies and cynicism experienced by the Americans brought out the worst in them, tore men like Hector apart, and made them eminently forgettable by the remainder of the society in its postwar phase of cynical narcissism.

Americans by and large do not want to hear from Hector in any case, no matter how skillfully he may juggle, since he belongs to a racially despised, i.e., imperialized, ex-peasantry. But when, in patriotic fondness, he descended into the hell of a Vietnamese jungle to await an endless night of fog, pestilence, land mines, and shots in the dark, he was made into a cipher lest he stain the national consciousness with awareness of his existence. By the time the Viet Cong bullet caught Hector from behind in his shoulder he had ceased distinguishing with regularity between his fantasy and factual reality. The sense of mutilation, of concrete vulnerability, put the finishing touches to his state: he became ravening, delirious, assaultive to those who could help him. And after Hector calmed down, a month later he was ready to be turned over, disabled, to the Veterans Administration, with the Purple Heart and an envoi from Bob Hope as a remembrance.

Bureaucracy is the location of social forgetting. It is society's way of wringing out irregular feeling in favor of rationality and impersonal fairness. This has numerous advantages, and is, in any case, necessary to the running of complex institutions. But in an antagonistic society, where feelings are likely to be negative ones, bureaucracy does not simply introduce a rationalized fairness; it no less importantly serves to suppress the negative feelings, or what might remind us of them. By packing Hector off, disabled, to the VA, American society was asserting that it cared without really having to care; it gave Hector a formal justice while burying him under forms.

For the next eight years Hector was swallowed up by bureaucracy. The only discernible development was a gradual shift from veterans' agencies to more purely civilian ones. It seemed to Hector as though half his life were spent in grimy fluorescent-lit rooms, standing on line or sitting impassively on rickety Day-Glow plastic chairs. Periodically, as we said, he worked, usually on a last-hired/first-fired basis or in some mob-run enterprise; and when his work was not prematurely interrupted by some vagary of the market, it was broken off by his perpetual inability to "adjust." There was nothing wrong with his mechanical performance, but squabbles inevitably intruded. Hector just could not seem to get along. The boss was screwing him, or the other workers were ganging up. Sometimes he quit; sometimes he was fired; ultimately, he scrounged.

Yet Hector hung on. He married Sylvia, fought with her mother, added an entire entourage of in-laws to his family of eleven. His own mother seemed to be weakening. When he was little, she, overcome with cares, would often go into frightening attacks of rage. Now as she aged she was becoming gentler but more withdrawn, absent, increasingly lost in prayer. The center of the family had shifted from her to Hector's siblings, cousins, and in-laws. When there was no work they helped each other out; together they figured out the system, played it for what it was worth, as people at the bottom of society will do in order to beat the bureaucracy. A year into the marriage Johnny arrived, trailing clouds of glory. Hector doted on the baby, refused to let him out of his sight, and became something of a local joke for his extreme possessiveness. But his affection was punctuated with moments of morbidity, as, for example, when for no discernible cause Hector got the idea that his baby, now two and a half, showed him no "respect." Sylvia, worried, tried to reason with him, but Hector silenced her with a chilling look, muttered, and walked out. The bad moods seemed to be gathering like dark clouds. Hector lost another job, and took to wandering the streets more and more. He borrowed Pedro's car, drove to Bear Mountain, drank some beer, and toyed with the idea of taking the car over the cliff. He rode awhile on the shoulder of the road, then thought of Johnny and headed back to town. The next day he saw the old woman and the youths.

When talking with Hector, one easily becomes convinced that whatever formal label is applied to him, he is a deeply troubled—not to say, mad—man. Upon our first meeting, no single remark of his met the criterion of psychosis. All of the sentences were logically constructed with proper subjects and predicates. His speech was idiomatic but not idiosyncratic, and employed no bizarre words; and he was capable, if queried, of adequately distinguishing between what he thought to be so and what was really "out there," beyond the perimeter of his subjectivity. And yet, though Hector used the common language and had a hold on common reality, it became obvious once he spoke that common realistic matters were not what was on his mind, except as they must be bent to his will.

To listen to Hector—not to address him with mundane concerns of one's own as in conversation, or to try to fit him into a bureaucratic mold, or to get work out of him, or even to try to love him, but just to listen to him, openly and simply—immediately gives one an unpleasant sensation that is akin to being harangued by a fundamentalist preacher who has long since lost hope of influencing his audience but nevertheless believes with a relentless certitude that his sole mission on earth is to expound the gospel. Except that in Hector's case, the gospel has no salvation but is instead an interminable litany of threats, injuries, counterattack, and revenge, a monologue delivered impassively yet with such a driving inner force that it sweeps up any stray line of thought into itself, like a stream raging in a flood that pulls silt down its banks.

As we noted before, often the scenario consists of Hector's coming to the aid of a helpless victim who is at the mercy of a pack of marauders. At other times, however, he is the victim who then turns on his tormentors; while at still other times, the perpetrator is a lone wolf and he, Hector, rallies the support of a group of vigilantes, who wreak vengeance upon the miscreant. No one theme emerges as dominant, yet the whole is as tightly interrelated as a fugue by Bach. The ideas do not so much add up to any central fantasy as cluster about it, surrounding it and revealing its shape the way deeper geological structures are revealed by a collection of surface irregularities. Nor, of course, is it a matter simply of ideas but rather of a tissue of thoughts about real as well as imagined events, woven together into a fabric in which the distinction between fact and fancy is irretrievably lost. Just as Hector muses about what is not yet real—for example, "getting" those people on the train who will harass Johnny when the boy becomes old enough to go to school—so does he ponder real events determined in part by his will to become involved in them, events such as the ganging-up on soldiers who were supposedly harassing his brother Angel, or, to be sure, the so-called "precipitating event" of his current crisis, the attempted rescue of the old woman mugged by the gang of toughs. Nor, finally, can the scenario be exempted from calamitous real events to which he was passively subjected, either those over which he had no control at all, such as witnessing his father slash his mother, or those, such as in Vietnam, where some elementary choice of his (for Hector went to "get the gooks who were out to get us") became swept up into a reality that apocalyptically exceeded his worst imaginings.

The decisive point in Hector's musings is not whether they are real or imaginary, but whether, insofar as they are real, he is able to actively master them, to prevent himself from being inundated by a hatred and terror that, given no outlet, could lead only to madness. We can never know Hector's response to the slashing scene, which took place when he was eighteen months old. But it would be inconceivable to assume that it was not traumatic—i.e., more than he could master—and being so, it became radically shut off from consciousness so that it festered in him, shaping the disposition of his wants as well as his thoughts and drawing to itself future events of a potentially like sort, each of which would become a fresh opportunity for him to be overcome. If his mastery of a situation failed, as in Vietnam, where the Viet Cong in fact surrounded him, or with the old lady, where the assailants proved too much for him, Hector would stand to become overtly psychotic, invaded by unbearable, world-destroying feelings.

Pursued by ill-fortune all his life, Hector has never been all of a piece but rather a collection of part-selves living in mutual terror of each other and the world. There is a black Hector and a white Hector, organized along the lines of the racism that has shadowed him: the black part being that which is dark and clotted in him; the white, that image of himself in what he takes to be the white man's eye. This he aspires toward, cannot be, but sometimes pretends he is. There is also a male Hector, identified with the murderous and absented father, as well as a female Hector, identified with the slashed, maddened, and abandoned mother. This, too, he cannot be, yet it is all that is available to him. None of these Hectors can be reconciled with any of the others, and at no time has a coherent identity been able to form itself out of the welter of their contradictions. Rather, existence for him has been a juggling at the margins, a playing-off of possibilities against menace, all against the backdrop of a never-too-accommodating world.

Madness for Hector would be a collapsing of everything into itself, a breaking of walls. This occurred in Vietnam when the hated black part had been heaved up by world history and placed in the jungle opposite him in the garb of the Viet Cong: black Hector there to kill white Hector. The result: manifest madness, redoubled when his wound, the surgeon's knife, and the resulting scar led to a collapse of one split—between black and white—into another—between male and female—which for Hector always means the father-assaulter and the mother-castrated. Since that time, Hector the vigilante, clinging desperately to shards of an alien whiteness, has had to ward off the persecution attendant upon any manifestation of the black-castrated self. But since this part is Hector, too, and the real trace of his past, there will be no peace for him, only an uneasy walk on the edge of dissolution. And since Hector is so preoccupied with the imminence of a catastrophe that has to be overcome in order to stave off this dissolution, he becomes suspicious, wary, vigiliant, ready to attack before the situation gets out of hand, in short, *paranoid*: a maker of walls.

When I first saw Hector, his paranoia was manifest in his glittering eyes and his obsession with danger, rescue, and vengeance. He did not have to articulate any full-blown delusion about persecution; the preoccupation with threat, the suspiciousness, the profound sense of estrangement, were testimony enough. Hector was so fixed on his various notions that one soon began to feel that there was a delusion after all beneath them, perhaps not recognizable to himself, perhaps held back out of fear for the consequences should it be revealed, but nevertheless there, a core of madness in relation to which his uttered speech was so many iron filings in a magnetic field. If we were to piece together its elements, Hector's delusion (or delusional system) might have read: "There is a malignant force out to get me. The force seems to settle now in one person, now in another, who becomes my enemy and who must be stopped first. Sometimes this person is after me, and sometimes—more often, in fact—he attacks someone who is so near to me that it might as well be me. This other person attacked may seem a stranger, but once assaulted, she or he becomes as dear to me as my own kin, and I must stop it or face the end." And Hector would have had to add, in order for the ideas to become delusional, "I know this is so; there is no point in persuading me with so-called proof that it is otherwise. I know better because I have an inner certainty of the truth, more important to me than any facts to the contrary." And this delusion, for all its unreason, makes a definite contribution to the structure of Hector's reality—and, by implication, ours, for, recognize it or not, we all live together.

What was I to do with Hector? Our "contract"—the informal yet necessary agreement defining the scope of a psychotherapy—was a highly limited one, not because of his needs, which were immense, but as a function of the class gap between us. This gap had been absorbed into bureaucracy and rationalized, but it was nonetheless material, for all that I tried to transcend it. My clinical work is apportioned into two phases, public and private; and the public phase is itself subordinated to educational purposes. In general, the private patients get my time, which, though bounded by the clock for each session, opens indefinitely into the future. However, Hector was not, to be sure, a private patient. Therefore, I was to see him for "brief therapy" —in practical terms, an evaluation—then turn him over to a resident psychiatrist, Dr. Telemann, who would work with Hector as long as possible, i.e., until the end of her training, at which point she was going to take a leave of absence to have a baby. Though I was prepared to treat Hector with no less care than my private patients in any given moment, I was also aware that the impersonal constraints of our class situation had introduced an alienation that no personal heroics on my part could overcome. This was no excuse for laying back—one had to do what one could; and though I could not see myself clear to opening enough space in my life to meet Hector's needs, I was not about to succumb to therapeutic nihilism either, which would have been a moral massage in the guise of breast beating. But so, too, would have been the assertion of a nonexistent commitment on my part. If I was not about to see Hector for more than ten sessions, come what may, then it would have been hypocritical for me to indicate that I was totally there for him. Good therapy is predicated on truthfulness. If all therapy is necessarily a kind of instrumental relationship, then one has to be truthful about instrumentality. I could not go about proclaiming some kind of existential unity between the two of us when our reality was ten sessions, which would not have taken place at all were it not for a training program that needed disturbed patients as raw material. These things stand between people, and one should not pretend them away—for anybody, but particularly for someone of a paranoid disposition marked by extreme sensitivity. The defensive remoteness of the paranoid is a boundary against the vulnerability of boundless desire.

Practically speaking, I had to beware of stirring up too much in Hector. I found myself in a familiar vise. Good therapy always mobilizes desire, simply because, for all its instrumentality, it is more authentic than the rest of everyday life. But desire is dangerous. Dostoevsky's Grand Inquisitor pinpointed it: in the historical world people all too generally prefer security and illusion to a freedom that awakens desire. Paradoxically, the wretched bureaucratic bungling to which Hector had been long subjected offered a kind of reassurance. It was always there, an ungiving mother whose stone breast forestalled longing. It took no vanity to claim that I could do better than this, simply by listening to him. But if that amelioration was combined with a premature separation we would be in for a difficult time of it. Yet Hector was desperate, and the luck of the draw had thrown us together. There was no dropping the case; one had to see it through.

Given the limited range of alternatives, my preliminary goal was to keep Hector from becoming more disorganized. He had already calmed down in expectation of getting help and was no longer suicidal. The VA had been pushing tranquilizers and antidepressants on him for years. I decided at first not to change the regimen, though the long-range goal was certainly to wean him. As is typically the case for the chronically disturbed at the lower end of the social scale, the only bounty to come forth from the stone teat of the mental-health bureaucracy is a hail of pills. The puffed-up science melts like cotton candy in the mouth of actual practice, where countless individuals are passively doped by faceless psychiatrists. Such was Hector's condition upon our first meeting; but rather than tamper with it, which would have introduced too many variables and aggrandized me to boot, I decided to hold the line for a few weeks and just listen.

At first all went well. Hector told me the story I have recounted here while I listened and helped him clarify his situation. In the fourth session, however, he began to inquire about myself in an intimate way; and in the fifth, he opined that I was quite an expert who might have the answers he had been seeking for so long. You see, there were questions, special ones, whose existence he had not breathed to any psychiatrist.

"I'd be interested to hear your questions, though I have no special powers to answer them."

"Yeah, but you went to school a long time; you must know a lot. . . . Too bad I didn't get a doctor like you from the start. Maybe I could have cleared a lot of this up years ago, who knows?"

"You must be wondering, and perhaps worrying a little, about what will happen when we part in a few weeks."

"Nah, not me. I understand all that. You're a busy man, a professor, right? I'm just glad to be of help to you in your teaching.

Maybe the young doctors who learn from me will be able to take better care of others than what I got. Maybe I'll come downtown to see you at your office. . . . Just kidding."

"The idea of our sessions stopping is painful to you."

"No way. I'm just grateful for what I get. Did I tell you about how Angel got hassled by some spades the other day?"

And he was off again. No further word was heard of the "special questions" between us.

Hector missed the next session. When he appeared for our seventh meeting his eyes were darting wildly and stayed so for the entire hour. Finally the story shamefacedly emerged. He had been afraid to come the previous week. The day before the session he had met one of the youthful muggers of the old woman. He chased the boy into an alley and beat him with a two-by-four until he whimpered in pain. Hector was suddenly overcome with remorse. He dropped his club, gave the boy his last five dollars, and fled. After wandering for two days he returned home.

The next week Hector had sealed over and nothing came out of him save a string of denials and rantings about how Puerto Ricans had to learn Yankee ways to survive. He failed to show up the following week and never returned to the clinic. When finally reached on the phone, Hector said that our services were no longer required.

I learned of what happened next from Dr. Telemann, who saw Hector in the hospital emergency room six weeks later and took care of him on the ward. For about three weeks after our last meeting, Hector seemed to settle down and even got a few odd jobs. Then Sylvia's younger brother, José, was cut up in a fight. Two days later, Hector's mother was hospitalized for a recurrent asthmatic condition. Although she was discharged shortly afterwards, Hector seemed to enter a downward spiral with her first wheeze. He barely ate and would spend hours staring out the window. When Sylvia tried to draw him into conversation, he would snarl back at her and say that he had "special questions" on his mind that were none of her business. Once he shoved her away rather violently, then began weeping with remorse. He turned to the Bible and began praying, despite having been quite irreligious until then.

One day Sylvia went out shopping and left Hector in charge of Johnny. When she returned, she heard the child screaming from two flights down. Bounding up the stairs, she smelled the gas before she reached the door. Inside, the following spectacle greeted Sylvia: the oven door was open, and before it Hector had assembled what appeared to be a small altar out of milk cartons and the child's blocks. On the altar were two candles, a few blackened leaves of lettuce, and some incense. Johnny was in the corner, howling; and Hector was kneeling, glassy-eyed, in front of his makeshift contraption, mumbling to himself and trying with trembling hands to strike a match. A small heap of bent matches lay beside him, testimony to a life-saving incapacity to do so, ascribable not only to his tremor but to the violent rocking of the upper half of his body. Sylvia screamed, grabbed the matches, then Johnny, shut off the gas, and tried to reason with her distracted husband. All of these acts were successfully performed except the last, for Hector was beyond reason. She then fled to her mother's and called the police. When they came Hector was gone.

Big cities are densely articulated places, and no one can be seriously mad for long within them without crossing some public boundary and creating a nuisance. The police function to winnow out such detritus from the social body and to pass them along to the appropriate mechanism for disposition. Thus, when Hector was picked up eighteen hours later wandering along the subway tracks and mouthing what they took to be gibberish, the authorities knew immediately that his destination was that kidney of the social organism: the psychiatric emergency room. There young psychiatrists patrol the boundary between ordinary and extraordinary madness. The latter is deemed unacceptable for everyday discourse and therefore gets passed through the filter of the emergency room into the processes of the hospital itself.

There could be no question that Hector had crossed that line. His wild appearance was sufficient evidence of that, as was his habit of alternating abruptly between periods of agitated ranting and a stuporous self-preoccupation. But it was what Hector said that aroused the keenest interest.

Hector kept shouting that he had the "special answer." Long had he studied in secret the ancient ways of his people, cast down in bondage to the white devils of the North. Now he had the illumination. He, Hector T., was not really a dumb, broke, out-of-work, and fucked-over Puerto Rican. He was the heir to the magic of his people, their tribal blood knowledge. Yes, Hector was the Prince of Darkness, and Darkness had come to overtake the Light. For centuries, so he said, the Lords of the Light had ruled the earth. But these were instruments of Satan. Originally, Light and Darkness were one, but the wicked principle that was to rule the mundane universe pushed them apart from each other and created earth as a domain of false light. One knew this light was false because the shadows it cast had no substance and all went in the same direction. (Hector excitedly demonstrated his thesis at this point with the shadow cast by his hand beneath the naked 150-watt bulb that was the sole illumination of the emergency room office, where he was expatiating for the benefit of Dr. Telemann and two wide-eyed medical students.) The true light, light of Hector's Lord Ahura-Montezuma, cast a material shadow in all directions at once, which was really part of the thing illuminated. The world had lain under the bondage of the bad light for four millennia, its darker people in bondage to the lighter ones, until this day, when Lord Ahura-Montezuma had chosen him, Hector T., to preach the principle of Darkness-in-Light and to lead men to salvation through higher knowledge. Why was Hector chosen? Because he was the greatest stranger of all mankind, and because of the magical structure of his genitals, which permitted an experiment to be performed on him to render him into the first person ever to combine the male and female generative organs in one. The hole at the end of his penis, Hector alleged, had been expanding for some time. This was a magical sign to him. In a blinding insight that came over him one day at a papaya stand, Hector realized that the by-now gaping hole was meant to tell him that a vagina was trying to be born in the middle of his penis, and that his was meant to be the first genital of the new sex. But the first of a long line. Through his organs a new race would be born, as androgynous as he, to undertake the great work of unification demanded by Ahura-Montezuma, the true god, the god above the god of Christians, Jews, and Moslems, the only god capable of uniting humanity, long cast down by the false lights of their particular gods, lights that confused people and enabled them to be enslaved by the white devil-master. These little gods, including the greatest of them, Jesus himself, were only mirrors of men in the fallen world. Ahura-Montezuma, on the other hand, was ultimate and beyond all description—until, that is, a man, himself, Hector T., became so changed that he might further aspire toward him. And that was why Hector was glad to be in this hospital, where he knew that the surgeons were excellent and could set to work immediately to complete the transformation of his genitals.

"I think you're asking for help to control your impulses," said Dr.

Telemann and packed Hector upstairs posthaste. "Did you catch that thought disorder?" said one medical student to the other as soon as the madman was gone.

THE HUMAN ABSTRACT

Pity would be no more
If we did not make somebody poor;
And Mercy no more could be
If all were as happy as we.

And mutual fear brings peace,
Till the selfish loves increase:
Then Cruelty knits a snare,
And spreads his baits with care.

He sits down with holy fears,
And waters the ground with tears;
Then Humility takes its root
Underneath his foot.

Soon spreads the dismal shade
Of Mystery over his head;
And the caterpillar and fly
Feed on the Mystery.

And it bears the fruit of Deceit,
Ruddy and sweet to eat;
And the raven his nest has made
In its thickest shade.

The Gods of the earth and sea
Sought thro' Nature to find this tree;
But their search was all in vain:
There grows one in the Human brain.

—WILLIAM BLAKE, *Songs of Experience*

In those days the ward to which Hector was sent was under the overall direction of Dr. Acheson. Beneath him was spread out an orderly chain of command and division of labor: various consultant-attending psychiatrists, a chief resident, junior residents (of whom Dr. Telemann was one), psychologists, social workers, and activity therapists, and finally the shock troops or infantry of the whole operation, the nursing staff. For some reason, the nurses and attendants, or nurse's aides, were all black or Third World, in contrast to the exclusively Caucasian composition of the professional staff proper. And, as with the army, they had their own noncommissioned chain of command, led by Head Nurse Watson, a black woman who combined a residual humaneness with traits of officiousness suitable for rising in the hospital bureaucracy. As a result, she was known for her WASP-ish temperament. Beneath her was, among others, Aide Jiminez, assigned the special duty of being with Hector, who from the beginning was an especially difficult patient to manage. Jiminez was a stolid and taciturn individual who professed to understand nothing of Hector's raving and had to be frequently chastised—even threatened with "charges"—for reading *El Diario* at the staff meetings, which occupied about half the working day. Nonetheless, when Jiminez was with the sick man, Nurse Watson observed that Hector became less agitated; and when Jiminez was off duty or preoccupied with other patients, Hector's behavior deteriorated to the point of requiring—by the canons of hospital psychiatry—massive doses of Thorazine, or even the more dreadful seclusion room. This chamber, which had a lockable steel door with a tiny peephole and was furnished with a bare mattress, was located at the end of the hall. The ward as a whole resembled nothing so much as an abattoir—the patient's quarters like so many pens; the severe walls, paved with dull-orange ceramic tile, seemingly made for hosing down; and the whole space converging or, rather, being passively absorbed into, long, dimly lit corridors leading to a central yardlike structure. And the seclusion room, at the end of the longest of these corridors, seemed the place for dumping offal, a place out of time where those end-stage individuals who had proven themselves unfit for even the community of the ward could be sent until they mended their ways. Hector must have secreted some matches on his person, because one day, having been banished to seclusion for urinating on senile Mrs. Nussbaum, he succeeded in setting fire to the mattress and so brought consternation to the uneasy hospital society. The resulting alarm brought the whole hospital to a stop until the fire department could extinguish the blaze. Nurse Watson had to work overtime filling out incident reports, and Dr. Acheson was called before the hospital administrator himself to answer for the matter. Coming on the heels of a few other episodes that smacked of lax ward administration—and so shortly before the annual inspection by the state hospital commission—Hector's fire nearly led to a full-scale hearing, such as would have embarrassed the Department of Psychiatry greatly and further bogged down its already overburdened staff with a truly horrendous amount of paperwork and surveillance. As a result, Hector's case was given even more scrutiny, and Aide Jiminez rarely left his side thereafter.

There was also in the hospital those days an elderly psychiatrist of British extraction, Dr. Taunton. Taunton had a colorful though somewhat obscure past, which included a spell as commando during World War II and a longish period of knocking about the corners of the fading empire afterwards. Somehow he had managed to get certified; and although without the formalities of psychoanalytic training, Taunton had gained a reputation among a segment of the psychiatric community as a perspicacious, if unorthodox, student of psychosis. It was Dr. Telemann's fortune to have been assigned to Dr. Taunton for supervision on Hector's case. Most of Taunton's week was spent downtown with his private practice; and the few hours given to the department were exclusively given over to the art of supervision, a weekly ritual during which cases could be reflected upon under conditions vastly more calm than those of the often chaotic ward.

Dr. Telemann regarded her supervision with Taunton as the high point of her week, partly because she was taken with the old gentleman, but mostly because she was so confused, albeit fascinated, by Hector. She recalled Hector as a brittle, remote, and highly suspicious individual, and was therefore all the more perplexed to see him as a ranting wild man who uttered unintelligible thoughts and who could, at the same time, affect her so deeply. Hector aroused in her an ineffable feeling compounded out of tenderness and extreme fear; he seemed to be reaching out to her even as he repelled her, and all of her previous experience and substantial personal gifts were proving impotent in the face of his madness.

Dr. Taunton listened for a long time to Dr. Telemann's account of Hector. Then he advised her:

"I think the first thing here is to get a better perspective, so with your permission I'm going to ramble a bit about some general features of the case. To begin with, the worst thing you can do for Hector is to assume that his thoughts are "disordered," as though there were some kind of benchmark of normal, ordered thinking against which they could be measured. If you do that you convert Hector into an inanimate object, a machine that spews forth standardizable thoughts as though they were merchandise. At the very least, you've thereby lost the opportunity to understand him. But the second-worst thing you can do for him is to romanticize his troubles away and assume, because his delusions are so appealing, that there is nothing the matter with him. Whether or not his ideas are a rational response to unbearable conditions is a fascinating and profound question, but we cannot begin to answer it until we appreciate how badly Hector has been damaged. We have to outgrow the kind of naïve antipsychiatry that flourished in the sixties, simply because its logical assumptions deprive the person of agency and make him into a passive victim without responsibility for what has happened to him. And it deprives him of a body, too, by denying in effect that we are complete organisms in which no mental event can transpire without a concomitant somatic event. Remember, *nobody* knows what psychosis really is; there are only better or worse types of ignorance, and the best type of ignorance is the one open to all the real dimensions of the situation, including that of the body, which is palpably involved.

"But first things first. We have to deal with the worst type of ignorance, simply because it happens to be the one in charge around here. It seems that the official categories of psychiatry, especially those of diagnosis, have been set up to expunge everything that is interesting about Hector and arouses our human concern. I don't know why, but it seems to be so. But anyhow, remember—perhaps you needn't be reminded, having spent so much time grappling with him on the ward—just how sick Hector is. Whatever 'sick' means in an ultimate sense, you know that Hector can be impossible to deal with and that he enrages you no less than he appeals to you. Yes, he is fascinating and at times charming, but he is also stubborn, spiteful, destructive, and filled with an unimaginable hatred. Psychosis is like the creative act in that the world is broken down. But unlike creativity, it's not really put back together again. Destructiveness has the upper hand; and the person, instead of uniting with others through the creative act, is driven further away from them. Hector will break your heart if you think you can magically transform him; and when you get close enough to him to begin seeing what he is about, you will quake with fear to be brought up against the abyss of terror and emptiness that he suffers every moment. Maybe we can call Hector's 'sickness' a kind of rupture with the ordinary human universe, so that everyday reality, as ungiving as it may be, is lost to him and he has to live in a chasm filled with eruptions from the deep along with whatever shards he can salvage from his ruin. I say this to emphasize what you know already, that it's very cold in there, and very scary. And that's where medical psychiatry comes in. I know it's a lot more complicated, but look, if you can for a second, at this side of it: people have to guard themselves against the terror that Hector undergoes. He has to be contained and excluded, and that's just what the psychiatry you're being taught does, with its container-type thinking."

"Yes," remonstrated Dr. Telemann, "but isn't that a little besides the point? What I experience firsthand every day is not the terror from Hector but the pressure from the ward to take some kind of immediate action with him. I mean, he is creating an uproar and we're over census as usual. And anyhow, I'm a doctor, trained to make precise diagnosis and to take action to help sick people, so I demand it of myself on those grounds."

"That's just the point," Taunton continued excitedly. "You see, you've got this alternate reality with its own standards of rationality with which to consume yourself. And supposedly it's there for Hector, but actually it's closed to him. That's how his madness gets sealed off, by having you—who are, after all, like a membrane between Hector and the official world—become preoccupied with its standards and not his. I mean, your whole work, which is supposed to be *for* Hector, is really a barrier *against* him; and that barrier is medical reason and the demands of the hospital bureaucracy, which I suppose represents society at large.

"If we're going to get back to Hector, we must take him from where he is; we can't go about putting him into boxes of Otherness that distance us from him. I'm not being nihilistic here. We must learn how to make useful differentiations; otherwise, reality is an ooze into which we all sink. And there's science in that, with careful observation, clear thinking, and testing against evidence. But there's all the difference in the world between real science and the stuff you're being taught as diagnosis, which denies the very object of its study.

"To put it another way, you can't isolate science from the social conditions of its use. Take drugs, for instance. As you know, I don't favor them much. The kind of problems I deal with usually don't require medication in any case, and I have a lot of respect for the harm they can do. But that's not the issue. The fact is, I also have a lot of respect for the good they can do; there are indeed some situations where talking and listening just aren't enough. If you really care for someone, you must resort at times to medication. But the point is, drugs have to be used as part of a caring social relationship. What's going on nowadays in psychiatry is too often just the opposite: drugs are used as a substitute for care and as part of a social process that is fundamentally dehumanizing. That's what gets to me, for when drugs are used in that context, they turn from something potentially quite useful into another technological nightmare.

"Let's get back to Hector. I don't think he should have drugs right away, and maybe not at all. He's been too bombed in the past, in any case, and we'd only be communicating to him that his problems are intolerable. The basic point is to get through to him, to establish some basis of care. And for that you've got to listen quite seriously to what he's saying, something that drugging him up won't facilitate just now.

"Look how interesting Hector becomes once you stop trying to label him and begin to differentiate out what is going on! Notice how his thought, which was so constricted and monotonous in the days when he was trying to cling to everyday life, becomes unfettered when he goes mad. Maybe—sadly, most likely—he's going to burn out, but meanwhile he lights up. Observe, too, how much richer and more suggestive his thinking is than the dried-up stuff you work with. Why not go with it? Again, I don't mean that Hector is in a higher state but rather that, driven mad, he is made to think at the edge of existence, forced to think through the fundamentals. It goes way beyond his immediate personal life with his family—which psychoanalysis, to its credit, brings up—it has to do with his partipation in all of history. History is inscribed in the individual, and it's just in states of madness like Hector's that you begin to see the connections re-emerging. Jung, who was a very gifted man, although in my opinion a bit of a charlatan and a reactionary to boot, intuited this in his theory of the archetypes and the collective unconscious. He sensed how, in dreams and psychosis, the history of a people became expressed in the individual.

"Look closely at Hector. See how, out of his anguish, he has had to reforge so much: the ancient Gnostic legend of the higher god and the alien messenger, for example; or certain ideas about the unity of existence that only very extraordinary geniuses like Blake have been privileged to work out. All these systems have been common attempts, each at a particular historical juncture, to work out the real dilemmas of existence that the complacency of bourgeois science has obscured. So, too, does each psychotic work out the problem of existence in his own, historically situated and damaged ways. Hector, for example, has quite profoundly reflected the history of the racism to which he has been subjected in his delusion by making himself into the blackened stranger hidden by the false white light; and he has done so by weaving the history of the race with his own, personal experience of mutilation and his search for the missing father. There is no separateness to these themes; they are dimensions of one fabric. But we shouldn't pretend that Hector's story has only two dimensions, like an actual piece of cloth. I'd go further: don't even try for closure in working with patients. To try vainly for a total comprehension is only a search for power on our part. The most we can do is to pick out some filaments from Hector's delusion of his broken interconnectedness with the human community."

"I'm suspicious of this precisely because I find it fascinating," said Dr. Telemann. "It seems something like a complicated post-mortem, an intellectual trip for us. I mean, how is it supposed to help Hector?"

"I'm glad," responded Dr. Taunton, "that you're so sensitive to the intellectual trap. No, we don't go through this for our own heads but to get us into a position to establish a life line to Hector. I'm not claiming that this is the only way, but if we can relate Hector to a truth we share precisely because we have undergone the same history, too, albeit from a different position, then some measure of that community has been at least potentially restored. But it has to be through us—because we are the ones positioned next to Hector—and not *in* him nor bounced back to him. It would be misleading and harmful to think that Hector can learn anything in an immediate sense from the riches of his own thoughts. If he could, then he wouldn't be where he is. Hector can spout some pretty amazing stuff, but he can't reflect on it and can't himself turn it into a project with others, in Sartre's sense. It's too much a matter of survival for him. You might say that Hector's not a subject . . . yet; even if he shows us the elements of a deeper and richer subjectivity than do so-called normal people, he's in no position to appropriate it. For us to take Hector where he is means we have to be faithful to the whole sundering of his own self, to the fragmentation that terrifies us no less than the profundity that links us to him. And this faithfulness is both very simple and very, very difficult: you have to simply *be* with him. I mean, you bear witness to what is going on with Hector by a calm acceptance that respects his reality yet offers him openings to develop it in a more creative way, by using the life that is in him. And yes, no matter how low people seem, there is a healing force within them so long as they breathe. Your attitude toward Hector should be a bit like that of a mother toward her very young infant. The baby is cosmic but helpless, and she simply takes it where it is. The aide, Jiminez, for example, who might not care about what we are saying here, is somehow in touch with Hector: he is there, he bears witness to Hector of his existence. In his way Jiminez gives *care*, which is what is ultimately necessary to heal the rupture, that is, to let Hector heal it. Isn't it ironic that Jiminez, who earns less in a week than we do in an afternoon, is able to give that care? I suppose it has something to do with spending so much time with Hector; though he's paid for the time, of course, the very lowliness of Jiminez's position lends a kind of maternal, unstructured quality to it. That sort of time, you know, is considered shit work; it's a woman's job, like changing a diaper; or a black's, like being a porter. But you know, if somehow I could build a setting where that kind of acceptance were spread around the clock and through the space of the unit, we'd get Hector back on his feet again. Not all better, to be sure; scarring is scarring, no matter where in the organism it takes place. But I know he could be allowed to bring himself back if he had some real care, and he wouldn't need those horrid drugs either. In fact, he wouldn't—couldn't—need this kind of institution at all. Then where would we be?"

The day that Dr. Telemann had her meeting with Dr. Taunton was also the day that Dr. Acheson was called before the hospital administrator to answer for the irregularities on his ward; and the next day was that of their weekly meeting together. As was his custom for this occasion, Dr. Acheson had doffed his tweed jacket in favor of his medical man's long white coat. Because of his apple-cheeks and somewhat slack lower lip, he had a juvenile look in profile; while head-on his exceptionally thin, flaring nose gave him a pinched and miserly appearance. But there was nothing odd about his career. Dr. Acheson was what was known as a "tiger" in the profession. Only in his mid thirties, he had already published four noteworthy books: *Principles of Hospital Management in Psychiatry; New Pathways in Ego Assessment; Psychiatry for the Twenty-First Century;* and, as a primer for medical students, *The Human Factor in Psychiatric Case Management.* Acheson's aim was, as he put it, to "tie up the whole ball of wax," i.e., to put all the levels into one system. His discipline and energy were awesome. He found time to pour forth his cornucopia of writings while running his ward, doing clinical research (which mainly consisted of drug trials), conducting a busy private practice, and taking part in innumerable professional activities. Acheson was surely bound for a major departmental chairmanship; it was said that he was only biding his time in the present position until the right opportunity arose. Meanwhile, he even had time to teach Dr. Telemann a thing or two, and through her, to reach Hector.

"So, Nancy, how are things going? I mean, with Hector. I think we should discuss him today."

"Fine. That is, he's really very sick, but I'm beginning to get a feeling for the case."

"Fine, Nancy, fine, but meanwhile, in case you hadn't noticed, he's going to burn down the whole goddamn ward. Nancy, let's face facts. You might have a feeling for the case, but you sure as hell don't have a grip on it. Who's supervising you? Taunton? I thought so. Look, I hate to interfere in somebody's supervision, but you're too promising a psychiatrist to let yourself get mesmerized by that old faker. I mean, what has he published? I'd like to see what a good refereed journal does with his romantic mysticism. He's thirty years behind the times, and, besides, look at his personal life. Well, let's not get into that. Let's stick with the case. To be honest, I think Hector's being out of control is a manifestation of your lack of control of his case."

"That's not fair. The man is shattered, and I'm trying to make some contact with him, not to bulldoze in with some instant gimmick. Why isn't his disruptive behavior a response to how alienated he feels here?"

"There you go with that mystical talk again. Look, we used to be called Alienists back in the Dark Ages of the profession, and I have no need to go back to that sort of jargon. I'm not telling you not to talk to your patients or to observe them closely. The doctor must meticulously observe the phenomena he is to treat. But we've got to have diagnosis if we're giong to treat anything rationally, and if you lose sight of this in all the mumbo jumbo you've been so taken with lately, you'll get so lost inside your patient's head that you'll never be able to relate to the latest scientific advances in therapy. Look at Hector. The man's been here two weeks already, and there's not a single precise diagnostic note in the chart, just some vague speculations about time and schizophrenia. You know the hospital commission is coming by for its accreditation visit in a week. We're busting our chops trying to put this place in order; and how is it going to look if they come snooping around, pull Hector's chart—which they're likely to do because of all the trouble he's been—and all they find is a lot of metaphysical ramblings without any treatment plan? This isn't the seventeenth century; and, more important, you're not on this case alone. We have a community of workers here, and the chart is a legal document that has to be communicable to all of them, both now and in the future. And it has to be in a language they recognize, not Hegelese. It's not just the doctors who are involved. There's Watson, too, and her supervisors, as well as the social workers, the activity workers, and the psychologists. And that's only the beginning. Don't forgot the hospital administration itself, as well as the downtown agency that funds us, the Department of Human Correction—you know, they need a diagnosis to reimburse us—not to mention the state bureau of mental hygiene, which has this brand-new centralized computer that's going to get precise clinical data on the whole population. You know there's no entry for 'alienation' in their system. What are you trying to do, throw a monkey wrench into the works and set research back to the Stone Age? And, finally, that chart might well be used in court some day. You think the average judge knows from 'alienation'? He'd laugh that one right out of court.

"But let's set all that aside. You know I'm more concerned with how Hector does here. And I must say I find it shocking that he's not on any drug. Would you deprive somebody with pneumonia of penicillin? Look, I'm not doctrinaire. Personally, I wouldn't mind a controlled experiment or two to test out drug-free treatment. But we're not set up for that. This is a public institution with limited resources and definite rules and expectations. Make Hector into an exception, and he'll mess up the whole ward, use up a disproportionate share of the resources, and behave like a spoiled brat, which is just what I think he's doing. You know how often Jiminez works alone. How is he supposed to take care of the other patients if he's got to hold Hector's hand all day? We're running over census as it is; and with the recent budget cuts, we've had to lay off so much staff that we can't even take care of a normally drugged ward population. Do you want us to make the rest of them comatose so we can bear down on Hector? Think of the resentment your policy is creating! Anyway, it's been scientifically proven by now that drugs are essential for the management of psychosis. My God, there've been ten thousand research articles published on Tofranil alone! With the weight of that kind of evidence, there's no turning back the clock. You've got to spend every last minute keeping up with the literature if you want to do right by your patients—and your career. There's no time to squander in outmoded speculation!"

Dr. Telemann was proving surprisingly resistive to Acheson's exhortation. "You know I don't want to harm the ward," she resumed. "But Hector has been so zonked for years that it seemed humane to let him dry out a little when he arrived. And the more these drugs are used, the more side effects turn up, often years later. But mostly, the drugs keep Hector from himself. To dope him up so quickly is like telling him that he is unbearable to himself. What you're saying is that we have to take this person, Hector, and turn him into something mechanical because society can't come up with the resources to provide care for him. You want to confirm his psychosis to him by treating him as a thing and not a person. It makes *me* sick to see us repeating here just what he's gone through his whole life."

Dr. Acheson was unfazed. "Now you're getting sentimental and, worse, overinvolved with your patient. This isn't some kind of soap opera. Nancy, you are a professional now, and that kind of mushy woman's-magazine reasoning just won't wash. Here is where a good, firm grip on theory would help you along, and help you to really help Hector instead of playing the bleeding heart. You said he was sick, right? Well, let's figure out his sickness. If you had taken the trouble to do a precise diagnostic interview and test him according to reliable rating scales, you would have discovered that Hector's got a pretty rotten ego there; and instead of complicating the case you would be able to precisely direct our limited resources to those ego functions that need building up. Be realistic: we can't fight the world; we're doctors, not revolutionaries, and our job is to help the sick. If a bunch of unions throw the city into crisis with their demands, that's not our problem, except as it puts a premium on the most efficient and scientifically reliable modes of treatment. I can live quite proudly with that, thank you. And if you'd stop worrying about vague and indeterminable issues, such as being 'unbearable' to one's self, and started concentrating on *measurable* ego functions, then you, too, could get down to business. You can drive a garbage truck through some of the holes in Hector's ego. Look at his reality testing, for example, or his moral judgment, or the way he can't neutralize his aggressive instinct. Now that's science. Those are precise entities, and you can treat each one rationally with specific therapies, the way any good doctor would: you can teach Hector what reality is by precisely pointing out the difference between his delusions and what is really there; or you can deal with him morally by setting firm limits and using the ward group to make him ashamed of his antisocial tendencies; and as for the aggression, you might want to clobber it with this experimental drug (I'm doing a little study on it for Farben Laboratories) Euphoryl. They say it works wonders with violence-prone individuals. Then maybe Hector will stop pretending that he's one of the F.A.L.N."

"You talk about 'aggression,' but maybe he's really trying to tell us what it was like at the Battle of Hue."

"Look, we all know that behavior is overdetermined, and we can't let ourselves get sidetracked by issues like that. As far as I'm concerned, what's *really* happening are those factors I can step in and control. But this is pointless, Nancy. I can see you're a really stubborn lady. Here's how we should settle this. Let's present Hector on Thursday to my old professor, Dr. Jaxon, who's going to be the special visiting clinician for this month. He should be able to handle the case, and then we'll decide what to do with it."

Dr. Acheson was genuinely interested in developing Nancy Telemann's career, and was particularly eager to rescue her from the clutches of Dr. Taunton on that account. She was an uncommonly gifted resident and a student well worth having, all the more so for being female. There is a kind of male academic who sets great, if unacknowledged store in having a covey of bright young protégées, finding in them the pleasures of the harem sublimated with the moral satisfaction of the liberal spirit. It galled Acheson to think of his prize coming under the spell of that old reprobate, and so he congratulated himself for his shrewdness in asking Nancy Telemann to present Hector to Dr. Jaxon. He knew that while she could bravely parade her Tauntonisms in his office, she would have to present a different face before such an august personage, and in a large group. Jaxon had not only been a mentor to Acheson; he had opened a few key doors for the younger man as well. To be a favorite of Jaxon's was to have success ensured in American psychiatry. He had at various times been president of the accrediting board itself, and chairman of the psychiatric association. And his most recent book, *DSM-IV and the Psychiatric Future*, testified to his central role in the panel that had recently updated the profession's sacred text, *The Diagnostic and Statistical Manual*, producing in its fourth edition the ultimate in a rigorously codifiable enumeration of mental disorders. DSM-IV had greatly augmented psychiatric power. The trick had not been merely the elaboration of a code to relate every individual disturbance to a computerizable item (Sexual Masochism was 302.83; Hector's Para-

157

noia was 297.10); more importantly, it meant getting the system accepted by the various state agencies with their computers, the insurance companies that disbursed the funds, and the central federal mental-health bureaucracy itself as the universal schema for naming the various mental illnesses. Once these categories had been materially nailed down by medical-psychiatric interests, it would be a relatively simple matter to ensure that medical psychiatrists were in control of the mental-health industry, and first in line for reimbursement. In practice this was not too difficult a task for Dr. Jaxon, since the men who commanded these institutions were mostly old pals of his. It did, however, require a lot of traveling and visibilty, which was a good reason for him graciously to accept the department's invitation to preside at their monthly special conference, where he was to consider and dispose of the case of Hector T.

Psychiatric case conferences, or Grand Rounds as they are perhaps more aptly called, are in fact usually banal affairs. This is a reflection, however, of the mentalities who conduct them, not of their essential symbolic structure, which goes much deeper than the simple instrumentality of evaluating a patient. At the deeper, mythical level, which operates regardless of the wills and shortcomings of the participants, Grand Rounds are settings of high drama, especially when featuring protagonists of the stature of Dr. Jaxon. If you were to compare them to gladiatorial combat of the kind where the warrior met a wild animal, or to the modern equivalent of the same, the *corrida*, you would get something of the flavor. But Grand Rounds hearken to an even more primeval encounter. The therapeutic rationalization that reverses the carnage at one level allows for a more direct engagement of power at another. The *torero*, after all, is usually a peasant boy and the gladiator, a slave. Dr. Jaxon, on the other hand, who stepped into the ring with wild Hector, could be regarded as the Warrior King himself. Grand Rounds are therefore a filiation extending back before the origins of the state, with its interposition of representatives between the sovereign and the people: it is the encounter of the archaic hero-chieftain with the Otherness of his tribe. By quelling Hector, Dr. Jaxon is to integrate the Otherness that is his psychosis into the rituals of psychiatric discourse. Grand Rounds are nothing less than a rite of authentication.

This might explain why Dr. Jaxon kept Hector waiting so long while he exhorted the assemblage, who included members of every level of psychiatric society, from Aide Jiminez to Dr. Acheson, and beyond him even, to the inpatient director, Dr. Pomerantz, and the department chairman, Dr. Agarman. Only Dr. Taunton was missing, for the conference had been scheduled on a day he worked in his private office. Even the kitchen workers, porters, and ward clerks, who comprise the nonpsychological infrastructure of the unit and so are denied, according to the prevailing division of labor, the opportunity of conversing with patients, were milling about the entrance to the conference room, drawn by the air of excitement. Dr. Jaxon was not just strutting and preening, although it seemed that he was to Nurse Watson and a few of the medical students and residents, including Nancy Telemann. His twenty-minute preamble on diagnosis, which included—once he had heard Hector's name—a digression into the newly discovered subtypes of Schizo-Affective Disorder that afflicted the Puerto Rican population, was meant to stake out the perimeters of that legitimacy into which the beast of Hector's madness was to be driven.

At length Hector was brought in. The several months since we had last met had effected a drastic change in him. His face had grown puffy; and his eyes, once furtive and vigilant, now expressed a dreamy raptness. He was mumbling to himself and shuffling as he went, with an agonizing slowness that became as eloquent a statement about the contours of his universe as Dr. Jaxon's disquisition on diagnosis had been of his. At length Hector ascended the platform.

The doctor broke the silence: "So, tell me, young man, how are things going?"

It was two minutes before Hector, with closed eyes, responded: "The thing is a visitation of the Lord."

Dr. Jaxon was not one to be nonplussed. Decades of practice had honed his reactions to peculiar speech into a fine, ever-ready edge. "I see you are a religious man."

In contrast to his previous remark, Hector's now fairly lashed out at the interviewer: "The Lord has spoken."

"Spoken, eh?" And here Dr. Jaxon ever-so-slightly tilted his head toward the gallery, as if to wink knowingly at them. "Sounds like you might actually hear him sometimes. Tell me, does God ever speak directly to you? I mean, do you sometimes hear a voice when no one's there? You needn't be embarrassed to talk about these things. We're all professionals here."

"You are standing in God's shadow."

"Ah, his shadow, eh?" And here the doctor swiftly recalled the

159

history of Hector's delusion as spelled out in Dr. Telemann's presentation. "I understand you have a lot of interesting ideas about shadows. I wonder if you could share them with me."

Hector's next statement came out suddenly, violently, as if he were vomiting forth words. It was all the more remarkable for being spoken impassively and without any change in Hector's rapt expression. "I sell ideas . . . high cash . . . the Lord takes, He makes, He breaks, beats upon poor spics and spades . . . jungle bunnies all, the Lord taketh maketh slaketh under His mountain breathing life. Angel will get fucked, sliced . . . you must go to the rajmantan, there shadows bend so white devils can't steal them from poor spics . . . the shadows are bradooring there. Sir, tell me, are you a surgeon? I have to have my prick stripped down. It has too much shadow on it, too dark. I'm tired of these sad shadows, men in the bush, mountains of inner-going men to sell tubes, words, I've got skid-row-feemia, junk in the streets my mamma will get cut up. Good sir, I want to go home. Can you get me out of the hospital?"

"Well, now, my young man, you'll have to talk a lot less crazily than that before you get out of the hospital. And I hear that you set fire to the mattress in your room. How can you be let out into society when you act so destructively?"

"The streets of the higher god washing to home. Blood fills the city. They are burning the mountain. I want to save you from yourself."

"Save me?"

"Lightness shadow on you falls. Amhurenop powers you."

"Amhuren . . . who? Now you're just making things up. I wonder whether you know where you are or just who is out in the world. I'd like to ask you a few practical questions to check this out. I'll start off simply. Tell me, who were the last four presidents?"

Hector suddenly appeared more lucid and his face became animated. "Kind sir, do not bother me with trifles. I sincerely want to save you, and you can let me go from the hospital. It's a deal. I have peace inside me now; and you, señor, and all the rest of you"—and here Hector slowly scanned the room—"are lost souls. You live in the higher depths of the shadows of lightness. You surround yourself with war, violence, and the fucking of my people. Excuse my language, but I must tell you the truth. That is why I came here, to escape the war and to save the people. I am ready to go back now, all well, higher spiritually. You are a great man, sir, and you all are compassionate people who want to help. Perhaps you are pleased with my performance and will join with me. Sir, with your power in Washington, you must be able to help. Between your power and my peacefulness we can transform the world."

"Hm . . . this idea that you can change the world, is it stronger in the morning or the evening?"

"Aker-Macker," said Hector, blank-faced once more. "Huggermugger . . . gardens open graves to bilsy. Jelmeck regurds to encrusteon. Jabber, geeks grow with gook . . . my nose flows with ooze. Weeds here . . . cut me down. . . ." And then he proceeded to mumble and pray.

There is no need to describe the rest of the interview, which dragged on in a frustrating manner for all parties. The only flurry of excitement came at the end, when Hector fell silent and refused to leave. He went limp in Jiminez's arms when the aide was summoned by an abrupt signal from Dr. Acheson, and had to be carried out like a baby.

"Now we can discuss the case," began Dr. Jaxon in a businesslike manner. "As you could see, we have a very interesting mix here of megalomania and catatonia, with abrupt outbursts of an underlying excitatory process, perhaps of cerebral origin. Are there any comments from the staff?"

A brief spate of speculation ensued. One of the bolder residents even ventured the suggestion that the patient might have been having a little fun at the expense of the doctor.

"That may indeed be one of the manifestations of his illness, Doctor," Jaxon said imperturbably, "for it was obviously psychotic of him to do so. The psychotic is often led into negativistic behavior by his disease. The question for us begins at this point and is to analyze the particular form of negativism shown here. That way we can understand the disease more exactly. And it is an interesting picture he presents. Fascinating case. What do you think, Dr. Agarman? Is it an atypical schizo-affective or a bipolar process superimposed on an underlying schizophrenia of the catatonic type? Sometimes, as you know, paranoids crack further in this direction. Then there's the organic factor. You know how these people are. I wouldn't be surprised if he picked up a little syphilis somewhere in his background, or blew his brain out with a bit too much angel dust. What do you think, Frank? Smells a little organic, doesn't it?"

"Hmmmmm," mused Dr. Agarman, who had a Continental background. "Sounded a bit like *pseudologica fantastica*, with those neologisms. Fantastic specimen of speech, that. Wish I'd brought my tape recorder."

"You can be sure we've thought of organicity, Abe," interjected Dr. Acheson bluffly, thereby displaying his first-name footing with Dr. Jaxon. "We've run him through every test in the book. There's a little bitemporal slowing on the EEG, but otherwise neuro has given his squash a clean bill of health. You know, Frank, in line with what you just said about his speech, I've been thinking the same way. We should get a little project going, tape some of it, then run it through the computer to do a factor analysis. I think it's doable. Might even be some seed grant money there."

"Not a bad idea, Ned," returned Dr. Jaxon, "but we've got to figure out what's wrong with the man first. You see, I have a hunch that this may just turn out to be one of those schizo-affective types that cluster in Puerto Ricans. That's why I emphasized the organicity, because this sub-variety has an organic feel to it. Of course, you have to rule out the effects of cultural impoverishment, which can lend a pseudo-organic flavor to the data. But this lad looks fairly intelligent to me, so maybe he has one of the special types. Of course, with his inappropriate affect and four-plus thought disorder, one has to think of schizophrenia as well. But if you observe closely, you'll see that the chain of ideas is actually linked as in a mania with pressured speech; and then the persecutory ideas have so much free-floating hostility attached to them that I'm really inclined to put my money on the good old schizo-affective, manic type. But what I'm leading up to is this: you've got to do more to find out. When I heard he was not on any drugs I was a little appalled—that's why the interview was a little hairy, by the way—but then I figured out that you wanted to clean him out so you could start him on some fresh protocols, which is just the right idea. Now, what he needs is a therapeutic trial, first on lithium alone, then on lithium plus that new Valium-type drug Elysium. If the first course doesn't calm him and the second one does, then you have pretty strong evidence of the Puerto Rican subtype. And if that one flies, I might even be able to get him down to Bethesda for some full-scale studies. And as for the interview, don't feel badly that the patient acted up a bit. Just the opposite. The crazier they are, the more there is for us to take care of."

And on that note the conference ended.

Things did not turn out for Hector quite as Dr. Jaxon had outlined —not that it would have mattered to the latter, for he left the hospital immediately and was far too preoccupied with national matters to give the case another thought. Dr. Acheson knew that Jaxon had merely suggested the drug trials as a coda to his performance; and so when the order came down that afternoon from Dr. Pomerantz to lower the ward census by 30 percent in anticipation of the dreaded accreditation visit, he did not think twice before consigning Hector to the category of ballast. Accordingly, the next day the still mute madman was led off to an unknown future at the state hospital. Fortunately, his wife had time for one last visit before the transfer was effected.

Dr. Nancy Telemann was enraged. She had held her tongue at the conference out of a lingering fear of male authority, and now she blamed herself for Hector's fate. She could hardly look at him as he left; and soon afterwards she fell into such a depression as to have to begin her own analysis immediately instead of waiting a few years as she had planned, at which time she would have been earning a reasonable doctor's salary, had her own private practice, and been able to begin repaying the $45,000 debt accruing from her medical training. Now she was really strapped. In order to meet her analyst's fees, she had to work an additional night a week at the local prison, and this placed added strain on her marriage. Fortunately, she now had her analyst to turn to for the resolution of the intrapsychic conflicts that arose about these dilemmas. But her conflicts were about to become morally accentuated even as they were alleviated economically, for soon thereafter Doctors Acheson, Pomerantz, and Agarman took her aside and offered her the prized chief residency on Dr. Acheson's unit for the following year. The prize in the short run—an immediate bonus in salary—was a trifle compared to the long-term prospects opening up before her as a result of the offer, for chief residencies are regarded as stepping stones to key academic positions, a fact underscored by the explicit promise made to her by the troika of departmental powers that they would respect her need to have a baby by holding over her job opportunity for an additional year.

Nancy Telemann knew well how scarce really good jobs are in today's hard times, and she did not have to be reminded of how long and arduously she had struggled for her toe hold in the male-dominated world of medicine. Though she despised Dr. Acheson and had yet to forgive him for what had happened to Hector—and blamed him, too, for the fact that Dr. Taunton had only a few weeks after the conference resigned in disgust from the department—still, she was not about to reject their offer out of hand. Indeed, something told her that though she might hate herself thereafter, she would eventually accept the offer. Taunton had no jobs to hand out, she thought bitterly, nor could she see herself getting along in times like these on her psychotherapeutic skills alone. Yes, that day she was especially glad to have an analyst to go to, and from the mists of her confusion for the first time seriously entertained thoughts of a career in psychoanalysis.

> A truth that's told with bad intent
> Beats all the lies you can invent.
> —WILLIAM BLAKE, Auguries of Innocence

There was one significant figure whose action—or, rather, inaction —has gone unrecounted that day in the room with Hector and Dr. Jaxon. Why did I, who, after all, knew Hector clinically and might have been able to say a few things as well about the charade that was going on before me, hold my tongue? Was it a feeling of bad faith about my own shortcomings where Hector was concerned, a twinge of guilt that rendered suspect the morally superior feelings that were welling up inside me? Perhaps. Perhaps, too, I was afraid to place myself outside a community that had been the scene of so many associations for me over the years. We are taught to be suspicious of "rescue fantasies"; and here I was, wanting to take Hector's side as sacrificial victim. However, for me to authentically rescue him from the role of beast—and from the beast I saw in Dr. Jaxon—would this not have required a commitment to provide an alternate reality for Hector, and at the least to accept him myself? But I could not shake from my heart the feeling that there was something truly *wrong* and *menacing* about Hector, even if I considered myself above the folly of trying to define him by the categories employed by Dr. Jaxon *et al.* And I knew that no matter how much I might rail at the goings on, ultimately I had to make peace with that order represented by Dr. Acheson unless I could advance an alternate one. And here, too, I felt stymied by frustrating experience over the years. It seemed self-evident that only a revolutionary transformation of society would suffice if genuine care was to be given to people in need. Yet it was one thing to envision this need and another to articulate it in a given setting. There, in that setting, I had frequently spoken out, until it became plain that the radicalism had itself become integrated into the ritual: it, too, was part of the spectacle; part of the good, pluralistic, liberal, all-absorbing reason that was psychiatric discourse; part of the very institution that it pretended to transcend and that processed Hector all the same. Just as there was no madness of Hector's that could not be absorbed into the positive reason of Dr. Jaxon, there was no critique of mine that could not have been equivalently absorbed by the institution so long as it remained plain that I was speaking as an *insider*.

Hector's madness had contained a valid critique of the existing world but had destroyed that world for him and isolated him from others in it. I, by contrast, was searching for a discourse not mad but *transcendent*, one that would indicate a better world born from the old. And yet I too feared isolation. Had I found words to express my mental groping; had I been able to say, for example, that Hector's madness was the *labor* of the Other and that his diagnosing was the production of an exchangeability that created value for the industry of mental health, and that the positive reason of mental health therefore contained the seeds of its own negation, so that it was destined to fail and increase suffering and meanwhile to become ridiculous—had I said all of this, or more, or any one intelligible part, then I too would have been blankly regarded as a stranger.

But it is true. The reader may be puzzled or disappointed to see Hector, who seemed so intriguing, sink like a stone from our narrative. However, that is what the mental-health industry does with people. His work done, Hector leaves. In this industry some people produce madness for others to work on, and so become Other to them. In the making of the diagnosis, exchange-value is created out of the human subject. It is not so much the end product as the mode of rationality, and the social relations contained in it, that provides the magical enumeration to turn a person into a set of gears to engage those of the institution. By being diagnosed, Hector is split from his madness, which enters the field of commodity relations. Meanwhile, the human part, used up like Styrofoam cups at a fast-food counter, is discarded. Or perhaps recycled at the state hospital. Whatever, Hector is gone, processed by the same rationality that structured the imperialism and racism which determined his past: the reason that renders the human into a thing. Hector has, in fact, come under the "shadow of lightness."

There was once a young man I tried to care for during my training, one of those "brilliant schizophrenics." His obsession was to rewrite the dictionary, trying to create, as Freud put it, "word-presentations" out of the "thing-presentations" of the unconscious world.[2] But we slipped away from each other; and I only heard tell of him thereafter from some friend at one or another institution through which he was passing. Then one day I saw him—or rather, passed him on the street. At first I took him for another vagrant, with his ratty clothes and matted beard. But there was something familiar about the eyes, and so I turned for another look. Sure enough, it was my old patient—but it was too late for greetings, for while I was recognizing him he vanished into the crowd.

10

THE ADMINISTRATION OF MIND

Bureaucracy, in effect, is the Other erected into a principle and a means of government: it means that the decomposition of the group has totally enclosed men in the internal field of the practico-inert. It is not that man has ceased to be the future of man, but that the man of the future comes to man as a human thing.

JEAN-PAUL SARTRE, *Critique of Dialectical Reason*

We may go on. It was said that Hector labored on behalf of the mental-health industry. But what was produced? His madness, true, but is that all? There was a fission product as well, a positive to the negative of Hector's madness: a reason produced along with unreason. This reason cannot be separated from the mental health industry itself; indeed it is more basic to it than the physical pills dispensed or the concrete substance of the psychiatric ward. Psychiatric reason is the *being* of the mental-health industry—the pills, wards, conferences, and so on, the objectification of that being. We may therefore assert that Hector, working in concert with Dr. Jaxon, *et al.*, produced, along with his madness, the mental health industry itself. The fact that he labors on behalf of the industry from the position of Other, i.e., as one who is not part of its dominant identity yet claimed by it, is but a measure of the extreme degree of alienation that obtains in his situation. Hector's relation to the mental-health industry differs in degree but not in kind from the position of the average worker whose alienated labor produces the industry where she/he works no less than the commodities sold by that industry. And like the average worker—but again, to a much more degraded extent, as befits his role of Other—Hector is provided for by the mental-health industry: given three square meals, a roof, some hospital clothing, and even a chance to earn some money in a "sheltered workshop."

The mental health industry, however, is no freestanding entity. It belongs to the totality of capitalist society, and more particularly to that organ that stands over the rest of society and regulates it: the state. The state is the integral of society's Otherness, inverted to become a ruling principle. Therefore, insofar as Hector and the rest labor to produce the mental-health industry, they also labor to produce the state.

To the eye of common sense, the state is materially there, vested in definite institutions, paper forms, granite buildings, and sundry regalia. Nothing, however, could be more misleading, albeit suitable to the ends of the state, which must strive to present itself as seamless and eternal. In fact, the state exists only as the integral of a set of ongoing social relationships. If people would stop working to produce it, the state would vanish. True, it comes to stand above the rest of society and seems to brood over it omnisciently. However, this position is actively and continuously sustained by an endless series of such acts as we have recounted in the case of Hector, not necessarily acts in which madness and reason intertwine, to be sure, but acts in which Otherness departs from the human form and is alienated into institutional form. The state is produced, then, in the course of an engagement of desire; but in its production, desire is lost, to reappear, inverted, as an awesome and mystifying legitimacy. And once this legitimacy is applied to a command over the means of violence, then the state has attained its being and takes on an ever-expanding yet spectral quality.[1] However, no matter how far it seems from human activity, the state remains dependent, like a queen bee, on the daily prodigious labor of its denizens . . . except that in contrast to the world of insects, the more people labor to produce and sustain the state, the farther do they get from it. All this has been told in the works of Kafka.

The state should not be regarded as a homogeneous entity. It embodies a basic contradiction: that it represents both society as a whole and the dominant class within society. This contradiction appears in Hector's case as the combination of a basic need to *care* for him with the fact that the men in charge of that care were all thoroughly tooled to perpetuate bourgeois class interests. Because of the contradiction, states can never achieve a complete integration of society. They therefore take vastly different forms depending upon their position in history. The particular history in which we are engaged, however, has been one in which state structures tend to converge toward a particular type of rationalization, drawn from the capitalist mode of production. We have witnessed this rationalization in various manifestations. Now we may discern it in institutional form. Having already observed that Hector's Otherness became alienated into a state bureaucracy, we may generalize: the state that arises in late capitalism is itself a *bureaucratic* state. And as Hector's madness was administered, so does administration threaten to consume all of reality.

It is said that the bureaucrat, like the insect, will inherit the earth. To this point there seems no hope of arresting either form of existence. It is difficult to say what will be the most chilling legacy of the twentieth century: its record of holocaust and genocidal slaughter, or its cancer of bureaucracy. But we need not choose; the two are different sides of one movement, for the slaugther has been carried out coldly and efficiently, i.e., in the bureaucratic mode, while the mode itself is the negation of what is most violent and chaotic. Bureaucracy picks up the pieces; then sees that things are shattered in a different place.

No romantic rejection of order or expertise is implied here. Any social process must institute principles of rationality, simply as a function of material vulnerability. And this requires division of labor, skill, predictability, even a hierarchy. A ship, for example, would never get across the sea if it were not carefully controlled. And even creative activity demands a rational scaffolding; to take a particularly radical example, the transcendent vision of Blake was grounded in an exacting technical mastery of the craft of engraving. As the play of a healthy child readily evinces, there need be no dualistic opposition between reason and the imagination. On the other hand, there is a sensitive dialectic involved, watered by desire and easily disrupted by domination. Bureaucracy is always subject to the totality of which it is an element; when domination takes over a society, the ordering within it becomes lifeless and opposed to desire. Twisted desire then begets twisted rationality; and the result, evident where a certain degree of agglomeration takes place, is a *strangulating* bureaucracy.

We cannot simply locate this problem today in capitalism, unless one wishes to call those allegedly socialist societies that are strangling in bureaucracy, capitalist under a different name. This is an arguable proposition but not one that concerns us here. What does concern us is the particular burden bureaucracy places on late-capitalist society. We have come to accept the *rationalizations* of bureaucratic administration as *rational* and to succumb all the more easily to them on that account. Yet they are rooted in the specific type of domination under which we suffer: the capitalist mode of production.

Bureaucracy in all its forms is essentially a depersonalization of social action.[2] The immediate and inevitably arbitrary will of an individual is replaced by an impersonal and general code. The merely personal cannot stand long before this mode of rationality and its greatly enhanced command of resources. However, bureaucracy is only seemingly autonomous. Beneath its disengaged surface of rationality, it remains subject to the deeper contradictions of society even as it seeks to iron out the disorder they provoke.

Consider a simple and seemingly neutral example: the necessity for traffic lights in a big city, "rationally" timed to ensure the flow of traffic. Traffic "naturally" tends to be chaotic, since the human organism cannot itself regulate the great power of the automobile. Enter a bureau of traffic and a traffic engineer who impersonally studies the flow of traffic, figures the problem out mathematically, and sets up a system of lights. And behind him enters the traffic police to impersonally enforce the law which, by saying one has to stop for lights, caps off the whole process of traffic rationalization. Now everyone is happy, for no one can force his way across intersections without paying a penalty. Even the tycoon, who can buy his way out of anything, pauses before the impersonal majesty of the traffic law, partly to forestall nuisance, partly out of concern for the dangers inherent in violating the law. People readily internalize the discipline of traffic signals. The most unruly lout will, in the vast majority of instances, stop at the red and go at the green. Even psychotics readily obey.

But when we focus on the rational need for bureaucratic intervention into the social complexity of traffic, we can lose sight of the reality behind the complexity. The flow of traffic in a city is primarily determined by the needs to get workers to and from the workplace and consumers to and from the stores; and secondarily, but equally deeply, determined by the need to keep markets expanding for the corporate behemoths who fatten on traffic: oil companies, automobile manufacturers, road builders, et cetera. Therefore, the complexity of traffic is a direct function of the exigencies of capital accumulation. And capital accumulation can never relent; its every success only feeds its chaotic tendencies. The more "efficient" traffic lights make this system at one level, the more uncontrolled they will make it, and the society it defines, at another level, the level of pollution, of energy squandering, inflation, technological unemployment, mechanization of work, imbecility of culture, and so forth. As I write, the people of Los Angeles are experiencing the city's worst smog alert in many years. Did they have this problem before? Yes, the announcer on the radio proclaims, and adds that traffic officials in California are somewhat pleased . . . for although the number of miles driven in the city is 30 *percent greater* than a decade ago, the maximum level of pollution has gone no higher, thanks to all kinds of bureaucratic improvements in traffic flow and antipollution devices. Such is progress under capitalism: permitting a 30 percent rise in commodifiable activity, while keeping the level of asphyxiation constant.

In a like manner, the maintenance of health, including that chimera "mental health," has become a massively bureaucratized affair. Here the situation is considerably more complicated than in the case of traffic flow. One source of complexity is the fact that health, unlike traffic, cannot be defined or, rather, is the setting of a continual struggle over definition, a struggle arising from the need to gain control over the realm of the transhistorical, i.e., nature, or the body. Health is the sphere in which nature is immediately historicized. By drawing boundaries around disease processes, medicine and psychiatry are telling us where history's control over humanized nature has become tenuous. All societies prescribe notions of health and disease according to what they can do and feel they have to do about the transhistorical. At this juncture arise the ever-fluctuating names and structures of disease, ranging all the way from the fatal encroachments of nature to the manifestations of historical dys-synchronizations. (As an example of the latter, consider "minimal brain dysfunction," a disorder of children manifest essentially by the fact that they *move around too much*—too much, that is, for school authorities. Because the child occupies the wrong kind of space in too little time—in other words, is failing to bind time properly—she/he is considered to have a *disease*, complete, you may be sure, with "underlying" brain disturbances and treatable with drugs.[3])

Capitalist society, however, departs from all others in that the sphere of health cannot be contained.[4] The root cause of this arises from the fundamental contradiction between the estrangement from nature inherent in capitalist relations, on the one hand, and, on the other, capital's need to expand personal life. As a result, the living body becomes a machine out of control, suffused with power yet mysteriously alienated. And as the forest becomes a field which becomes a lawn which becomes Astroturf, so is the human organism converted into a zone of commodification.[5] The notion of "health" is then applied to this field with a double intent: for health is at once the control of the organism as commodity and machine, and a longing for contact with a lost natural spontaneity. Health becomes an inherently contradictory state, then. It expresses both the forward movement of capital toward iron technical mastery and a look backward at the primitive condition left behind. And when this self-contradictory cultural meaning of health is combined with the noxious reality—the pollutants, the noise, the adulterated food, the workplace hazards, the conditions imposed by the traffic just described, and above all, the wear and tear of the basically predatory way of life under capitalism and the inability of people to find a transcendent path out of their condition—it is little wonder that the sphere of medicine grows so chaotically. And as it grows, it brings the curse of bureaucracy down upon it.[6]

For long the maintenance of health was solely in the hands of an army of private entrepreneurs, the doctors. That health remained such a fundamentally individual matter while so much was undergoing concentration testifies to the ideological value placed by capitalism on the well-being of the individual person. But medicine—and psychiatry, for here the development of the two runs essentially parallel—could not forever remain outside the net cast by the state bureaucracy. And when this happened, what had been merely disorderly went haywire.

Recall the basic contradiction of the state, between its representation of society as a whole and its subservience to the dominant class. This may be rephrased: The capitalist state has two contradictory functions: it must ensure the *accumulation* of capital; and it must provide for the *legitimation* of the given society, including itself. Health care clearly belongs to the second, legitimation function of the state but it is no less on that account under the aegis of the accumulation function. In fact, the legitimation function, though indispensable, is always the weak sister relative to the state's need to preserve, and expand capital accumulation.[7] Late capitalism is also, however, a time of protracted state crisis, for the economic needs of the system continually undercut the state's ability to make good its promises of legitimation. In short, the ever-expanding needs of health are met by a state with increasingly limited resources. A serious impasse results. While health care is necessary for the maintenance of the work force and also to some degree serviceable for the expansion of capital (notably, of course, in the machinations of the drug and medical equipment industries), in its essentials health can never fully repay capitalist society for the resources it expends on its behalf. From the standpoint of political economy health has to be a bad investment for the basic reason that it trades in something—organismic functioning—that can never be adequately subsumed into the form of the commodity. The "commodity," wrote Marx on the first page of *Capital*, "is, in the first place, an object outside us, a thing that by its properties satisfies human wants of some sort or another."[8] The commodity must have "thing-form"; it must be perfectly objectifiable and ultimately quantifiable so that it may be put into a system of exchange and given a dollar sign. One can do this pretty well with Valium, steel, or transistors (or driving on freeways), but very poorly with the whole of health, for health is the search for an estranged *inner* nature, fundamentally unquantifiable. Health can never be "in the first place an object outside us." In chasing after health capitalist society is chasing its own phantoms and creating more phantoms to chase in the process. It is bad business, wasteful of fiscal resources, and in the eyes of capitalism it requires a watchdog or governor to make it work more efficiently.

Hence the proliferation of bureaucracy, the only way capital knows to effect the order that is sacred to it. A fantastic swarm of regulations, administrators, utilization codes, reimbursement forms, peer reviews, HMOs, PSROs, site visitors, and computerized printouts descends on the health worker. Professional activity becomes more and more compartmentalized, rigidly stratified, and encoded each year; and the professions themselves become increasingly dominated by no-nonsense technicians, people whose allegiance is to "hard" science and the sound principles of management.

The utterly predictable result is an increase in estrangement and a renewed search for medicalized well-being. The depersonalization intrinsic to bureaucracy runs counter to the basically personal nature of health. The system moves to its next phase, with a fresh infusion of bureaucratic wisdom and another round of increases in malpractice rates. Along the way, politicians enter, the state becomes more and more immediately intrusive. Gradually the professionals lose their autonomy and become a crowd of fancy proletarians working for a state that defines the terms of health and disease. Soon enough the erstwhile professional learns that she/he is not only a mere worker but unproductive as well, and wasteful of the state's resources (called, for purposes of propaganda, "the taxpayers' money," as if individuals had freely chipped in). The next day a new form appears in the mail, a new checklist, a new diagnostic scheme, a new protocol for the central computer that houses all the patient's records in a nice safe place. The age of administered health is upon us.

Bureaucracy is more than a politico-economic arrangement. There is also bureaucracy in relation to desire, bureaucracy as Other, the bureaucracy of Kafka. And then there is the bureaucracy *of* desire: the mental-health industry.

Few more barbaric or grotesque terms exist than "mental health" or, worse, "mental hygiene." To take them by their own logic we would have to assume that there is a freestanding entity, "mind," that is capable of health or cleanliness.[9] In reality what is meant turns out to be the correct, i.e., conformist, behavior of individuals. And in the terms of the discourse we are developing here, mental health should be taken to mean the positive image of Otherness; it is the ideology of health directed to negate the negation of the estranged Other. As we have seen, this Other necessarily collects among the citizenry of capitalist society by virtue of the tension between a bound reason and an alienated desire. The mad—Hector/Bartleby—are lightning rods to draw the general Other to themselves. They become thereby the Other-in-itself and are deemed unproductive members of society. There is a logic to this, for the mad cannot, in fact, work according to the tenets of capitalist rationalization; their lack of productivity, however, should not be ascribed to a defect in them so much as to a *function* they are made to perform, namely, drawing to themselves that which is antiproductive.

Psychiatry is the ritual wherein the antiproductive is fixated by the positive science of technocratic medicine. Since this is its deeper logic, we should expect its manifest ideology of promoting real human well-being to be a sham—and indeed it is. For all of the notable individuals who labor within it, the basic, i.e., institutional, function of psychiatry is much like that of mass culture: both foster a degree of illusion and mediocrity consonant with the crippled level of capitalist relations. The balance struck is similar to that of the schools, which try to educate people well enough to be adequate workers and consumers but not so well that they cease being docile. This is not to say that the schools, or any such institution, succeed in achieving this balance; in fact, they usually fail and, owing to the fiscal crisis of the state, in such a way that they turn out substandard workers. Similarly, the U.S. Army in Indochina had to promote enough drug use so that the men would not kill their officers but not so much that they would stop fighting (of course, this failed, too, and then the war was over); and the same may be said of the ordinary use of drugs among the American population.

This general mechanism works itself out in various ways. In the case of psychiatry, the conventional wisdom holds that insufficient fiscal resources are turned over by the state for the care of the mentally ill. Undoubtedly there is truth to this, but it is a truth at a low level of validity. In the case of Hector, for example, were there more funds there would be more staff for fewer patients, and the logic of Dr. Acheson would have proportionately less sway. But to stop at this level is fatuous, for the logic of Dr. Acheson and the low level of funding are neither accidental nor unrelated. Each is an essential element of the totality, his logic being that of the class in charge, while the fiscal shortage is an inevitable consequence of the kind of state it runs. In an upswing of capitalist fortunes (which, of course, is usually gained at the expense of the rest of the world), some of the surplus will be plowed back to humanize its basic tendencies. And while this is a good thing—mainly because it fuels revolutionary expectations—it should by no means be confused with an elimination of those tendencies. At its best, the flower of capitalist humanization is gained at the price of a hypocritical denial of its own poisonous roots, and those roots will prevail so long as the capitalist system maintains its hegemony.

A related simplification would see things at the level of particular individuals. It would look to replace the villains—Doctors Acheson and Jaxon, for example, or the numerous real people they represent —with people of virtue—Dr. Taunton or a properly trained Dr. Telemann, or Aide Jiminez, or the numerous real individuals they represent. But this is to miss the point entirely. On the basis of my experience I would warrant that a goodly number, perhaps the majority, of psychiatric practitioners are, if not villains, certifiably out-and-out hacks. However, the point of interest here is not to weed them out and replace them with better elements (needless to say, I am not denying the need to do this in practical situations even if it should run the risk of seriously depleting institutions of manpower) but to determine what it is that has made the average practitioner so wanting. We are dealing here with a well-established and widespread entity, *bourgeois stupidity*. Though this may not be all that easy to explain, it is surely not a matter of genetic inferiority. The psychiatrist who suffers from bourgeois stupidity was not born stupid. More than likely he was a bright and carefully nurtured youngster who turned dull only after years of immersion in the tarnishing bath of bourgeois professional life. Nor is his lackluster quality simply the result of poor training, and for the same reason that inadequate funding is not the real cause of poor patient care. All the money in the world can be thrown at bourgeois training institutions, and they will only turn out perfect bourgeois psychiatrists, not because better training is impossible but because training is never abstract, and the money thrown at it will have to be bourgeois money. No training process can transcend its concrete material conditions; in Marx's words, who is to educate the educator?[10] Therefore, all established efforts to upgrade psychiatric training, including that lucrative farce known as continuing medical education (wherein graduated practitioners have to certify that they have taken—usually at considerable expense—so many credits of ongoing professional training), do nothing to reverse the tide of stupidity that characterizes the profession precisely because it is *professional*, i.e., remains within a stupefying social practice.

The human failure of psychiatry must be located, then, in what is loosely referred to as the System. Nobody plotted it to be so, although very definite interests are served by it, and real individuals participate, wittingly or not, in its impersonal workings. Though wrapped in the mantle of bureaucratic depersonalization, the psychiatric System is in no sense outside the human world. It is carried out by some persons and shapes the destinies of others. But it offers up the human, as Sartre wrote, in the form of a thing, and so introduces thing-qualities into human existence. This is the bedrock of our quarrel with the prevailing mode of diagnosis and the source of the lifelessness that characterizes the profession.

The System consists of a set of sedimented practices—an opaque specter rendered mysterious, like the commodity itself, because cut off from the living sources of its value. In a very elementary way, what Doctors Acheson, Jaxon, *et al.*, i.e., the psychiatrist as Big-Time Professional, have done is to build for themselves an edifice of power out of the estrangement of madness: alienated desire. The firmer and more institutionally developed their reason becomes, the more remote will psychiatry be from the humanity of its clientele, who must increasingly become objects to its discourse. There is no way out of this predicament so long as the profession keeps its theory and practice within established channels. Therefore, the psychiatric System simply cannot permit the reversal of self-alienation, which is the authentic condition for the overcoming of mental disorder. Because the System self-contradictorily contains an imperative to care for people, it is happily not seamless, and numerous examples of a healing practice can be found in the real world. These are, however, characterized by being *personal* efforts; i.e., they run against the current of bureaucratic *depersonalization*, and so are disenfranchised from the moment of their birth. Except as window dressing, care has no point of engagement with a bureaucratic system. It simply does not "take." Meanwhile, those who play along with the prevailing power are made stupid through the lifelessness of their practices. Indeed, stupidity is a necessary by-product of a bureaucratic industry, whose main commerce is in madness.

Official psychiatry is created actively at the point of alienation, as described in the hospital stay of Hector. Once germinated it is propped up by the ideology of science and rooted in the soil of the state bureaucracy, whose larger purposes of social integration it serves. Thus, a number of contradictory processes are joined to form its systematization. We may isolate them out for purposes of exposition—the encounter with the personal Other of madness, the mystique of science, the needs of the state, careerism, and so forth. What counts is not any individual element but their mutual incompatibility, for such an inherently contradictory conglomerate creates the imperative for bureaucratic rationalization. And bureaucracy is like the Man Who Came to Dinner: it digs in, a pest sustained by the further contradictions it creates as its deadly impersonality goes to work on human needs under the aegis of the capitalist state.

It is, to repeat, human participation that keeps the System going and grinds down its participants. The mental-health practitioner becomes caught in the extreme degree of negation between the Otherness of the mad and that of the state. The high rate of breakdown characteristic of the profession—as well as the fact that the clientele of psychoanalysts is largely composed of other mental-health practitioners—is a logical outcome of the daily encounter between the poles of unhinged desire and alienated rationalization. And the dullness of mind evinced by so many becomes further comprehensible as a defense against the madness inherent in the toil of mental health. It is an occupational hazard, just like asbestosis.

The sedimented mass of bureaucratic practice has amongst its properties a significant alteration in the experience of time. Recall that history works itself out in different orders of temporality. We have already distinguished two such modes: the bound time, introduced in capitalist production; and the unbound time, revealed in psychoanalytic practice and postulated as the historical negation of bound time. Bureaucratic systems reveal yet another, tertiary order of temporality. Let us call it by a fittingly ugly name: *dysbound time*. There is no good word for it (one might just as well use the term "secondarily bound time" or "secondarily unbound time"); yet it is a definite entity.

It was noted above that bureaucracy, by introducing a degree of rationalization, frees up resources. And along with resources, desire is set in motion. Yet bureaucracy also depersonalizes; and to the extent that it entails domination, i.e., in most practical instances of interest to us, causes desire to be further alienated. Neither bound nor unbound time is adequate for bureaucratic needs. Too rational and fair for the direct domination of the former, and to remote and alienated for the erotics of the latter, bureaucracy is forced to turn its cold eye toward the production of a tertiary temporality, conjugated from bound and unbound time. Dysbound time draws upon the linear qualities of bound time and conceals its domination beneath the free-floating quality of unbound time. Practically speaking, this may be translated as follows: bureaucratic organizations—and the entire spectrum of social life as it comes under the sway of administration—are settings of disciplined unproductivity. Workers goof off and nobody really cares, perhaps because so little pleasure is taken.[11] Things are controlled but not much happens. Ennui, fatigue, and lethargy reign; and imagination and the critical intellect alike wither. Desire, loosened, asphyxiates in the stale bureaucratic air. Dysbound time *hangs*: it drifts like unbound time, but instead of alighting on the subjects of desire, it chokes on the clock of rationality.

Dysbound time is far more than a matter of the bureaucratic workplace; it exists wherever everyday life is touched by administration. And it most certainly affects the objects of bureaucracy: its clients. Nor do we wish to confine the orders of temporality to that which is subsumed by clocks; rather, they are entire modes of social experience. Therefore, the endless lineups characteristic of end-stage bureaucracy—the post office; Hector's VA; the clinics of inner-city hospitals, which "serve" the poor—are also manifestations of dysbound time, its *spatialization*. This spatialization is not fleeting but becomes embodied in the actual architecture of bureaucratic structures. And where these are supposed to relate to human needs, such as in the public mental hospital, dysbound space becomes the means of social forgetting and the further turning of the human into the animal, and eventually the inanimate. There is no need for physical brutalization in such places, although the setting invites it and brutalization often occurs. The process of administrative ordering through the medium of dysbound time wreaks more havoc in its silent way than could the most ardent sadist with his naked hand or the simple tools of cruelty.

Therefore, the abattoir-like atmosphere of Hector's ward was neither an accident nor a simple outcome of the economic fact that it is cheaper to build things with tiles and right angles. Nor is it incidental that nowhere does time hang so heavy as in the mental ward. The psychotic staring off into space is caught in an agonizing dilemma: the self, become Other, can further its Otherness by mirroring the dysbound time and space characteristic of its environment or, pushed to the wall, can immediately negate that time and space in a chaotic outburst of madness or violence, thereby also furthering its Otherness. Hector's ignition of the mattress in the seclusion room was just such a negation, with just such an outcome, although, as Dr. Telemann had accurately intuited, it was also an attempt to recapture another time, in Vietnam, when endless waiting became suffused with terror—and, indeed, all those times of terror and waiting he had known: the terror of waiting for his father's knife to descend, the waiting for his father to return, and more, no doubt. All these times are summated in the dysbound time of the bureaucratic institution, where they receive their apotheosis and where any spontaneous affirmation of Hector's becomes only a proof of his Otherness. Surrounded by the ice of bureaucracy, there is nothing for him to do but freeze. So it is that mental patients may be said to have careers.

The time that Proust invoked as the medium of human existence varies both historically and transhistorically. At the transhistorical level of the organism, time varies dramatically at different phases of life;[12] while historically time varies according to the prevailing mode of freedom and unfreedom. We are saturated in time, and we experience the totality through a multiplicity of temporalities, summed up in late-capitalist society by a movement from the bound time of production to the dysbound time of bureaucracy, with unbound time lurking about the edges. This movement is not a steady or harmonious one but the result of struggle. Dysbound time therefore has its own concrete history, with roots extending well back into the misty origins of capitalist rationalization. It may be said to have broken out into the open with the movement toward scientific management initiated by that warped genius Frederick W. Taylor. Taylor's contribution to culture was the top-down administration of effort. He came along at the moment of transition to monopoly capitalism, when the rationalization of the factory—which is, after all, a kind of bureaucratic organization—had proceeded to the point where worker inefficiency could become appreciable and hence under managerial control. Inefficiency from the standpoint of production can of course be desire and resistance on the part of the worker; but Taylor, who epitomized the emotionally blocked individual typical of capitalist relations, saw none of that.[13] Rather, he envisioned the possibility of quantifying effort. His means of doing so, the time-and-motion study, was the leading edge of the modern form of domination entailed in the reduction of sensuous activity to lifeless categories of time and space. The same type of maneuver that resurfaces in psychiatric diagnosis was seized upon: the reduction of sensuous conscious historical participation to a dead objective category that can be placed into a system of exchange for the benefit of a ruling class. Management is domination become bureaucratic, and the conversion of the time of experience to the dysbound form. Taylor's innovation has ramified throughout the totality, from the workplace to the supermarket to the psychiatric hospital. It is the sign of late capitalism.[14]

Yet struggle continues. Desire, being transhistorical, cannot be done away with. More, bureaucratic practice, by introducing labor-saving devices, continually provokes its emergence and in turn creates imperatives for new forms of control. Mad Hector is the extreme that illuminates the hazy middle ground. His conflagration of the seclusion room represents desire turned to hatred reacting against the blank confinement incorporated in the mental institution. It is a real, if self-defeating, form of political resistance. And the psychiatric practices that arise from the binding of Hector's desire—his diagnosing, the ritual of Grand Rounds, the training of Dr. Telemann, the careers of Doctors Acheson and Jaxon—are all materializations of the control that had to be gained over him just as Taylor had to take control of his underproducing workers. The rigmarole of established psychiatry is therefore a species of scientific management. It is Taylorism of the mind.

However, the administration of mind goes far beyond the binding up of the mentally disturbed. Of greater importance is the prevention of social unrest among the normal. Hector has fallen over the wall of Otherness. Those of us who live on the productive side of that boundary also have desire breathed into life and are each potential outbreaks of resistance. Therefore, this desire too, must be administered and dysbound lest it become irksome. Here, of course, mental health is no longer the designated means of administration, although it bears a close relationship to that which has been given the job.

In its most general sense, the administration of mind in late-capitalist culture is the province of what is called mass culture. Despite its self-image, then, the mental health industry is closer to mass culture than it is to science. A brief consideration of this sphere may thus repay our interest.[15]

By "mass culture" we mean not only entertainment but also the dissemination of news and, indeed, the entire managerial manipulation of symbolic reality (crudely termed "information"). Therefore, it plays a critical role in whatever fortunes psyche may have in capitalist society, and indeed is crucial to the survival of that society.

Capitalism's *means* to influence culture systematically came with the development of technology, especially that of communication, while its *interest* in doing so derived from a twofold source: the basic need of every system of domination to quash resistance, and capitalism's very own need to universalize the commodity form, in particular to convert labor-power into a commodity. For example, E. P. Thompson has beautifully shown how the culture of linear time (which is itself a kind of firmament for so many other cultural activities) became forcibly imposed upon the peasant population in the course of industrialization.[16] Here the technical means were acquired in the form of (manufactured) mechanical timepieces, while the interest was clearly that of shaping up a work force who had to be paid hourly wages in order to have surplus value wrung out of them. The workplace in capitalist form was a setting whose spontaneous cultural roots had been destroyed.[17] This was not incidental but a basic ingredient of the capitalist mode of production and one that has reverberated down through the years. The loss of the connection to productivity left behind a cultural vacuum that would not long remain unfilled.

Throughout the nineteenth century, the ruling class set itself the task of cultural colonization of the individual no less than it undertook the political colonization of the entire globe. The goal was to secure and advance the particular structures necessary for capitalism: to make the world a market, the workplace a setting for the alienation of wage labor, and personal life a product of the nuclear family. The idealization of the family and the sentimantalization of women were among its main inroads. Another was the codification in a patriarchal repressive mode of popular legends into "fairy tales" by, for example, the Brothers Grimm or Hans Christian Andersen. Yet another was the widespread popularization of the pulp romance. And the effects of such cultural penetration upon individuals became sufficiently striking to draw the attention of artists, most notably in the first great novel to depict critically the personal ruin wrought by cultural domination, *Madame Bovary*.

As a result of these machinations and their interrelation with other features of political economy, it becomes possible to talk of a new, specifically capitalist entity: mass culture. And it becomes necessary to talk about another entity, the masses, as the object of mass culture. Unlike high culture, which preceded it, mass culture establishes itself not by opposition to popular culture but by a penetration of it. The sweetest result of this, so far as ruling class interests go, is a serious undercutting of resistence to capitalist domination. Class consciousness is unthinkable without an authentic popular culture from which to materially articulate its existence. Mass culture invades popular culture as a cancer-producing virus invades host tissue; and as it does do, the articulation of a class for itself dissolves into that of a formless homogenized social mass incapable of real resistance. Popular culture fights back, i.e., the host attempts to reassert its resistance; but the lesson of this decay is not lost upon the class of capitalists, and in the twentieth century a concatenation of elements combines to render the mass culture of the nineteenth century relative child's play.

It is not our purpose to detail the workings of contemporary mass culture except to indicate their point of entry into the psychology of the individual. It is sufficient to point out here that the whole affair has been made possible by the concentration of capital in its monopoly phase and by the rise of a massive state apparatus to superintend society as a whole. (In this respect the mass media, the advertising industry, et cetera, even though they belong primarily to the so-called private sector and may take positions at variance with the government, are, with that government, parts of the *state*.) At the same time, the process has been made necessary by the imperatives of late capital, which *must* subdue the personal life it has created if commodity consumption is to proceed and work is not to break down. Furthermore, the images and information purveyed by mass culture are symbols that at one and the same time register on the individual mind and take on an objective existence of their own. In their latter aspect, these symbols become commodities themselves, and their production and sale is the vast preserve of a very large and complex enterprise, the *culture industry*, which is obedient in the highest degree to the laws of capitalist development. The culture industry is doubly important to capitalist society, as both the generator of mass culture and big business in itself. In fact, the inexorable development of political economy, just as it has abstracted the exchange function from solid gold to blips on an electronic screen, has made of information, i.e., materialized symbols, the prime commodity of late-capitalist society.[18]

Finally, the whole development would have been inconceivable without major technological advances. Here once again technology is no neutral force but a chosen servant, a Caliban to express the will of its Prospero. In any case, the advent of first electrical and then electronic transmission of symbols has been, together with nuclear technology, the decisive technological move of the twentieth century. For example, broadcasting, like no other event in human history, drastically changes the structure of personal experience and lends to the particular contents of mass culture a radically new force. With mass media, mind is everywhere and anywhere. The disembodiment initiated by Plato, elaborated by Descartes, and materially anchored in the capitalist mode of production could not achieve its full realization until the age of broadcasting. Print, to be sure, was a near equal to broadcasting in its usefulness as a medium for mass culture. However, it was not until print and broadcasting became hooked up to each other that the vision of total control over communications could become a palpable possibility. The electronic transmission of symbols, abstracted from the immediate presentation of their source, instantly disseminable around the glove, and infinitely malleable, is not just a

representation of capitalist relations; it is the apotheosis of those relations, a pure form of capitalist abstraction, seemingly freed from the
brutal alienation of labor that infects the real capitalist totality. The
media is capital's dream.

The ideology of mass culture has a simple core: to present capital
as a timeless universal instead of as a historical phase. It strives to
present the world of capitalist production and consumption as both
rational and gratifying, and capitalist society as a domain of fundamental consensus livened up by occasional squabbles instead of one
beset with fundamental antagonisms. Viewed from a critical standpoint, therefore, it fails wretchedly in these goals, and so winds up
with a demented and banal view of reality. But smug dismissal is not
in order. What counts about mass culture is less its judgment by
critical standards than the fact that it seeks—and virtually succeeds—
to eliminate the ground from which a real critique can be made. Mass
culture is realized then not so much in any of its particular contents as
in the process by which it moves to absorb all opposition. Banality—
the result of loss of critical tension—is therefore not incidental but an
essential condition. Mass culture constantly searches for and appro-
priates spontaneous manifestations of culture, including oppositional
ones—and just as constantly works to render these living shoots of
popular culture into standardized fodder for the masses. The chain
from the Homeric legend and the authentic folktale to the Brothers
Grimm to the early "artistic" Disney cartoon to today's computer-
realized cartoon on Saturday morning television is an inexorable and
paradigmatic one, downward and debased as far as human possibilities go, just fine from the standpoint of capital. It would be a grave
mistake to think that the aim of the culture industry is to produce
objects of real utility, enlightenment, or gratification. Rather, its concrete goals are to mystify, to titillate, and to frustrate; to take from
people the organs of their own cultural resistence and to keep them
hungry, restless, and confused, frantic in search of leisure, greedy for
new commodities, and incapable of understanding, much less changing, their world. So successful has the culture industry been in its
various campaigns to subdue human mental capacities that to it we
owe one definite if dubious favor; it has so far spared us the need for
fascism. Or, to be more exact, it spares us the need for hard, authoritarian fascism, moving instead in the direction of a *soft fascism* more
in line with the needs of late capitalism. As the late Italian filmmaker

Pier Paolo Pasolini put it for his own country and for the culture industry's most successful medium, television:

> No one doubts that television is authoritarian and repressive, as no other means of information in the world has ever been. The fascist newspapers and the Mussolini slogans on the farms are laughable in comparison and are (tragically) just as ridiculous as the plow when placed alongside the tractor. Fascism, I repeat, even in its very essence, was not capable of scratching the soul of the Italian people, while the new fascism, thanks to the new means of communication and information (especially the television) has not only scratched it, but torn it, raped it and befouled it forever.[19]

It is tempting to hunt this monstrosity down its various paths, to study its several institutions—television, journalism, advertising, tourism, et cetera—and its particular contents. But this would distract us from the task at hand, and so we leave the job for others. The problem for us rather is this: How do all these tremendous developments in social control intersect with the subjectivity of individuals? How does the administration of reality just outline act upon a consciousness nurtured by the nuclear family?

The answer lies less in the manifest content of ideology than in the form by which it is conveyed. The phrase "administration of reality" means that every communication takes on a dual quality, being on the one hand a statement about the world and, on the other, an instrument of administration. These two qualities are always conjoined, but they need have nothing to do with each other so far as their content or qualities go. Nonetheless, there is a definite relation between them: the former, i.e., the statement about the world, is manifest and carefully wrought but remains subordinated to the latter, the instrument of administration, which is hidden.[20] What is concealed about this instrument—which we may call a supermessage to the ostensible message transmitted by the medium—is any explicit declaration of meaning. Nonetheless, the content of the supermessage is perfectly interpretable, being always a variation on the theme "made—and controlled—by the culture industry," or "administered to you in the interests of capital," or "you may think this is for you but it is made by an unseen me who wants you in my power"; in other words, the supermessage may be summed up by the formula [*For It*], where the brackets convey its hidden quality, while the *It* is the unseen power of capital controlling the culture industry. The supermessage is a unitary structure made at the point where the culture industry seizes control over spontaneous culture. Hence, it is always present, built-in, as it were, to the medium itself, so long as we remember to consider the medium a social practice and not an inert piece of technology.

It is characteristic of the culture industry to produce a limitless set of representations of the universe, from sublime explorations of novae in space to asinine television game shows. Yet the very prodigality of its messages renders more stark the grimly contrasting supermessage [*For It*]. Indeed, the very totalizing character of the media, their relentless pursuit of any conceivable topic and theme, is less the sign of a robust diversity than of the omnipresence and omnipotence of this *It*, which indifferently views the universe as fodder for its needs.

There is a basic contradiction ingrained then in all mass-cultural products, between the visible and luminous profusion of the message and the monotonous, concealed power of the supermessage. Therefore, the more the manifest message within mass culture has an emancipatory or universal content, the less true it becomes. For example, the recent television serial *Roots*, which depicted the resistance of a black family to hideous oppression through several generations, was widely hailed as a sign that "America" has outgrown its racist past. Of course, the series never mentioned the roots of racism (or slavery) in the logic of American capitalism, and indeed showed the Haley family eventually overcoming its *denigration* through absorption into mainstream capitalist society. However, the actual message was more pervasive than that: it was simply the immersion of the saga in the medium of television itself, most notably in the frequent "breaks" wherein the audience was told, in brutal effect, "Now a word from your master, the commodity," but equally present in the adherence to all the conventions of administered televised discourse, the timing, the structure of language, the total immersion in packaged technology, all of which make the programs themselves into commodities and so negate at the deepest level the manifest message of universality. In sum, then, the totalized message of any mass cultural product that purports to emancipate its audience is not "freedom" in the abstract, but *"Be free [For It]."*

What is this mysterious *It* to which mass culture hews? Capital is its ultimate referent, but the ultimate meaning of something does not exhaust its intermediary forms, which are after all what comprise actual reality. Capital, moreover, is no thing but, as Marx put it, a social relation that inheres in various things and gives them their quality. The quality of spectral omnipresence and omnipotence deriving from capital is perhaps best revealed when it appears as the "thing" called money, which combines intrinsic worthlessness (thereby permitting its omnipresence), mystery, and awesome ever-expanding power. The spectral power of capital also appears more generally in commodities themselves, where it gives them what Marx called their fetishistic character. Now we locate it again in the super-message of mass culture.

But we have also seen *It*, have we not, in the guise of that Other characteristic of pathological narcissism? We have explored this Other as it appeared immediately in the mental life of our Sarah and inferred it as the characteristic form of inner estrangement set going by the bourgeois family in the late stages of its historical agony. The omnipresent supermessage of mass culture allows us to close the circle between capital and its objectifiable forms (money, commodities) on the one side, and subjectivity on the other. Now we may surmise more clearly why little Sarahs stay glued to the television screen—and why the appellation "narcissistic character," though it may be applied in a full-blown, pathological way to only a tiny fraction of the people, is nonetheless a historical development.

Viewed from the other end, the culture industry itself is the work of this kind of narcissism. It is the "narcissistic character of our time" manifest as a force of production. Our Sarah, with more "mental health" and less integrity, would have worked well in any of its numerous outposts. The empty sensibility of the narcissist serves perfectly as a zone of mediation between the unbound time of desire and the bound time that controls the culture industry. The narcissistic consciousness is a transducer that converts the primary temporalities of capital into the dysbound form by which culture is administered in the world of bureaucracy. The culture industry must water the bitterness of reality with desire, and for this purpose only the narcissistic character has enough empty desire at his/her disposal and enough indifference as well as detachment to employ it as the master requires. By this mechanism, the most "advanced" sensibility produced by the bourgeois family in its state of decay is plowed back into the apparatus that regulates the family. And the multiplication between this psychological loop on the one hand, and, on the other, the technological explosion of the means of transmitting symbolic reality results in the omnipresence of mind characteristic of mass culture. We can no longer talk of a universally and humanly internalized personal world, a mental world that can be localized in persons themselves. The self never existed, as the medical and psychoanalytic models had it, as an entity within the individual: it always included its Other, was always essentially grounded in intersubjective naming. But this Other, though it led to the divine or to nature, was, no matter how oppressive or mystifying, always mediated by a human presence. Even Jahweh, the not-to-be-visualized godhead, was demonstrably linked to the father. The decisive difference in advanced capitalism is the loss of human mediation—in other words, the loss of popular, spontaneous culture—and its replacement by administered mass culture. Now the symbol itself is multivalently rooted in the person and the commodity, two antithetical worlds. Mass culture has succeeded in bringing the commodity into the psyche even as it has blunted class struggle through a corruption of proletarian desire. As any television screen shows, the Other and the commodity are united, and all struggle is predestined as futile.

I do not wish to imply that the actual cultural situation is as one-sided as the foregoing account indicates, only that the account is true to a certain basic and essential tendency. In the actual world of culture (which goes beyond the industry itself, i.e., to include the so-called independent media community, just as a substantial portion of emotional care is delivered outside the bounds of the mental-health industry), pockets of resistance flourish. It is not our purpose to describe this inasmuch as our theme remains personal and subjective life.

And here it may be said that mass culture, for all that it is not everything in the cultural domain, has become so powerful an influence as to have structurally altered the relations between psyche and world in advanced capitalist society.

The television screen shows us only the external symbol of the Other. Our concern is what happens when the symbol is ingested, as it must be in the desociated, deparentalized world of late capitalism. Once incorporated, the symbol settles like a drowned sailor till it comes to rest on the deepest mental strata, which lay unprotected by the mantle of authentic human activity. "Full fathom five thy father lies," sang Ariel to Ferdinand, telling him of the wondrous "sea-change" that was Prospero's art. Today the change is no longer wondrous, owing to the passage of the control of the symbol from Prospero to Caliban: the culture industry. A defeated, desensualized representation penetrates psyche; and the disembodied notion (*For It*], invades the subject and sets itself alongside the weakened parental imagoes. The individual craves this buttressing, for she/he is unable to complete the arc of personal development without it. We would minimize the influence of the [*For It*] if we saw it as simply a matter of providing personal guidance or sustenance to the self. No, the symbol of the Other offers no such warmth; all it promises is stabilization, the battening down of hatches, a numbing anodyne against the terrors of existence.

To succumb to this system—that is to say, to grow up in our society and turn out normal—is to become pacified. And pacified should be read in two interrelated yet distinct senses: removed from class consciousness, and spared neurosis. Freud was a profound dualist and postulated a sharp split between the id, a portion of "immortal nature," and the ego, representative of the given social world, with superego a differentiation within the ego that dialectically fused id energies with morality as encoded in parental imagoes. This schema was presented as a transhistorical given and has been accepted as such. In it the weight of history was confined to the superego, and to the kinds of identifications within it and the ego. A sharp split between id and ego was held to be as natural as the supposed split between ego and outer world. It was a potent conception and helped to account for a great deal; but with much of psychoanalytic theory (and bourgeois thought in general) it shares a characteristic denial of history, a freezing of the psychological relations peculiar to a given time into a timeless and supposedly natural mold. The ego/id split, with its exciting implication of a seething and potentially revolutionary core ready to burst through at any time, is historically apt only to that age of humanity characterized by direct conflict between social classes. It is not the representation of a psychological structure so much as a metaphor for the rage of the slave or proletarian, ready to strike at the master and restrained only by force from doing so. It does not describe well the psychology of the primitive, or that of a classless society. And it does not help us think very clearly (which is the best thing a theory can be called upon to do) for an age such as ours when the instruments of mass culture continually cross the boundary between ego and id.

The power of the media to locate mind everywhere breaks through ego boundaries that hitherto only a psychosis could breach; and the interests of capital in asserting total social control intersect profoundly with this technical capability. The combination of interest and means allows for a new round of alienation, that of id. Late capital does not have to rely exclusively upon police or the father or ego to impose domination. It now has the option, which it finds increasingly necessary to employ, of so magically transforming the very air of reality that desire can be exhaled directly into it. In this way the self expires into history.

Even with this degree of penetration, there is resistance. It is in people to fight back. The self is born in negation, with the infant's refusal of the parental Other and his/her coordinated assertion of individuality. On the far side of that transhistorical refusal, the mental Other takes shape and challenges the organs of administration. Desire and the state enter into a dialectic that determines the content of mass culture and shapes the contours of individual lives. We do not yet have the calculus to comprehend how individual lives as a whole are determined by their relationship to a historical process such as bureaucratic administration. The psychologic discourse at our disposal concentrates on limiting the perimeter of the personal to the family. How such limits are breached, as they must be, is a matter of major concern and deserves the exposition of still another life story with its specimen of "pathology."

Consider Frank, a worker with whom I recently became acquainted. Like all workers, Frank lives in the shadow of necessity and contributes to the reproduction of capital: his everyday existence is conducted according to the prevailing notion of necessity. He is obedient to the clock, drives to work on the right-hand side of the road, and despite impecunity has two television sets, one for the kids and one for himself and his wife (sometimes their quarreling over prime-time programing makes them think of purchasing a third). The oldest child goes to school, where the official system of symbolic representation is drummed into her head; and his wife reads pulp magazines and watches soap operas during the day, whereby a certain amount of desire is bled off and mixed with the canons of consumerism.

I did not, to be sure, see Frank for these matters, but because of his folly, or "emotional illness." Frank, to put it bluntly, is a wife beater. A bad one, in fact: he has recently been given to knocking her silly and even made her to go the hospital once, which was the immediate occasion of his seeking help. There is no elegant way of putting the matter, which is an unhappily common occurrence and one justifiably considered deserving of condemnation in everyday life. If Frank differs from other wife beaters, it is in a heightened sense of remorse. He wishes to repent, i.e., be cured, of his vice, and so brings himself to the clinic. In this way we come to know him, if not to forgive his sins, for forgiveness is what he wants but is not within our province to offer. I lack the power to absolve sin in an ecclesiastical sense and refuse to exercise it from the standpoint of that tepid liberalism, which holds that an individual like Frank is to be relieved of moral responsibility for his acts because he is "emotionally sick" or so victimized by life in capitalist society that he could not behave otherwise. I say this on philosophical grounds. There is an intrinsic and essential split between the individual person and abstract necessity, historical or otherwise. Therefore, we always have a choice, and the notion of moral responsibility exists because of this reality. It should be added that if we cannot offer moral absolution, neither can we condemn, which is a great relief. And though there is no point in either excusing or blaming Frank for what he does, I found myself touched by him the more I got to know him. It is one of the saving graces of psychoanalytic work that the most outrageous scoundrel becomes less malevolent and more sympathetic when one understands him from the vantage point of desire. This is due less to an understanding in an intellectual sense than to the reconnection we make with our own maternality in the course of clinical work.

In any case, Frank is no scoundrel but someone who, like Jane, suffers from attacks during which hatred gets the better of him. It is tempting, in fact, to regard him as a victim, one who reconnects the abuses he has suffered over his twenty-six years into hostility toward his wife. As we shall see, Frank had a pretty harrowing childhood; and his adult work, instead of bringing some autonomy or satisfaction, barely entitles him to subsistence. Frank works as a laborer when he can, which has turned out to be on the average of two or three days a week. As the housing industry has taken a beating recently, due to those "impersonal" forces of capitalist political economy, Frank has found himself on the margins of the "reserve army of the unemployed." He is in a constant state of anxiety about whether he will work; and when he does work, he suffers an alienation that results in a general stunting of his powers of craft, a lack of genuine involvement in the task, and a weakening of bonds with his fellow workers. Only in the last year has Frank managed to acquire enough seniority to keep the wolf from his door—but of this, more later.

Assume for the moment that times go badly for him. Can this be the reason why Frank behaves as he does? Hardly, even though the most reliable epidemiological prediction of mental breakdown is the rate of unemployment,[21] and though it is well-known that the ordinary pursuit of work in the United States is deadening when it is not maddening.[22] However, neither of these generalizations describes the vagaries of any given individual. For the individual person it is personal history that counts, and personal history is shaped by desire as it meets historical reality. "Psychology" is necessary and yet must be superseded if we are to grasp this juncture, which we may begin to understand if we sense the meaning of concrete particulars. Exactly how does the "outside," historically manifest world of productive institutions intersect with the "inside," domestically organized world to which desire has been relegated in capitalist society? To figure this out we must take a fairly close look at Frank.

Frank comes for help—as do most—because he has lost control of his situation. And he is afraid of what he might do the next time. Matters have deteriorated so much that he has voluntarily moved out lest he do further harm. Frank stays in frequent touch with his wife, Mary, but for safety's sake he confines his visits to an hour or so in the evening. For all his self-imposed limitation Frank lives for his visits home. He loves Mary, and even more than her, loves his three children—to be exact, his two children and Mary's three. The oldest, eight-year-old Gail, is the child of a liaison between Mary and a now-forgotten lover, Emil, a man she never married and knew only briefly in the interstices of her hectic courtship with Frank. Frank raised Gail from birth and cares for her as one of his own, as much as four-year-old Kathryn and baby Frank, Jr., only five months old.

Curiously, it is with Frank, Jr.'s arrival that Frank's problem became unmanageable. Until then he and Mary had had a fairly turbulent but basically equilibrated life together. Their many quarrels never proceeded to anything more serious than screaming, an occasional slap, or at the most, a night at Mary's mother's house. Since the infant's birth, however, Frank has felt a kind of incoherent fury at Mary welling up inside him, which is triggered whenever Mary nags him. All she has to do is to suggest that he is not taking good enough care of her and the children, and Frank feels a shudder go through him. When she does not relent—and it is not in Mary's way to do so—something snaps and Frank strikes, not with a slap but with a closed fist, and he does not stop until he realizes she is no longer yelling at him but whimpering. Only then does Frank relax; and with the return of his senses he becomes aware with horror of the children, wide-eyed with fear, cringing in the corner.

Frank accepts violence as part of the normal routine of life. But this is different. "Something comes over me. I don't know what I'm doing. It's not normal." Agreed—but this "it" happens. What is "it"? Translate back to the Greek and we have Freud's id, that which is unnamable, unnaming, and peremptory, the bidding of desire, here turned to hatred. We do not have a force that builds up, hydraulically, because of accumulated frustrations in life until it explodes and bursts through its barriers. If this were so, if people merely reacted in proportion to their insult, then oppression would have halted long ago. Id, or desire, is part of the world, yet disjoined from the rest by an incapacity to name, to describe in language. The common-sense view—which is, it may be added, politico-economic in its structure—assumes a balance sheet of exchangeable, real events: so much "trauma"—hard luck at work, "stress" from the infant, bills to pay, the beers imbibed on the way home, and so forth—in one column, so many "coping mechanisms" in another, until column A outweighs column B and violence is "released." It is easy to see the homology of such discourse with the cost-accounting methods of the modern corporation or Pentagon. It makes Frank's personality quantifiable, so that too much of a bad thing pushes out the accumulated hostility that has been stockpiled like unrealizable merchandise in the warehouse of his mind. The reproaches leveled against Freud's original "hydraulic" libido theory[23] are therefore more properly directed toward the kind of economic logic that lies embedded in it. This is a truer characterization than the one of "nineteenth-century biology" ordinarily used to describe Freud's libido theory, for if nineteenth-century biology was mechanistic, it was because of its subordination to the forms of nineteenth-century capitalist culture.

In any event, politico-economic discourse applied to matters psychological tends to rationalize what Frank does, to make him understandable in terms of point-to-point reasoning. But this contradicts his own self-perception: "I go crazy," he says. "It doesn't figure at all. Why should I act this way? I love my son; he's what I've wanted all my life. And these spells, they seem to take me over completely by surprise."

The baby is not the only good thing that has happened to Frank lately. He has also been able to make amends for an ancient source of humiliation. Here we return to the betterment of his fortunes, noted above. Only shortly before the birth of Frank, Jr., did Frank's seniority on the job enable him to finally marry Mary legally and to establish an officially recognized residence. I say "officially recognized" with some cause, for what had kept them from legalizing their relations was one of those mad flights of bureaucratic rationality, namely, that Frank's marginal position in the labor force made it more expedient for Mary to go on welfare as an unmarried mother than to live in legal wedlock with him. Mary—and her sister and mother—had become quite skilled at playing the welfare game. Her virtuosity as a welfare pirate had given Mary as much pride as it had chagrined Frank; and he sensed a heightened irritability in Mary once she was lawfully his wife and he was at last removed of the burden of evading the welfare caseworker. It seems as though Mary preferred her *impersonal* dependency upon the welfare bureaucracy to *personal* dependency on Frank. No doubt his increased economic power at home led him to make greater demands on her. It was as if she had four children now instead of two, with one of them claiming sovereignty over the household. The old arrangement had left her closer to her mother, more able to bridge the gap between the families. Mary was not at all sure she liked the new arrangements; she felt paradoxically unemployed, and not being able to recognize this, she transported her attack to more conventional ground and needled Frank for not giving her more.

We now have the setting for Frank's outbursts of rage but not its immediacy. If we are to break with politico-economic discourse and admit the agency of a desire that wishes but cannot name, we must stake out the ground of subjectivity itself. And subjectivity, or "psychic reality" as Freud held it, has its own mode of being. There is no way of reading directly from the world into the mind. As far as the commodity has penetrated, it only drives subjectivity back farther like a wild animal, Blake's Tyger, into the jungles of desire. Frank's subjectivity, the location of his outbreak, is something that is his alone. Put into first-person terminology, it is the "I," not the "me," that is the subject's alone and not included in any province of the object.

A road into this zone (not the zone itself, but a platform for observing it better, a safari of sorts) is given by personal history revealed in the shards of language it has left behind. Such was Freud's central hypothesis. Put into logical terms, if one is seized by something that is real but unrecognized, it may be that the altered state—the "it" or id—is a product of some earlier time, a returned, or *revenant*, as Freud called it. Desire becomes folly through its hold on illusion, its investment in the impossible and the nonexistent. As we are unalterably historical, each impossible nonexistent is carried forward as the search for new illusions. What we consider to be "immediacy" in its freshness and vividness is never wholly irradiated by the objective present. Its appearing to be in the present is the product of forgetting; while that which is forgotten, i.e., repressed desire, is what applies the quality of immediacy by pressing forward toward consciousness. All present objects—including, to be sure, the commodities and wages of political economy—are gained then by a process of forgetting;[24] and the eruptions of desire that flare into the various species of madness are, as Freud decisively pointed out, a kind of remembering, past desire coming closer to the present and hence defining the heightened awareness that is gained, even at the price of madness, when the interior and the exterior, subject and object, move toward one another.

So must it be with Frank's rage. Our query then is: What is he trying to remember, and what happens to him as he tries to remember it?

Frank is the fifth of six children born in rapid succession to second-generation Irish and Italian immigrants. Ethnicity is an important datum here, as it signifies that Frank's mother, who was from the Italian side, was marrying out of the clan by joining with Frank's Irish father. Though the conditions of capitalist upheaval have made such intermarriages commonplace among the working class, we should never underestimate their significance. "Marrying outside the family" means that the exchange function played by the woman is violated, an event that the family cannot take supinely. In the case of Frank's mother, however, she never got very far outside her family of origin. Concretely, this meant getting caught between father and husband, the former a violently patriarchal man who refused to tolerate loss of control over his females, and the latter, a passive, mournful sort, given to drink and evasion. Frank's father was to have much opportunity to exercise these characteristics, particularly the second, in the conditions of life thrust upon him by his tyrannical father-in-law and his complaisant wife. Soon after the birth of his last child (and when Frank was two), the enmity between the two males flared into open combat. The older was the more powerful, not physically so much as authoritatively, which flowed from the lingering embedment of immigrant families in highly patriarchal precapitalist culture. The old man banished his son-in-law from the house and threatened to kill him if he returned. Meanwhile, Frank's mother, tied to her father, did not leave. Little Frank may have witnessed this dramatic denouement; and if he did not, he had considerable opportunity to experience its sequelae. After his flight, Frank's father began to live a shadow existence, hidden from the wrathful yet nodding gaze of the patriarch. A part of the house was more or less sealed off, and here Frank's father would repair at nights, padding about surreptitiously to avoid detection. So complete was the subterfuge, and so thorough his humiliation, that he was denied access to the bathroom lest his presence be discovered. Instead he had to resort to bedpans and the portage of his wife to satisfy bodily needs.

In this way Frank grew up. Yet matters were not always so. As often as not, and with increasing frequency over the years, his father would simply fade away for weeks, even months, at a time. Occasionally Frank would get wind of his presence and meet the old man at a playground or nearby bar. A few words, a few trinkets, and his father was gone again. Finally the visits stopped altogether, and Frank learned that his father was dying of cancer. He saw him one last time at the hospital. The funeral had to be kept secret from grandfather, who followed his son-in-law into the grave three years later. But by then Frank was trying to forget in the navy.

What Frank tried to forget was his desire for his father. Desire does not know *what* it wants but it knows it *wants*. Frank forgot even this. However, desire forgotten is quiet but not quiescent. Frank sustained his through the basic process of identification. He became the father-who-stays when he gave up Mary to Emil, then accepted their child; and then, the father-who-leaves when he repeated the father's ways and stealthily moved in and out of his wife's home under the eye of the welfare caseworker. Being like the father absolved Frank of the imperative of wanting him, especially as the subterfuge involved a suppression of Frank's activity, a complementary humiliation in this case. Desire is best held in check by stunting, inertia, and passivity, i.e., victimization, the time worn fee of the oppressed.

What threatens the oppressed is not victimization but its undoing, the upsurge of desire whether as hatred or love. Frank's danger came when he decided to move forward, to grow—in other words, to place himself in the way of his desire. For the most part, growth does not occur consciously or deliberately, like a New Year's resolution. It happens as people assert the life that is in them. And life is blind at first; consciousness is hard won and tolerable only to the lucky. Frank was not lucky. When he released his wife from her bondage to the welfare bureaucracy, he was trying to reconcile father and grandfather within himself, and to gain thereby a wife-mother worthy of his dreams. Not a chance. The desire for his father necessarily contained too much hatred for this illusion to be sustained, hatred that belonged between father and grandfather, and his own toward each of them. Meanwhile, his wife, instead of turning into the mother he dreamed of, became what she was—a real woman, herself caught in the tangles of patriarchal possession, and rankling, as we have pointed out, from the loss of her own autonomy. In this deformed world desire requires illusion for a sense of realization, i.e., pasteboard figures, not real people with their own, often contrary, illusions. In any event, Frank's wife reminded him once too often that he was not the man he had hoped to become. This might have been tolerable under the previous circumstances but was not so in an arrangement that had ignited Frank's desire. The fall—shall we say "narcissistic injury"?—was too great and the crash too explosive. What was released was a pent-up murderousness toward the real mother, now palpably present in the guise of Mary. And here a peculiarity of desire occured, which students of the phenomenon know quite well, and women under patriarchy have come to rue: that the rage toward mother knows no bounds. The male who uneasily attempts to assume the power of the phallus is exquisitely sensitive to his desire for the woman who was with him at his beginning. This desire can lead to the customary Oedipal consequences of castration by the patriarch. Such is the main outcome when the patriarch, or his direct representative, a strong father, is present. It is often enough a fairly murderous situation, as recorded in fable, myth, and innumerable case histories. As for Frank, this dimension existed but was fatally complicated by the fact of being presented with two mutually destructive male images: a father who is destroyed and a wrathful grandfather who destroys him. But there is another twist to the relation, one that can coexist with the Oedipal situation and comes to dominate it in situations where patriarchy is preserved, where the conditions of hatred are established, yet where the real father is absent or weak. And this ensues from the fact that the small boy is mainly in the care of the very woman from whom he is to differentiate himself as possessor of the phallus.[25] If the real father is not there, what the boy-Frank has to contend with is a current toward *merger* with the mother, i.e., a subjective union with her or actually becoming her. Critically, this occurs at a stage of development much more primitive than that of the ordinary identification with the father. Now merger is experienced as a liquidation of the self; and if hatred forms much of the picture, the liquidation is experienced as annihilation: a murderous chaos to be relieved only by a hasty, radical, and equally murderous differentiation. It is in such settings that women from Clytemnestra (who was slain by her son, Orestes, after having engineered the murder of her husband, Agamemnon) to Frank's Mary have received their violence. While Orestes goes mad after the revenge-murder of his mother (a condition that Aeschylus represents in the *Oresteia* as the pursuit by female furies, i.e., internal figures of the Bad Mother), he is ultimately redeemed by Apollo in a reconstructed patriarchy for which the Mother God becomes tamed and phallic Athene. Frank, on the other hand, being a proletarian in late capitalism, can expect no such salvation. All he has at his disposal is a mental-health clinic with a good-sized waiting list and shifting, inexperienced personnel. Meanwhile, to be sure, he has seen to it that he is once again out of the house, as was his father. This may put his desire at bay once more, and bring him a little closer to the image of the wrathful grandfather, but it is definitely not what could be called an optimal solution.

The murderous violence against women that extends all the way from Aeschylus's *Agamemnon* to Frank should not lead us to believe it is transhistorical, for it occurs only under specific historical circumstances such as patriarchal domination. And it is made much more likely to occur when patriarchy is threatened or in decline, and the male is faced with the simultaneous task of dominating via the phallus and differentiating himself from the primitive mother. But if this murderous outcome of desire is historical, then it must also be implicated in shaping history. The person Frank is an occasion in which political economy and desire intersect at a historical conjuncture. His retreat from the family is occasioned by the weakness of his actual father vis-à-vis his grandfather, i.e., by a historical gradient of declining patriarchal authority, one which, I believe, would be quite generally confirmed by widespread personal experience. Whether the "old days" were good or bad, it must be recognized that fathers, generally speaking, had a lot more uncontested authority in them. At the same time, Frank's retreat reproduces that gradient but with a decisive difference. The gap that Frank inherited was between two real men, grandfather and father. The gap that he passes on to his children, on the other hand, is between a man—himself—and an impersonal bureaucracy. The linkage point from the standpoint of desire is the equation made by Frank between the grandfather as patriarch and the welfare bureaucracy as repository of impersonal undifferentiated power. Translated into infantile terms, the bureaucracy inherits the patriarchal mantle and combines it with the nameless primitive power of the mother. The real living figures of Frank and his father, who hold intermediate status from a psychological standpoint, are simply by-passed by this historical connection. Thus, desire enters history without a psychological construction, yet it shapes "psychology" every step of the way. At the same time desire plays a role in shaping historical institutions, such as welfare bureaucracies, that are conventionally thought to be pure functions of the capitalist state's attempt to iron out contradictions in political economy.

The end product, after all the psychological and economic factors cancel out, is the strengthening of bureaucracy. Frank's violence is the self-negating protest against the total process in which he is enveloped, even if it strikes, as protest so often does, against a co-victim, his wife. And Frank's folly drives him, as father, farther from the family, leaving wife and children behind. As for these latter, the state has its mental-health consultants on hand to back up the welfare caseworker. Meanwhile, their free time may be spent watching television, for whose Other life has already well-primed them.

According to Marx, an inexorable condition of capitalist production is the "rising organic composition" of capital; that is, the proportion of capital given to fixed nonliving components, such as machinery, rises in relation to the living component, labor. Capital is inherently self-expanding: if it does not grow, it dies. In terms of its monetary form, the rate of profit must be maximized in capitalist society or else there is hell to pay and all elements of the apparatus of societal control are set into motion. Spurred by this remorseless governor, capital increasingly replaces living human labor with dead machine labor. In other words, it automatizes the production process. Since machines do not metabolize, i.e., exchange with the environment, and since they have no desire as humans do, and so make no demands, the capitalist can cut his costs per unit productivity by automatizing. He therefore is irresistibly drawn to machinery by the threat of extinction at the hands of competitors. However, at the same time it is only human living labor that adds value to any social activity. Hence, the rising organic composition of capital thrusts the capitalist into a mare's nest of contradictions. The complex outcome of the capitalist's dilemma need not concern us here,[26] except as it highlights a profound and evidently ineluctable contradiction in capitalist society: that capital promotes dead labor over living yet needs living labor as its own lifeblood. But if the life that is in labor be allowed full expression, the domination by the capitalist class would come to an end. Therefore the manifest outcome of this contradiction, which is to say the dominant form of history as revealed in political economy, is an icy attempt to assert total administrative control over the world, from the workplace to the most intimate location of personal life.

But the "life that is in labor," does this not include the desire of the worker—of Frank, Hector, and indeed Sarah, inasmuch as she, too, became caught up in the life of the class of workers? To what extent does desire enter into the concrete activity of the working class?

Desire is transhistorically part of the labor process, since the human capacity to make new objects, praxis, is always to some extent influenced by desire. We shall return to explore this relationship in a concluding section. But desire's transhistorical role is modified decisively by historical forces, in this case, by the fact that the working class has been in thrall to capital and has had to define and reproduce itself through the internalization of capitalist relations. Labor is therefore internally split and thwarted, in other words, self-alienated. And consequently its desire also becomes self-alienated.

We have explored the alienation of desire as it appeared in various individual manifestations of "psychopathology." There is, however, a more general manifestation common to the working class as a whole. Recall that desire as it works its way through the psyche does not spontaneously attach itself to the formation of new objects but rather dwells on the body, and immediate personal relations in general. In other words, it becomes psychoanalytical or, in general, psychological. We may say, therefore, that desire tends to flow away from the object and toward the subject, that is, it tends to become *narcissistic*. The object becomes the Other, which collapses back into the self. But this process is a historical process and must coincide with the self-alienation of labor. It is inscribed historically by those developments, outlined above, in which the family became enucleated and the original unity of the traditional community was severed into the workplace and the home. Labor as an element in capitalist society, i.e., as wage labor, arose thereby. We now see that as it arose it was already stamped with that inward quality that would play havoc with class consciousness and give birth to psychology. What was only immanent in the early days of industrial capital becomes full-blown in the day of monopoly, during which time work has become technologically degraded and the narcissistic self predominant. As capital becomes more "organic," so does labor become more "psychological." The flow of symbolic input ebbs from the workplace and surges from personal life. This in turn creates the opportunity—indeed, the imperative—for the culture industry to set about its job of administering personal life and for the mental-health industry to tidy up the debris. The result in terms of class consciousness is not hard to predict and becomes one of the main reasons for capital's superannuation.

Capitalism may be superannuated, and it certainly is decadent, but it is nonetheless inhabited by real, desiring individuals whose lives are more or less full and contain zones of possibility. The inert state of class consciousness and the failure of the Left exist and need to be overcome. Meanwhile, people in fact experience their lives through the illusory categories of the isolated individual. We cannot therefore turn away from praxes that are situated in the world as it is and move people one way or another within their zone of possibility. Consider the practice of psychoanalysis which, for all its elitism and mystery, is as mundane as can be.

11

THE MENDING OF SARAH

This is the predicament of psychoanalysis: it protests against the un-bearable alienation of capitalist society and at the same time reinforces that alienation. The splitting of public and private spheres produces individuals whose social nature is distorted and artificial. Turned inward by alienation, subjectivity flowers like orchids in a greenhouse. The greenhouse is the bourgeois psyche, heated artificially, irradiated by energy outside itself, essentially cut off from the world. One should watch the metaphor: the psyche is full of rank weeds as well as orchids. In any case, psychoanalysts are its gardeners, and I am one of them.

Can there be a Marxist psychoanalysis or therapeutics in general? One feels compelled to answer with a resounding *no*. The only Marxist "ther-apy" is revolution. Change the relations of production, put people in charge of their life, let them generate their own culture, and then worry about psychoanalysis. I like this prospect. It appeals to my chiliastic side. I would like to envision a society where the flowers bloom everywhere, where the good that is in psychoanalysis suffuses everyday life, and where its bad evaporates. True socialism always stands for Bread and Roses.

What do we do now? What do *I* do now? In the meantime I am a psychoanalyst uncomfortable with his profession. I have always been uncomfortable with the profession, which may have had some bearing on why one of the psychoanalytic institutes to which I applied turned me down. I am not disputing their judgment within its own terms. Psycho-analytic institutes are interested above all in reproducing the profession. They want solid workers, team players, and loyalists; and as I could not vouch for more than the first criterion, they were correct in doubting me. I am sure that they saw—and would still see—excessive Oedipal strivings and a degree of intolerance for the pure, heady air of the unconscious, an intolerance they saw rationalized through an excessive tendency to look to the "outside," i.e., society, for a source of explanation. Nor can I dispute the existence of a frankly Oedipal side to my makeup. The antiauthoritarianism that forms so large a component of my character began, I know full well, in my relations to an authoritarian father; and I know well, too, that it is an attitude with a murkier side, one that has by no means been fully expunged from my present-day conduct.

But this leaves much unsaid. We are all stained with Oedipality so long as we relate to power in a class-dominated patriarchal society: it is simply the subject side of such a social relation, played out through the family. Since a profession such as psychoanalysis involves power, Oedipal relations will mark its practitioners as they go about their business. The question is not whether Oedipus or how much, but how Oedipus is to be deployed. The psychoanalysts have opted for an intense, all-embracing subjectivism: make it conscious, stay with it, don't act upon it, tell it to the Other-as-analyst, and you will be transformed, reconciled, you will both overcome yourself and become yourself, you will be healed, mended. "It" here is Freud's id, or the unconscious, or the drives, or, as I might prefer to call it, the "it-ness" of ourselves, the unspeakable, what desire has left in our being. I have never been sure of the ultimate value of such a model of therapy, but I have seen its effects on those who practice it. By and large these effects seem less the overcoming of the Oedipus complex than a translation into sectarian pettiness and fratricidal rivalry. Meanwhile, those who have no stomach for this sort of thing have no choice but to retreat into an amiable lethargy and intellectual indolence. The mediation for this unhappy development is the training analysis, which awakens all the student's infantility toward a figure who, because of his place in the training heirarchy, holds a very real power in the future analyst's life. Thus, transference and reality can never be differentiated from each other, with the result that reality comes under the sway of a transference weighted in the direction of submissiveness, inasmuch as the figure toward whom fantasy is directed actually has power. Since it is necessary for any number of reasons that a resolution of this impossible state of affairs be promoted, and since such a resolution must not contravene the authority of the discourse of psychoanalysis itself, the whole direction of psychoanalytic life veers excessively toward a spirit of mystery and authority. But to submerge Oedipal hostility beneath the waters of cultism is no more an escape than to maintain an attitude of rebelliousness. Indeed, the latter posture offers the greater possibilities for transcendence because it potentially points out of the institutional cage wherein all these relations are trapped, and raises the larger question of class interests to which analytic practice may be subordinated. This may be special pleading on my part, but if it succeeds in opening up a level of reality to which psychoanalysis has been grossly opaque, it will justify itself. A lack of curiosity toward a major sphere of reality is not a desirable attitude in a profession that prides itself on an unswerving fidelity to truthfulness.

Whatever, the relentlessly inward-looking attitude that is the obverse side of this lack of curiosity fosters a type of practice in which the main reference points become one's colleagues, and clinical work becomes an end in itself. Amongst psychoanalysts there is tacit agreement that only they can understand not only what each other does but indeed just what life is really all about. Other modes of explanation concerning the world are given polite consideration but no real credence, for *only* the psychoanalytic cognoscenti are recognized to have the discipline and, yes, the courage to face up to what really counts, namely, the unconscious. One must recognize the purity of purpose and ardor that can be associated with such an attitude. And indeed there is something noble in many of my analytic brethren, a kind of integrity that accrues to those who give themselves completely over to a task. However I may admire this, I must ultimately reject it as well, just as I would reject a career in chess or any obsession that turns a person's "genius and conscience" (to defer to the words of Blake) away from universality. More, the perversion of psychoanalytic passion exceeds that of the chess player or of any artist. Psychoanalysis is no game and has no aesthetic preserve in which to work. Instead, it deliberately traps the universalizing implications of its grasp of desire in a net of bourgeois subjectivism; and that it does so in order to lend legitimacy to its stature as a profession lends an aura of tawdriness to the whole business. It is this I have never been able to swallow and have been chewing over for a number of years.

Psychoanalysis is not a therapy with a neatly defined goal, such as the elimination of a disease. Rather, it is, a moral practice of a certain kind that people pursue because they value the life associated with it. So, as a matter of fact, are other therapies. Congress, insurance companies, and the medical-science establishment may not like this view of the matter, but their preferences have never had much to do with truth.

The most dismal science of all is the study of the "outcome" of psychotherapy. A comparable project would be a study of music that arrived at the conclusion that music was about tones arranged in a pleasing manner. I am convinced that psychotherapy and psychoanalysis belong to the arts or to culture in general. Given the facts of capitalist society, the painful truth is that its best practitioners are fine artists; while the majority are like those who turn out jingles on television commercials or computer-generated cartoon shows.

I treated a sea captain once—or, rather, tried to. The man was a bad drunkard, and his shipping company had sent him to me for help under the threat of dismissal should his habit continue. I was green then and imbued with the psychoanalytic ideal of truth telling as a liberatory force. I spent a few sessions with him "exploring" his hostility to his wife and so forth. And then without notice he suddenly came no more. A month later he returned, redolent of sobriety and seeking a clean bill of health for his bosses. To what did he owe his remarkable recovery? It seems to a better therapy, one more to his liking. He had found for himself a doctor of the new school, a practitioner of "cybernetic reintegration." This man took his story, pronounced him curable, and gave him the nostrum: a long-playing tape recording of the doctor's voice exhorting the sufferer to turn his back on drink and inspiring him with homilies concerning the correct conduct of life. The tape was to be played each night as he went to sleep and repeated automatically through the night as he slept. The captain pronounced it a miracle.

It takes a dull mind not to recognize the ritual nature of psychotherapy. Alienation has many faces, and one of them is this: with the loss, or failure, of community, the individual is deprived of coherent rituals of socialization. In functioning primitive cultures, these rituals are organized about the great transition zones of life, primarily puberty, with its passage from family to community. In the degenerate society of capitalism, this line is severed, and the individual either vaults full scale into narcissistic isolation or sinks backwards into the superheated atmosphere of the family. In fact, both movements may occur simultaneously and are inscribed in different zones of the psyche, hence the self-alienated, schizoid and narcissistic character of today's neuroses.

Therapy is nothing more—or less—than a bridge back, a ritual of repassage. That is why its content tends to center upon the family and why it tries to provide symbolic community, a promised land into which the sufferer, cast down too long in bondage to the family, is to be led.

Since there is no authentic community in capitalist society, each therapy is free to conjure one up as a projection of its praxis, i.e., "technique." In other words, the therapy aims toward an imaginary community, which it then tends to bring into existence through the way it conducts itself. Because therapists generally do what they do in order to make a living, their practice will gravitate toward the bourgeois side of things (into which they have been indoctrinated all their lives, anyhow), and so the imaginary community they project will ultimately resemble the actual pseudo-community concocted by mass culture. Hence the virtues of banality in therapy and the reason why one does not have to be a true artist at it in order to succeed.

In a supermarket society there will be a proliferation of commodities without end, just as there is no end to varieties of mumbo jumbo for channeling into therapeutic practices, and from there, pseudo-communities. This can be—and often is—regarded as healthy pagan diversity. Its benignity, however, is called into question by the powerful tendency of therapeutic movements to turn either into cults watched over by an authoritarian figure or professionalized institutions that jealously guard their arcane secrets and squabble greedily over shares of the therapeutic dollar. Often enough, the two developments are combined. And the history of therapies shows that the "scientistic spirit," which is periodically invoked to straighten things out, is all too often in actual practice but another ideological club. The history of Freudian psychoanalysis is a deplorable example of all these trends, and is unique only in being the most extensive.

Therefore, the people who want to scientifically standardize therapy so that it can be inexpensively administered according to criteria set by the federal bureaucracy will succeed only in authorizing a *scientific* kind of ritual. Since the abstract ritual of scientific discourse has been a means of repressing the archaic demons of the family from the days of the pre-Socratics and Plato, this type of therapy may seem to "work"; i.e., people who undergo it will obliterate enough consciousness to report themselves "better" at the end. It will therefore reinforce the authority of the busy researchers who received grants to study it. It will also, as a matter of course, reinforce self-alienation by further removing people from the prospect of an authentic community generated by their own life activity. Therapy can thus repress neurosis at one end of the social process while generating it at another. In other terms, it functions as a vertically integrated industry, controlling raw materials, production, distribution, and consumption. No wonder the mental-health industry grows despite the prevalent low level of productivity. Indeed, the very attempts to improve productivity—drugs, standardized therapy, new phantasms of diagnostic hair splitting, and the like—as ludicrous as they may be in their own right, paradoxically work, not by improving the level of productivity, which is a fool's game in any case, but by increasing the raw material of alienation while legitimating the entire system.

Lest we succumb to nihilistic despair, we should recall that the disastrous course of therapeutics outlined here applies only to the extent that therapy succumbs to capitalist relations—in blunt terms, becomes like Big Business. Only a Pollyanna would deny that this is an inevitable trend, measured by the march of psychiatry, psychology, and psychoanalysis toward a bureaucratic accommodation with the state. But the self-same inefficiency of therapeutics that leads positive science to gnash its teeth with frustration is a saving grace. There is no end of cracks that necessarily emerge as the ponderous and self-contradictory system grows. Between these cracks individual practitioners can slip, and, following this, find a better ground for reaffiliation. Ultimately, therapy must devolve through the human relationship. If the line is severed, only a human hand can join it; and that human hand, or voice, or gaze is the ultimate antagonist of bureaucracy's clammy embrace. Hence we should celebrate, and neither yield to nor obliterate, therapy's glorious unproductivity, for in it is located the desire that genuine healing must recapture.[1]

ANTISTROPHE

As for me, I must frequently remind myself of the above, for I find analysis a trying affair. Perhaps I question too much. But this is an idle inquiry, for I cannot help myself and have no intention of changing. I find myself still imbued with the psychoanalytic ideal of truth telling, although I have long since abandoned the thought that this possesses any immediate liberatory value. My only justification—and it is not an insignificant one—is that to struggle for the truth is the best long-term hope for liberation. And in the state of darkness in which all human projects exist, it is the most worthwhile course of action. A slender reed, no doubt, yet I obstinately cling to it.

In any event, a therapist who questions too much is sure to have a difficult, if interesting, time of it.

*   *

> *If the Sun and Moon should doubt,*
> *They'd immediately go out.*

> —WILLIAM BLAKE, *Auguries of Innocence*

No, I don't exactly *doubt*, for I find myself possessed of an insensate hopefulness which is unreasoning and must be the conscious surface of desire, life itself. This urging pushes down all notions before it as though they were stacks of lettered blocks knocked over by a rambunctious child. And so I've never been able to accept the words my teachers—including my teachers of psychoanalysis, and including *myself* as a teacher of psychoanalysis—offer up as explanations for what happens to people. It is this very peculiarity that leads me to provisionally settle upon the notion that psychoanalysis is the discourse of a desire that cannot be named, and to value accordingly that great artificer Jacques Lacan, for his arrogant courage in enunciating a theory that breaks through all codes.

But if one respects desire and holds as a practical corollary that we have an inexhaustible capacity for illusion, then what useful propositions beyond the banal can be made about the conduct of analysis, or any other therapy, for that matter? This has always baffled me and leads me, no matter how expertly I may be functioning, to feel per-petually at sea when faced with another human being in the guise of a patient. I enjoy fielding questions after giving a lecture; but there is one type of question I have never been able to answer to my satisfac-tion, and that is the following: "What practical therapeutic advice do you have on the basis of all this [social theory, etc.]"? Or "How can you reconcile a politically radical position with the practice of a con-servative therapy like psychoanalysis?" The fact that such questions are often asked by someone with gimlet eyes who is aching to break in with tales of *his* therapeutic liberation is no reassurance.

Perhaps it would be best to plunge *in medias res* into the disorderly actuality of an analysis to see where it leads us. Have we any choice?

OCCURRENCES IN SESSIONS

With Sarah it is not a matter of "attacks" or symptoms or any-thing focused. Sickened desire is spread all over her like an electric charge on a metal plate. She is simply—there is no other word for it—unhappy. Nothing pleases her, and nothing is good enough for her. This is not because she feels good about herself. Sarah scarcely ever feels good about herself, being rather pinioned between extremes of self-loathing and grandiose exaltation. In the former state her caustic vileness corrodes and annihilates all that comes within her perimeter, while in the latter, her power magnetically repels. And these states do not alternate but coexist, one occasionally seizing consciousness at the expense of the other, more often, the two canceling each other out into a hazy numbness. She experiences herself as a machine, a walk-ing automaton with two chinks in the place of eyes. Through these chinks a keen sensibility views the world. And Sarah is terrified to strip away the armor plate lest she dissolve. It should be added that the outside world knows little of this, since the automaton has been finely machined to resemble a functional human being—at least ac-cording to the terms of Sarah's milieu, which places a premium on a certain mechanical good cheer and efficient functioning.

We are schooled by medical tradition to think analytically, to ab-stract from a complex situation an essential feature and to dissect that feature into its component elements. The delirious, dehydrated in-dividual may be suffering from a virus or may have a diabetic ab-normality that is out of control, leading to an increase in his bodily acidity. The nuclear psychoanalytic conceptions are of the same kind.

If a woman is sexually frigid, we think in terms of unconscious fantasy A, say, a wish to devour the penis during coitus, that would induce anxiety were it to become conscious. Therefore A is met by defense B, repression buttressed by inhibition of function, yielding compromise formation C, which is the frigidity. We observe that C, contains within itself A as well as B, in that the wish to revenge herself upon a man is realized, however imperfectly, by it. And it also realizes another force, D, the guilt accruing as a result of her destructiveness.

This is analytic reasoning, and the program of a psychoanalysis is to bring in turn all these derivatives from a state of unconsciousness to one of consciousness, tracing the ideas to their actual sources in infantile history, and so permitting the mature woman, or, in psychoanalytic parlance, her "ego," to repudiate what had previously wracked her. And Sarah and I have been doing this for her, with some modest results.

The unhappiness, however, persists. Worse, it seems perversely related to the pursuit of psychoanalytic goals. For Sarah to learn that her sexual unresponsiveness is the product of repressed infantile wishes of hostility and revenge has no liberating quality whatsoever. It only reconfirms for her her sense of badness. She cannot, in short, repudiate.

"You see, I knew it all along. I am a killer at heart."

"But these are remnants of a past you could not comprehend at the time. They are not your real adult wishes."

"It is easy for you to say that, safe in your chair. For you, this is only a job. You listen, take my money, then go home to your life. But this is my life. I know I am rotten, and what I learn here only confirms it. So what if my hatred of men stems from a rotten father? The fact is, there is nothing illusory in my infantile hatred, unless you assume that the way women have been put down for centuries is also an illusion."

"But why take it out on yourself? You're so set on settling old scores that you deny yourself life in the here and now. And the way you see it is an illusion, even if it has a truth to it."

"It's not just old scores. Everything since has been arranged just the same way. Women remain objects. We exist to get fucked, used, and displayed. Then we're asked to console men for life's blows. Concede to me at least the lucidity to see the world as it is."

"The fact is, for all that what you say may be true, it does not exhaust your ideas on the subject. More, by dwelling on what is real outside the office you excuse yourself from the work of facing what has come up in here. To be blunt, you're afraid to face your real anger—here in the analysis no less than in life outside. Instead, you just get sullen and pout, all the while pretending to be the good girl. The pretense has become a reality of its own. When you were little, you were the good girl who performed, suffered, and then paid your parents back by falling down in the clutch, as when you had that attack at the dance recital. Now you're doing the same to me here by seeming to go along, suffering all the while, and claiming that the analysis is doing you no good."

"Everything you say makes perfect sense but doesn't touch me in the least. I'm getting sleepy. I've got to change. Life is passing me by. I itch all over. It's cold in here."

Sarah is trying to draw me in to repeat what her parents did for her: flutter anxiously around, tend the poor dear's hurts. This only confirmed her passivity then and seems to be doing more of the same now. I am troubled by the way the analysis itself reproduces Sarah's problem. No matter what I do, so long as I do it as analyst, I am there for her and no one else. Analysis has to feed narcissism even as it attacks it. Fire with fire. But here is a person who retreats from the world, who was pampered and coddled while young; and here is a procedure that is isolated from the world, a sanctuary in which every word is listened to and the analyst's entire subjectivity is open, gaping, attuned to her and her alone. This is why she pays me, and this is the way it must be for the purposes of analytic work, for unless the primitive ground of her experience is recaptured, there can be no change for her. It is necessary to go back, retrench, give her a chance to redefine the terms closer to their original ground. But in so doing, she is bound to retrace those steps of hers which we rightly regard as pathological, even if we use the term without sinking into medical barbarism. Neurotics retreat from reality and psychotics break with it. In so doing, they all lose the slender thread that the community, such as it is, still vouchsafes to us. We therefore regard them as ill and seek to restore them to social reality. It is clear that analysis can do this for some but it is also clear that in a sense it makes people worse in order to make them better. Sarah illustrates the problem sharply in that her disorder is itself manifest as a state of withdrawal. Another person might rebel with frantic activity, while still another might choose different stages entirely on which to enact his/her dreams. But the dilemma holds for all. It takes a certain faith in the regenerative powers of people to assume that they will spring back up after going so far down. I wonder about this. Why should faith turn out to play so large a role in a discipline that prides itself on belonging to the scientific tradition of the Enlightenment?

"I have a dream to report today. It is not my own. I was walking in a strange country with a crowd of people. There were piles of a precious white substance on the ground. Like ore. I was told it would be bad for me if I ate it. It had been rare but was now abundant. However, it was not available where I came from. Despite all this I had a great feeling of happiness during this dream.

"I have no idea why I disown this dream. That's weird. A group of us were talking last night about cocaine, which is what the white stuff reminds me of. Someone asked if it was used mainly to get high all around the world, but then someone else said that the Indians of Bolivia chew the leaves to dull the pain of working in the mines. I guess that's why the stuff reminded me of ore. I don't happen to like cocaine that much, so it must stand for something else. White reminds me of milk, of course, and the shape, in round piles, of the breast, though maybe it was animal droppings. . . . Strange I should feel happy and yet I couldn't have it. Sounds like mother, but she never made me happy."

"The country itself was strange, too, and so is your disowning of the dream."

"Usually when I have a dream I want to show it off to you so you will see how clever I am. Maybe this one I wanted to give to you. Then it wouldn't be mine any longer. I hate analysis sometimes. Nothing for me at the end of it, just pour it out to you and get nothing in return. You should pay *me* for what I have, not I you for listening. And it is like mining, too, plunging deep inside. I don't like that image, it's too violent. Also what we dig up here is much more like shit than milk."

"You've never had an image of happiness before."

"And I don't have one now. I said the dream wasn't mine."

"But you had to have the image in order to reject it. You're afraid even to imagine happiness, not to mention asking for it."

"Happiness, a college teacher once told me, is for pigs. I can't imagine being happy, and I resent you for even bringing up the subject. You do this just to torment me, to tantalize me. It is just like the Indians in the mines. I go down there for you and bring up these goodies so you can analyze them. But it's not for me. And I need to dull the pain."

Then followed a ten-minute silence.

"I don't know where you begin and I end. Or where I begin. I think I am part of this couch, and so of you. I hate you."

Sarah has never been able to feel any solidarity with anyone, much less workers. It was strange and, in a way, touching to hear her, the spoiled child of a bourgeois family, evince a common interest with Bolivian miners. Neurosis is the other side of perversion, Freud held. Maybe it is also the other side of history. What others enact, sexually or historically, the neurotic fantasizes. The real domination out of which the West has been built and a neurotic need for submission meet on the ground of the symbolic. I am not persuaded that this is only an accidental occurrence or that the whole thing can be explained on a purely materialist basis. Sarah is, after all, a child of the West; and other children of the West, intoxicated by mineral wealth, enslaved the miners.

But these reflections of mine do Sarah no good. It is no consolation for a neurotic to be told that she is part of a historical process. Neurotic immediacy is, precisely, locked away from history. It is a desire that has been lost to history except through a symbolic mediation that is necessarily distant. But Sarah wants something here, now; and that *thing* has been vested in me. What is demanding in analysis is to face that *desire*, so close to the pure form, without bleeding it into pale abstractions. Theory, necessary for grasping the totality, can also be a wall against immediacy. The work for Sarah as well as myself is to stay with that horrific, yawning emptiness, that hollowed-out subjectivity which is at the same time an epitome of late-capitalist narcissism and her own, real, exquisitely particular and absolutely unexchangeable suffering. But theory cannot be by-passed. It is one's vantage point. Through my theory Sarah knows something of me and locates herself accordingly. I suspect that she chose to build her dream out of the image of miners because of some apprehension of my politics. I never spout politics during the analysis, but she knows pretty well where I stand. It makes sense that out of the thousands of ideas that float by during the day, Sarah would develop dream thoughts from images for which I would have some sympathy. Freudian patients have Freudian dreams, Jungian patients, Jungian dreams, it is said; why should she not have a Marxist dream for me, one, moreover, that would accuse *me* of being the capitalist and place her, ever ready to feel victimized, in the role of proletarian?

One must take every idea of a patient's with the utmost seriousness. Is there perhaps a parallel movement between what we do in the session and the capitalist mode of production? And if so, is each a product of capitalist relations or a manifestation of a transhistorical current of domination inherent in *human* relations, a universal like Hegel's master-slave dialectic? The answer cannot be of the either/or variety. Nothing is historical without being transhistorical, and nothing is transhistorical without being historical. The infant develops a sense of self by negating separation. Yet, the loneliness and estrangement can be made to remain behind the mirror that the self presents to reality. Any relation with another which goes beyond pure instrumentality entails a renegotiating of the fundamental terms by which the self was constructed. In analysis, we see this drawn most sharply where the two parties come to stand for differentiated portions of the self. The differentiation is always asymmetrical, so that one partner looms over the other, the way a parent looms over an infant in a cradle, or, indeed, the way the infant's desire itself looms over her/him.

All of these relations are located in a specific time, however; and Sarah and I are nothing if not creatures of a society for which exchange relations have achieved paramount importance. She was always made to perform for the glory of her parents; and she perceived, not at all delusionally it seems to me, that their attention to her had all the qualities of capital invested for a future yield. It is true today that I do not see her out of love but for the exchange-value inherent in the fee. That I am genuinely interested in her and that I do care for her is a real part of the case but not at all the whole of it. The fact is, she, or her "case," is my work; and what we do for money, we do not do for love. I use her, no less than anyone uses anyone else in this society, for private, personal acquisition, whether of funds, knowledge, or, indeed, gratification. And this is because there is no real community in this society in which the schism between public and private can be abolished. Personal life is in the private sphere, period, and such community as exists is parlayed through this sphere. Therefore her parents, if reproached with their capitalist-exploitative attitude toward Sarah's achievements, might answer in perfect candor that their investment in her is, in fact, a communal gesture, since it pays off in the heightened esteem of their friends, her father's better standing with his customers, and a general all-around sense of self-satisfaction, which is absolutely essential for the smooth functioning of the bourgeois family and, hence, society. By the same reasoning, it might be truly said that I, through my private appropriation of Sarah, manage to live in my form of community, such as it may be. This has been, after all, but another way to express the well-known adage that psychoanalysis stands within bourgeois society. Like all therapies, it is a ritual of passage within that society; and because it, like all therapies, deals in dislocations, it will have a contradictory aspect vis-à-vis the historical movement of society.

Unless I were to become lost in pointless self-castigation, however, it must remain clear to me that my degree of appropriation of Sarah is not comparable in ferocity or inequality to that of South American mine owners to their workers. The difference between the inequities, lodged in Sarah's imagination, is the measure of her neurotic self-abandonment. It is the quantum of desire turned into hatred that is whispered out at the end of the session and that had passed before then through the varying forms taken by her discourse.

Neurosis is the trapping of desire, in the form of hatred, as reminiscence. But this reminiscence occurs along the great divides instituted by capital—between the family and the workplace, between the private and public spheres of existence. Denied outlet to the world of social production, desire slips backwards along paths determined for it by the pathology of the family. For Sarah, the "real" hatred cannot be grasped without reference to what I become for her: the miner is herself, as before; but the mine, as object, passes through the forms of analytic activity, then the setting of my office, with which she feels part of me, to rest itself on the body of her mother, into which she eventually and helplessly sees herself receding. And beyond the symbol of the phsyical mine, location of the exploitation of labor and minerals, the significant word "mine" becomes detached from its referents, or signifieds, to become the signifier in itself. At the level of dream, or more generally, the psychoanalytic discourse of desire, there is equivalence between "mine" as a wealth-producing hole in the ground, and as mother—in other terms, mine as indication of some object in the world; and, on the other hand, "mine" as first-person possessive-pronoun, signifying the subject herself in the moment of appropriation: miner of the mine. The work of desire, if such a term can be used, is the positing of such equivalences. Desire contains, therefore, a movement toward the dissolution of the subject in her/his differentiation from the object-world. And what happened to Sarah at the end of her dream sequence is paradigmatic for the psychoanalytic process as a whole.

Sarah's merging is not a blissful, Nirvana-like reunion, although it is often cloaked in the ideology of such a promise. It is only the other side of her active side, a side that she has come to regard as phallic and destructive, and therefore has denied to herself. She would indeed wish to blast, plunge, penetrate. However, the very wish seems unutterably monstrous to her. This is because, subjected to repression, infantile thought strikes the grown person with all the force it held in the beginnings of life. Repression is the subjectifying event; it is the mark of the turn inwards, the rejecting of a named object in favor of the undifferentiation of unconscious "things." Repression creates the pure "insides," the tissue of fantasies that inscribe desire's vain struggles. The mother whom Sarah hates and equates with a mine is not the real, objective mother; the mother caught up in political economy as useless ornament; the mother who propped up Sarah's father so that he could be a big shot, and coddled and overpraised her; the mother who held the breast at a certain angle, took it away, and conveyed the right and wrong things through her gaze and contact with her body. That mother was there and belonged to nature as well as to the history of the world. But this mother, the mother whom Sarah hates, belongs only to Sarah's imagination and is the creature of repressed desire. She is the Other. She never existed materially, though she was modeled after an existent mother and though she will prompt Sarah to re-create her likeness in the world of objects. In other words, the hate is based on something real and will be reproduced, in life no less than in the analysis. And if it is not directed toward objects (and, generally speaking, it is not, for Sarah is a model of decorum, except where certain men are concerned), it is freely expandable toward the self in accordance with desire's equivalency between subject and object.

But there is more to be said about this self-immolation of Sarah's. Desire can push matters either way, it being a matter of indifference to desire whether Sarah hates her husband, me, or herself, for desire is comfortable with the notion that all things are one, including the self and world. Desire is *primarily* narcissistic. It is the essential, omnipresent, transhistorical ground of narcissistic perfection. For historical reality, on the other hand, it makes a great deal of difference how matters are apportioned. The arc that Sarah's desire inscribes between her infantile and adult experiences is the highly specific signature of a stage of history. Sarah's self-preoccupation is not so much a reflection of the passivity of her historical position as it is a real ingredient of that position. Everything that was instilled in her—the endless lessons, parental hugs, long soulful talks with a maddeningly interested mother—engendered a double motion: an activity, to make, to change the world, to do; and a passivity, to be made for the Other that was bred into her. Existence was tilted inward for Sarah from the day of her birth, not by any isolated peculiarity of her human interactions but by the immersion of her family and child in a totality of late-capitalist "individualism," specifically, the type that afflicts the bourgeoisie of an affluent suburb. That she was an ornament for her parents; that they were passive instruments of guidance counselors and parenting-as-therapy guidebooks; that the school was therapeutically designed to bring out the narcissist in her; that she was immersed in a bath of administered mass-culture and technocratic meaningless work from the beginning; that, in sum, there was no transcendent path out of the particular selfishness of her class position and toward some kind of universal affirmation—all this provided the matrix according to which the infantile mishaps she became subjected to were laid down in a "pathologically narcissistic" way. The totality characteristic of a given historical moment determines the direction of the track down which a neurotic development will proceed. Not everyone in Sarah's historical position will turn out neurotically, or, if neurotic, neurotic in the way Sarah was neurotic. But Sarah's neurosis will move in the way prescribed for her by the configuration of those same real objects, that is, by history.

Sarah's neurosis attaches itself like a fungus to the self swollen by the failure of historical community. It infects that self with the grotesqueries induced by an excessive interaction of a family turned inward on itself. This same self, grown adult and trained to work in the vacuously administered world of work and leisure, can no longer recognize itself in others. It turns away from mutual affirmation with humanity as a whole, and particularly with members of other classes and races, for these are rightly perceived as threats to the hold that the early parental objects have upon the self. Indeed, the self in such a position will not even recognize the other gender except as a bearer of missing sexual organs for delectation. It is good only for consumption and technocratic work, and that is just the way the capitalist state likes it.

How can I get through to Sarah? She has walled me off so badly that at times I despair. Why bother, after all? There are sicker patients galore, people who cannot function at all, people who would be thrilled to move upwards, to a mere state of hollow alienation. Perhaps my antipathy for her social circumstances is standing in the way. It is hard to be, at the same time, for her and against her milieu and the appalling self-centeredness she manifests. Doesn't this very split convert Sarah into too much of an abstraction? Is there a "her" that remains after its attributes are factored out? Sometimes I think I am entirely too critical and ungiving for this kind of work. Maybe she needs Carl Rogers or a good rousing feminist therapist who will build her self-esteem a little.

Freud never counted on this sort of thing when he developed psychoanalysis; and when he awoke to it, the problem generated one of his most pessimistic pieces, "Analysis Terminable and Interminable".[2] This looks like one of the latter kind. The theory was originally worked out for a so-called healthy ego that suffers neurosis the way an otherwise sound organism suffers an abscess, and the therapy accordingly was predicated on the model of lancing a boil. But as time wore on it became clearer that such a model of neurosis and therapy did not correspond to reality. The "ego" itself—that is, the "I," or himself/herself—was found to be the location of the neurosis. And we have every reason to believe that in late capitalism, with its remorseless penetration of the family and personal life, this problem intensifies. Whatever the cause, there is no doubt with each decade that analysis becomes both longer and harder to define. And increasingly it looks as though our work is centered on problems that do not resolve themselves into a model of analytic discourse, i.e., into a praxis that can isolate causal factors, for example, an "infantile neurosis" or a repressed "castration complex," which can be attacked discretely with benefit to the patient. Rather, it seems we are dealing with matters that are mundane in their origins, "existential" in their structure, problems of belief or despair, of intimacy and givingness, of selfishness and coldness, problems for which an analytic dissection simply avoids the issue. One can analyze Sarah's (very real) castration complex until time's end, and she will still experience an inner deadness, an alienation. And yet, the alienation is a real psychological issue, even if the isolated mind in which it is supposed to take place is but a manifestation of the problem and not an actual location. For Sarah, whatever her environment, alienation is self-alienation: it is inscribed subjectively, and it is unresponsive to real objects according to the ways of repressed desire. The castration complex is a very definite part of the picture. To pretend it away does no justice to Sarah as a real person entitled to the truth about herself and strong enough to bear reality.

And yet she will not allow herself to be reached. What can I do?

I must remember that she has me where she wants me. She must make me feel despair, must try to destroy me with her untouchability. I have to be made to feel as futile about myself as she does about herself. Only then are we one. This is the transference we speak of so often and so easily. It is not the recollection of the past but its repetition in absolute immediacy. Analysis gets farthest into the past the closer it comes to the exquisite moment of presence. At that moment we are mirrored in each other. I too easily become discouraged by Sarah. She makes me feel as if my legitimate function, which is to awaken her from the dream of her neurosis, is a sadistic assault on her, ending not even in rape but proceeding to disembowelment. But this faculty is also my critical intelligence. I know something of the mire from which it arose but refuse to accept her verdict of universal damnation. That is not just false but unworthy, puerile. If Sarah's fantasy is correct, why does she continue coming to session? Why does her intelligence keep working? Why does she sustain some hope in the midst of her darkness, and why do I do the same?

Analysis is a ritual, fine; and it is like a struggle for a soul, fine. That is simply the way things are with us humans. We need that consolation that Freud professed to despise; we need to feel belief, something to help us find our way about in this darkness we create. There is nothing wrong with analysis for doing so, and something noble if at the same time it works in the spirit of an enlightenment proper to those who have given up on the gods. Patients do not need love; their guilt will not permit it. But they do need care and someone to make their life intelligible to them so they can get in touch with their own belief, their own desire. So back to work. At the center of that transference by which Sarah makes me feel so cruel is nothing but her own cruelty mirrored in me. But how to convey this? One thing is clear. All my social theory, whatever its independent merit, is of no use here. Maybe I simply have to be "emotionally" with her, get close up to her and just be there, enduring her deathliness. It might break the spell she has cast on herself. Analysis is not just a matter of belief but of sheer survival. I will not go away—and this may be the most I can do. She wants to drive me mad. If I stay with her and not succumb, it might show her the way out.

"I had another dream. You were in it and you had one breast in the middle of your stomach. I don't remember the rest of the dream, but it left me feeling low."

"Low?"

"I don't know why. You were so deformed . . . pathetic. I hardly ever feel sorry for you but I did a little, in the dream. I don't now. I was just thinking how you would interpret this dream."

"You want to save me the trouble?"

"No, it's just such a bore. Why should I tell you what the dream means? You'll just make some intellectual game of it, then we'll talk some more—or, rather, I'll talk into a vacuum—and then the session will be over. I think of the time spent here, drifting, floating, without any sense of direction . . . then those awful words of yours, 'We have to stop.' Why do we have to stop? This is where I want to be even if I hate it. Why stop? If you cared, you'd extend the session. So what if I don't make use of it. I pay for it, don't I? So I can pay you some more and stay some more, no? No. What's wrong with it? My husband's policy doesn't care. He gets nice insurance benefits so we can get shrunk. I think they figure it keeps us quiet, makes us better citizens. I bet that pisses you off, you with your socialist ideas. Well, it's true. We're all parasites. You feed off me, I feed off him, he feeds off his family just as I did off mine, and our families feed off the people from whom they get their dough in the first place. Back to you again, Doctor. So if we're all parasites, why not enjoy it?"

"Sucking off my one breast, right over my stomach."

"Which is halfway down to your crotch. This week, I can see, is going to be devoted to the penis, just as last week was to the breast."

"Your dream is trying to draw an equivalence between them, saying that I have both . . . and neither. And the same goes for your image of yourself."

"What am I supposed to do with that? What good is it to me?"

"You know, I just imagined then that I did have a breast and that I tried to feed you with it, and you bit it, real hard. Nothing is good enough for you because you hate yourself so badly."

"I never believed my mother, no matter how hard she tried. And with Alan it was the same way. He was always doting on me, before and after the marriage. He adored me, gave me everything, but nothing was good enough. So we soured on each other. With him, I think it was my fault. But my mother was bad."

"Yet you recall nothing except her excessive devotion. Was the excessiveness the badness itself, the fact you each had nowhere to go?"

"Simply being close to someone is intolerable. Yet I can't bear being alone. Closeness is worse. I'd rather have roaches crawling on my belly or claw my body to ribbons. So good to look at, so rotten inside. No one is to touch me. . . ."

"You are silent so long."

"I remembered something else about mother. The 'touching' brought it back. She gave me enemas. Not too many but I recall them well now. She hated my insides. Assaulted me, too . . . like with a big prick. To be trapped with her . . . and now with you."

"You have to present yourself as hideous to keep me away. Yet you keep closed, holding back, as you must have with her, trying to get me to intervene. And when I do you treat it as though it were an enema to be expelled."

"That's the way I feel about what you just said. Except it's like forcing shit up inside me. Well, I won't give in. I'll stay here forever or until you kick me out. The trouble with this analysis is that it's too real. What happens here is just like what went on with Mother. It only reconfirms my suspicions and self-loathing. For me there are no metaphors."

"I think you would like to be close. You think, though, that this means yielding to me, and fear that I would penetrate and rape you if you did. And that would mean your dissolution."

"Why must you always criticize me? Never anything good to say to me."

"I don't know that you can accept anything good I have to say. Never once have you told me that anything good was happening here."

"Well, why should I? You want me to be honest, and that's how I honestly feel. Anyhow, you're criticizing me again."

"But here's how I honestly feel. I do try to make some kind of emotional contact with you, to touch you somehow, but I despair sometimes of ever getting through."

For the first time in the several years I had been working with her something softer crept into Sarah's voice.

"Please don't feel too bad. I don't want you to give up on me. You're all I have right now."

APPROPRIATION

It would be fatuous to claim that this moment constituted a "breakthrough" for Sarah. I don't believe in the breakthrough concept, which seems to me to cheapen immeasurably the complexities of human discourse. But there was a change in Sarah—or, rather, us—after this session, so that it was impossible to think so hopelessly about her as before. We both knew that she would somehow "make it" without knowing exactly what "making it" meant. One thing it must have meant was that Sarah seemed to be a *different person* to me. I found myself unable to apply the diagnostic appellation "narcissistic character" to her afterwards, although it had seemed exceedingly lucid beforehand by all the canons of psychoanalytic reasoning. And this was perfectly reasonable, since one defines a narcissistic character by the type of relationship formed in analysis, and that relationship had in fact changed decisively from this moment forwards.

But if we can diagnose people by the type of relationship they form to others—and this, it seems to me, is a much sounder way of understanding them than by the dissection of a conjured-up mental essence —then it follows from this example that all diagnoses are forever provisional and will remain so until all historical possibilities are exhausted. If anyone seemed stubborn and intransigent, it was Sarah; month after month she proved herself a fixed, cold, "narcissistic character," and then, quite swiftly and effortlessly, became something else

—without, to be sure, ceasing to be Sarah. So a diagnosis is like a negative piece of history. It is not an entity fixed in space and time but a piece of history waiting to happen. Lest we get carried away on a wave of therapeutic optimism, we should recall that most history does not happen, and what happens often turns out wrong.

But what happened to Sarah and me was historical. After a long and obdurate struggle, during which we behaved like two enemy states balefully watching each other across a swathe of contested territory, we began to get along. And what had made it possible was a twofold motion that can be understood only as the consummation of the protracted and agonizing praxis that went before it: my opening myself to her by confessing my frustration; and Sarah's forgiveness of me for it. And this had to be spoken to be made explicit.

There is no reducing this event or analyzing it away. It is totality; and it *happens*, after which a new historical totality arises. It could not have happened without my frustration to confess, and this could not have happened without months of beating my head against her narcissistic carapace. Beforehand, Sarah and I are the narcissistic pair: strangers to each other. In the real event, a kind of contact occurs; we are each different and remain so afterwards because this event henceforth reacts with everything within and between us. I do not think we can contain this totality in the notion of "insight," although the kind of subjective enlightenment called insight is one of its concurrences; and I do not think we can account for it in terms of the past, by claiming, for example, that I provided her with "good mothering," though it must have been the case that her mother, larded with complacency and self-righteousness, could never have admitted to any human weakness, and that this quality in her contributed to Sarah's own inaccessibility. No, all these matters are real enough but none accounts for the decisiveness of my opening myself to her when I did, and her forgiveness. Sarah cannot be mended by any number of analytically correct insights: something definite and real has to happen *between* us (although it has to happen in a psychoanalytic way). If "insight" is the crux of psychoanalytic work, then it must be a material event, not just the play of ideas. Psychoanalysis is not a matter of breaking something down "analytically" into component parts the way a chemist approaches a problematic substance. Rather, it is the finding of differentiation within a totality without losing the sense of that totality, which always includes the individual's relation to history. What is differentiated is not lost but finds a new relation of *individuation* to the totality of which it remains an element. In other words, individuation is predicated upon a point of real contact being established within the analytic situation. There has to be such a point—which for Sarah is constituted as forgiveness —if change is to occur. Only then could her proud heart yield.

Weakness is the great danger for narcissism. If the narcissist is to grow, she/he must forgive not sin but weakness. At its root, forgiveness means the renunciation of hatred toward some object; and since loculated hatred is a defining feature of neurosis, it may be that a moment of forgiveness goes beyond Sarah's case to be a decisively healing event. Each must forgive as she/he was bent, and no two moments are alike. Sarah's moment of forgiveness—which was also, I think, a "moment of truth"—was hers alone; to be more exact, hers and mine alone together, for she had to forgive me in order to forgive herself, to renew contact with the social world and to reconcile herself with her own history. I am confounded by the uniqueness of this moment, which was, after all, predicated upon years of very painstaking work between two very definite individuals . . . confounded, too, by the contrast between this uniqueness and Marcuse's notion of "one-dimensionality", which describes a state of being that has passed beyond richly articulated individuality to become the atomized, homogenized, and shallow personages to whom we apply the term "narcissistic person of our time." Marcuse and those in his tracks were not wrong. Sarah was that kind of person, yet she became otherwise. A person is correctly seen as a member of a faceless mass because of lack of concrete relatedness to others in a historical project. It is not a matter of any in-dwelling essence or of an externally imposed condition, but of a real loss in consciously chosen praxis. From this standpoint Sarah was, in fact, a complete grain of sand, not because of any "ego defect" but because of the way she was locked into the total relationship between her and the world. Her lack of sociation, of participation and affirmation, was, I must admit, shocking to me. Yet for all the reality of her narcissistic desociation, it remained historically open to future praxis. Her analysis became a praxis of this kind, which restored through her forgiveness a real human tie and opened her onto history. Her power, we may say, was immanent and awaited its moment in such a praxis. And what is specific about the praxis called psychoanalysis is its austere and painstaking respect for and reconstruction of desire. It puts enough consciousness to bear on a neurotically trapped desire to create the condition for the forgiveness of desire's hatred. For this alone it must be credited for standing against the barbarism of its age.

I feel more hopeful about Sarah and psychoanalysis now. We should not delude ourselves, however. She still has to return to the entire reality for which coldness and a false self are nicely tuned mechanisms, and where aloneness has become a social imperative. Against that reality the gains of analysis may seem slender indeed.

Psychoanalysis does not do more, really, than allow a kind of "true speech" to take place. I do not mean this in a purely intellectual way. For speech to become true, it must connect itself with the material realities of life—the realities of the body, of desire, and of the actual relationship with the analyst. All this occurred in Sarah's moment of forgiveness, which was a precondition for the further development of true speech. Speech is but discourse, however; it is material and concerns objects, but it does not presume or include mastery of the object. And the therapy has not yet been invented that includes control of the object along with exploration of the subject. Given the alienation of subjectivity in capitalist society we can do no more at present than dream of such a therapy, which would, indeed, be better called some species of revolution.

But good therapy or analysis is not merely subjective, either. Because it is material, true speech is alive to historical possibility even if it does not conquer history. It is not passive contemplation, nor is it a matter of "adjusting" the person to fit the situation. This may be what the employer wants when he foots an insurance bill, but it does not have to be what he gets. The insurance policy that covers part of the treatment is itself part of the reality of the treatment and subject to confrontation by true speech. Sarah and I have begun discussing this usefully, too, along with the rest of the conditions of her life. To the extent that she can speak truly about them she is that much less alienated. The rest, however, is up to her, for the anlaysis is not located in her world but removed from it by the abstract exchanging power of the money that is her wage and my fee. This leads us somewhat closer to real historical alienation but cannot take us there, for the "there" must always be defined sensuously, and the only sensuous presentations with which we work are those of the analytic situation itself.

Am I influencing Sarah here, in violation of the canon of analytic mutuality? This is a tricky issue and cannot easily be put to rest. No doubt I do not lecture to her on my theory of society, nor do I take any definite position on what she should do with her life. But it would be utterly hypocritical to deny that I influence Sarah, even if this be done, so to speak, quietly. The "shock" that I felt over her lack of social participation was a real one; and even if I kept it to myself, it was bound to influence my response to her. And my preoccupation with the question of whether therapy helps one adjust to a crazed world is bound to induce me to "steer" Sarah in one way or another, again, only if quietly and by selecting from her own responses rather than by forcing my own solutions upon her. Beyond this there lies the nest of values that are transmitted silently, whether through unconscious and habitual reactions of speech or through the choice of magazines for the waiting room. Indeed, wherever the issue of "reality" intrudes, whether it is the reality of the analytic setting itself or the reality to which her discourse refers, I cannot help influencing Sarah. When she mentions her attitudes toward, say, work, or refers to her mother in a way that discloses some element of social class, I must respond through the categories of my own experience.

Once we push it to this level, however, it is obvious that the question of influence in analysis takes on a different aspect, for it is not a matter of whether one influences patients but of how. Since it is impossible—not to mention undesirable—to eliminate influence from any human situation, the problem becomes one of specifying it and bringing it under conscious control. Recall that therapy is a ritual, a rite of passage from the family to something else. Specifying influence means the determination of what kind of family is to be left behind and what kind of "something else" is to be set ahead. Are we to eliminate the family and turn individuals over to the state, as Plato suggested long ago and as certain therapies do now, albeit in disguised fashion? Or are we to allow individuals to overcome what is archaic and murderously destructive in family existence, that which has been instilled in the grotesque family setting of capitalist society, and at the same time to retain the moment of intimacy vouchsafed by the consolatory function of that same family? And, similarly, do we hold out a vision of reality that is at least lucid, if not transcendent, to the individual who is in our care? Must we accept the *value*, numbly espoused by the great body of psychotherapists, that the world to which the patient returns is both *transparent*—and therefore not in need of demystification—and neutral, and hence implicitly benign? More, need we flaccidly continue to endorse the prevailing "health ethics" by means of which one abolishes the moral complexities of living in a world where the unfree labor of the many permits the thought (and therapy) of the few and joins in with the clear and softly fascistic narcissism of the so-called new age, that narcissism of "healthy sexual performance" and the "how-to-live" technical manuals? One thing only is clear, even if it has become something of a cliché: we always take a position, even when we do not take a position.

Analysis has always chosen. Here, then, is another choice, not so different perhaps from what many have done implicitly all along but refreshed with the waters of emancipatory socialism that have flowed alongside for more than a century. There should be, after all, a unity of theory and praxis. A praxis, therefore, that is alive to the contradictory complexities of family existence, that regards reality as unfree and in need of demystification, and that lives with moral subtleties, i.e., that shows a concern for human freedom in an unfree reality. Is not such a praxis both psychoanalytic and dialectical? And if dialectical, must it not strive toward universality? Must not psychoanalysis appropriate Marx if it is to be itself?

Psychoanalytic theory is the metadiscourse of desire. Now, it may be established that psychoanalytic practice is the praxis of desire, its discourse itself. Desire is what emerges out of its historically material setting, the analytic situation. By fixing the time and opening ourselves up to the patient, we create a sensuous reality in which time becomes unbound and desire flows like maple sap in early spring. Desire is that with which we "work." Through our relationship together we find words for the brute things of existence and so arrive asymptotically at a true speech, or at least a truer one. And in so doing—if we do it well—we undo something too—that ancient lesion set going when capital severed production from the home and left the one to grow cold and the other to fester.

I think I was wrong before: there is love in our work, and something to be guarded in dark times. It is not trivial to open a person somewhat further onto history. I have grown more content with incremental and nonabsolute gains. Put dialectically, one deals with determinate negations. Each little bit helps and leads somewhere. The real good of the world can occur silently and inhere in countless small advances. Each one, as Blake would have it, is a particle of infinity and eternity.

Part Three

THE
RECAPTURE
OF DESIRE

12

DESIRE AND PRAXIS

At heart psychoanalysis knows only desire. This is the mother-liquor that crystallizes out into the particles of its discourse or, rather, discourses, for there is not just the discourse of Freud and the Freudians, but others: Sullivan, Horney, Klein, even Jung, more than we need enumerate here, all who have participated in this project to appropriate the depth of the individual, who have found there desire and have shaped it this way and that according to their predilections. Desire, being unable to name, has to be conjugated with some element of the historical world in order to be made an object of thought, and this the various schools of psychoanalysis have done after their fashion.

Yet despite the outpouring of innumerable insights into the real lives of people, there is an unmistakable tendency within schools of psychoanalysis to turn living desire into theoretical stone. There are partial exceptions, which I need not pursue here. However, by and large psychoanalysis has taken the vital center of the individual and encased it in one mold or another—in order, no doubt, to register the truth that the full individual is more than a vital center and has to live, stabilized, in the world. This casing of the individual, which becomes the template for the given system of psychoanalysis, is always a reflection of the way psychoanalysis has had to live or, rather, chosen to live in the world—as a bourgeois profession with a profound, if unspoken interest in reproducing bourgeois society. Hence, the routine petrification of psychoanalytic discourse is essentially a denial of history, a reading out of the historical dimension, so that the stabilization of the individual—his or her ego, identity, or whatever —becomes subordinated to the stabilization of the social order, of which psychoanalysis is a comfortable part.

The clearest, and yet most deeply problematic, example of this is in the biologization of psychoanalytic theory, best exemplified in the Freudian notion of instinct or instinctual drive. Instinct is the clearest example because by ascribing something to nature, one is reading historical development out of it. And this is what Freud and his school have tended to do. If women, for example, really have an innate drive that cuts across all historical circumstances and leads them into a self-defeating "penis envy," then anatomy is indeed destiny and female inferiority is written in the stars. Yet the concept of instinct cannot be dismissed as mere biologization, because in it Freud also theorized his abiding insight that we were not automatically civilized, that civilization does not take all of us, but that beneath its influence there is a wordless, "thinglike" stratum. Freud's concept of instinct, then, was more than a residuum of nineteenth-century mechanism and more than an ideological sop to bourgeois patriarchy. It was also a radical, even revolutionary concept, still the closest to the essence of desire itself of all the various attempts (with the possible exception of Lacan—see appendix) to theorize about the core of psychoanalytic discourse.

Freud's concept of instinct is a way of stating that desire has trans-historical qualities, that it is close to "nature," i.e., the body, and is therefore primarily erotic. This was his original and deepest insight, which became complicated later on by a development that can be read either as Freud's gathering pessimism or as his courageous effort to grasp the evident truth that the erotic was inextricably admixed with the hateful in the thinglike stratum of our existence.

Ultimately, Freud rooted his theory of the instincts in what he called the compulsion to repeat, a tendency he saw as fundamental to biological systems.[1] On this basis he constructed the grand dualism of instinctual life, Eros and Thanatos, or, as they developed into psychological manifestations, the instincts of sexuality and aggression. That the compulsion to repeat is a function of organic matter itself, as Freud held, is a dubious proposition. What cannot be disputed is the presence of such a compulsion inder the conditions of psychoanalytic work. Once desire is freed from the constraints of ordinary discourse, it reveals an unmistakable tendency to repeat itself in very elementary patterns that have an "organic" feel to them, much as the rhythms of hunger or sexual arousal. It is for this reason—a compelling one for somebody who has spent a long time listening to people in a psychoanalytic way—that the Freudian notion of instinct as a "borderline concept between the mind and body"² is not to be dismissed. For example, if we recall the case of Curtis, it is striking how he returned again and again to certain basic longings for his father. Nor can we accept the conclusion that his impulsions were simply for his father's attention or care, as Curtis's conscious thought would have; rather, they had a very definite sexual intention to them, in line with the fact that they arose in early childhood, when the body and its desire were conceived as a unity. Curtis has, it may be said, a "negative Oedipus complex" where his father is concerned. And if we also recall the early-childhood memory wherein Curtis watched the soapy water go down the drain, we will be struck once more by the sensuous immediacy of those things that go into desire and the lifelong fascination they hold; despite all the wealth Curtis joins in accumulating, all the worldly power he wields, none of it can replace, or even touch, the primitive and, by the standards of worldly logic, trivial attraction of the infantile image.

Therefore, if we are to be true to people—and grant them a dimension in which the penetration of the administered world of political economy is only partial—we need to retain an "instinct-like" concept; and this cannot be divorced from the realm of nature or the transhistorical.

Yet there is no such "thing" as *instinct*: there is no sexual instinct as such, and there is no aggressive instinct as such. There is only a person making history under the conditions of nature as revealed in the body. Men make their history, Marx wrote,³ but they do not make it as they please; they make it under conditions handed down from the past. And our body is paramount among those conditions handed down from the past, i.e., from nature, which always has the quality of "that which comes before."

The body is not "out there," "a piece of unconquerable nature," as Freud was given to postulate when he sank into dualism.⁴ It does not drive history onwards and, through its instincts, set itself as a brake to human possibilities. The body is not a brake but a limit, or, more deeply, a condition that is itself transformed in historical development. "The cultivation of the five senses," wrote the young Marx, ". . . is the work of all previous history."⁵ Or as Blake would have it, "that call'd Body is a portion of Soul discern'd by the five Senses, the chief inlets of Soul in this age."⁶ The body is never lost: it is either transcended, or repressed and split away. In either case it persists and is known through the filaments of desire.

What we call instincts are therefore *configurations of desire*. Instinct is shaped between the conditions of the body, on the one hand, and, on the other, the historically arranged disposition of the object world. Desire is the mediation between the transhistorical and what has been made of it in history; and it is configured according to the structure of these two dimensions into instinct-like patterns. The realization of desire as instinct involves then, in Freud's parlance, a source and an aim (the side of the body as subject) and an object (the side of the world, which includes, along with the bodies of others, one's own body as object). Since the "aim" of the body as subject is sensuous gratification, instinct as such is always pleasure seeking, or erotic. However, inasmuch as instinct is also a deployment of desire, gratification can never be contained within the literal, or real body. It must always expand to include the imaginary infantile body, which already contains within itself the mark of symbolic transformation through fusion with the Other. Therefore, instinctual gratification is not only imaginary, it is historical as well. Curtis's desire as conveyed in his childhood memory leads him to dirt, wetness, the feel through the hands—all of which is sensuous, to be sure. Yet there is no such thing as dirt in nature; it is a category of the human imagination. And water does not remain water but becomes bodily fluids—milk? urine? amniotic fluid?—which become sources of gratification not in themselves but as linked with the historical parent. Finally, that the water goes down the drain raises the entirely human problem of separation, not to mention human institutions such as plumbing, that mediate the object side of the instinctual organization.

True, the instinct is organized about bodily zones, orifices, innervations, et cetera. But this is merely one of its conditions, the side of the body as subject or as sensuous membrane, the body as "chief inlet of soul." The instinct as such is no thing but a structured deployment that contains the imaginary and the Other as well as the bodily membrane in its organization. From another angle, the instinct is the path inscribed by desire through the imagination between the exigencies of the body and those of civilization. It represents, then, the transformation of the body (and quite regularly, given the reality of domination, its deformation) in order to turn the infant over to civilization. The instinct represents not "biology" so much as what has been left over from civilization's march. It is what is denied in the notion of "progress," yet remains as a goad to further historical development, since it refuses to be fully gratified by any real thing. And full gratification is what it demands.

Desire cannot be all that is fundamental about being human. Indeed, in itself it is nothing, a mere wisp of imagination. There must be a reality-making side to people of which desire is the negation. Our reality is made by us; it is not inertly there. The object-world to which the instinct relates is constructed. The object that desire seeks and then rejects is a human object, appropriated from the natural world. The material nature that forms its substratum is not lost thereby. It persists, transformed, in the human product and remains a condition of its making. This is so whether the product is a meal we cook or the body that is the "work of all previous history."

We have already encountered this other fundamental category and now must explore its psychological ramifications. The side of us that makes reality is called, after Marx, praxis, or labor. Praxis may be defined as the creation of new objects out of old. "Object" here is not meant to be confined to grossly palpable things, for example, the cooking of a meal out of raw food. More generally, it is any perceivable entity with objective qualities, for example, speech, as in a psychoanalytic interpretation. For something to have objective qualities means that there must be a *subject* to regard them so. Therefore, praxis always includes a simultaneous transformation of the subject, i.e., the individual, who is making the object. Praxis includes play as well as work, and is present in any purposive activity. It may be observed from the first hours of life, as soon as the infant begins actively tracking objects with its gaze. Through praxis, the individual is made as reality is made. And since praxis is purposive, it is conscious and involves the emergence of consciousness. Finally, praxis is an inherently social process, since subject and object can be formed only under social conditions; that is, through recognition by another person. It might be helpful to mention here two properties I do not regard praxis as having:

Praxis is not, in my opinion, the same as "production," or, rather, it takes on the character of production only under the conditions of capitalist domination, inasmuch as production is the hallmark of the capitalist totality. There is a fair question as to whether Marx eventually collapsed his original "Hegelian" conception of praxis into a later one that was subordinated to production and workplace discipline.[7]

Be that as it may, I shall employ the notion of the early Marx, hold it to be transhistorical, and assert that an adequate theory of "human nature" must include praxis as one of its two leading categories, the other being desire.

Praxis should also not, in my opinion, be subsumed into a psycho-analytic theory of the ego[8] even though the ego is ordinarily regarded as the reality-making side of the psyche. The reason for this need not be belabored: ego has become perhaps the most extensively reified of all psychoanalytic concepts, the one most petrified and most freighted with repressive and bourgeois features. It was precisely to get away from the rigidities of the ego that praxis, which connotes an active, self-transformative principle rather than a static structure, has been introduced. This is not to deny the problem of mental structure but only to assert that it must be approached from a fresh perspective.

The basic relation of desire and praxis is one of negation. However, it is not a dualistic, splitting negativity but a dialectical, differentiating one. Desire and praxis negate each other but also define each other. Desire is the claim of the nature that is, so to speak, left behind by the object making of praxis, while praxis is an activity shaped by an imagination whose hidden term is desire. We see this relation in extremes of capitalist alienation, when the two terms are pushed so far apart as to be experienced as severed. Witness Curtis's relation to work, where his praxis is goaded by an unspeakable desire that is fanned by the loneliness induced through his public work-life. And we see this at the beginning of life, when the infant, goaded by an urging she/he cannot formulate, refuses the breast and seeks new objects at the price of separateness.

Desire and praxis are carried out entirely on the plane of what is human; they owe nothing to biology, except insofar as they define a nature that has been humanized. The concept of instinct, on the other hand, reaches into biology; it is a reminder that, as much as we transcend it, we are still flesh. The instinctual drive is primarily a configuration of desire. Nonetheless, it cannot be severed from praxis. The object of the instinct is a human object, created out of praxis, while the approach to that object—what the ethologists would call the appetitive and consummatory phases—is again, on the human level, a matter of praxis. Sexuality in its fullness is not just a matter of imagination and pleasure; it necessarily involves activity. And even if this seems of a passive or irrational kind, it is still praxis, albeit a praxis that is primarily placed at the disposal of desire, in contrast to the usual relation.

But there is another instinct—aggression—is there not? There is according to psychoanalytic theory, as Freud posited it in 1920.[9] But that does not mean there has to be an aggressive instinct in reality, all the more so in view of the ideological usefulness of the theory of aggression as a buttress to psychoanalytic conservatism. The repressive view of civilization is ideally suited to a conviction that man is an inherently predatory animal whose aggression must be controlled—by society, of course. And there is even less ground for assuming the existence of a *biological* instinct of aggression if its essential terms can be found to reside elsewhere. And they can—in the notion of praxis itself, whose terms can be mapped onto those of the aggressive instinct. Because praxis is transhistorical, it can be assumed as a part of nature, like an instinct. Also, praxis involves activity, like aggression, and, most significantly, entails the breaking down of existing object configurations and their replacement with new ones, as in the cutting up of wood to make furniture or, as the adage goes, in the breaking of eggs without which making an omelette is impossible.

That this view of the matter should have been missing all this time from traditional psychoanalytic theory is not the least bit surprising, for as much as psychoanalysis has had to gain from seeing aggression as a biological instinct, it has had far more to lose from the introduction of a category drawn from the unspeakable domain of Marxism. Think what a difference would be made in its discourse if human activity could be taken out of the shadow of predatoriness and placed in the light of a force with revolutionary possibility. But the issue is not to engage once more in an ideological critique of psychoanalysis. Rather, it is to see whether transposing the question of aggressive activity from the domain of biology to that of praxis gives us a superior grasp of the problem.

A central difficulty in this area has been to tease out the phenomena of hostility from those of aggressive activity as such. Hostility, which always involves malevolent intent toward its object, goes beyond aggression pure and simple, and, in any case, constitutes the vexing aspect of the matter. Nobody worries about aggression as such, but the intent to harm—to cause pain to another; to seek revenge, to expropriate what is her/his; to assert dominion over; to kill, rape, or mentally torture; or to take property away—rightly exerts the great-est interest. But these motivations are essentially *historical matters*, involving social position and, in each case, a concrete historical rela-tionship that gets played out in the act of hostility. And praxis, which is the history-making activity as such, can account for this, while the biological instinct does not, except, as mentioned, as an ideological club. Consider some examples:

A one-year-old infant comes upon her father's eyeglasses while he is napping and twists them out of shape. This is praxis—and it is aggressive, by the same token—but there is no hostility involved, unless, of course, the father chooses to turn the action into such. It is praxis because it is conscious and purposive, and creates a new object (that the baby is indifferent to the fact that she has created an object of less exchange-value than its predecessor is specific for her praxis). And being praxis, it is human and involves a social relationship through the Other, in which what is part of the father becomes readily transposed, through her desire, into herself. And finally, that the act is free from hostility is a function of the fact that her desire here regards the father and his glasses as a good Other. That desire will be un-realized, that in fact she cannot incorporate the glasses (which she has been angling to get for a number of days, knowing how the father values them), is therefore seen as no catastrophe or occasion for hatred, but simply as an incentive to go on exploring the world in her neverending quest.

By contrast, consider the following cases:

· A cat pounces on a mouse. The cat hunts the mouse as the baby hunted the glasses, yet here a biological instinct is at work. One might call this aggressive if one likes. However no praxis is involved because there is no purposive consciousness, no desire, and no notion of the mouse as Other (at least I assume so, Tom and Jerry cartoons to the contrary notwithstanding). And as there is no praxis, there is no hostility.

· Fascist thugs beat up a Jewish shopkeeper and break his glasses. Here, by contrast, there is an aggressive praxis involving hostility. A part of the fascist self is projected into the Jew as bad Other. Note, however, that the problem cannot be confined to such limits; it is not simply that a bad Other is invested in Jewishness, but that the whole fascist personality becomes subjected to a radical and chronic split-ting that requires a sustained, i.e., historically structured, relationship with the victim, who must be kept at a certain distance for desire (now as hatred) and praxis to work themselves out. In sum, the hostility cannot be grasped apart from concrete and essentially qualitative historical circumstances.

· Black rioters in an urban ghetto smash various shopwindows. Again a hostile praxis, but now a qualitatively different situation. The object of the praxis is a thing rather than a person, and the praxis breaks down that thing. In contrast to the chronic, radical splitting felt by the fascist (characteristic of the petty bourgeoisie who have a stake in society but feel betrayed by it), the rioter, having been by virtue of racism the Other who is nothing, makes the thing—the shopwindow—into his Other and exteriorizes a sudden rage upon it. The object is not the body of the shopkeeper and what is appended to it (e.g., eyeglasses) but the things—property—attached to that body by virtue of the exchange principle, i.e., the history of capitalism. More than likely, the store is part of a chain run by some spectral conglomerate, thus doubly removed from the body. Violence here is therefore the restoration to a kind of real existence of what had been abstracted into nothingness. At a certain level—unconscious, no doubt—the praxis contained the fragment of a movement to overcome the history of racism. To be sure, if the act remains individual, isolated, and unconscious, it will probably end up only by furthering the history of racism; the chain will not reopen the store, the rioter will be subjected to the greater alienation of prison, et cetera. The point, however, is that one hostile praxis cannot be compared to another by virtue of a lowest common denominator of instinct. Violent acts can have entirely different historical vectors, which can be understood only in their specificity.

· Alexander Berkman shoots Henry Clay Frick during the Homestead Strike of 1892. Here, hostility is directed at one concrete individual from another. There is intent to kill (which failed) and willingness to assume the consequences (which were fourteen years in the penitentiary). There is no way to grasp this act by reducing it to any of the given psychological categories of aggressiveness. Whatever Frick represented in the way of Berkman's father, et cetera, is subsumed in the choice of Frick, the particular individual, as the embodiment of Capital. (He was, in fact, Andrew Carnegie's hatchet man, directly responsible for brutally suppressing the strike.) No purely psychological category can comprehend a praxis constituted as a blow for universal liberation, for the universalizing movement had to be wrung out in order that psychology could arise.

· Dr. Acheson sends Hector to the state hospital. Here is a movement in the opposite direction. The doctor must have experienced some irritation with Hector for having thwarted so many of his well-laid plans. However, the praxis to eliminate Hector stands in stark contrast to those of the preceding three examples, for there is no violence to it and scarcely any passion; indeed, the act itself has been rendered virtually devoid of desire by the processes of bureaucracy. Though there is little hatred for Hector, there is less love, and the tiny increment of hatred is sufficient to trigger the entire ponderous machine of bureaucratic annihilation. And this machine has but one function: to turn a person into a thing and finally into a number.

· The troops observed by Tolstoy's Pierre at the Battle of Borodino were wild with desire for Tsar Alexander. Like the followers of Mohammed, they went off to kill and to be killed insouciantly, knowing that the all-powerful Other would embrace them if they did. American troops in Vietnam, by contrast, quite often went mad with ennui from a life dominated by the rhythms of dysbound time. When violence occurs under such circumstances it is likely to be sporadic, random, and seemingly unmotivated, or in accordance with racial planes of cleavage where desire can establish a concrete toe hold of hatred (consider Hector's response). Otherwise, it is merely button pushing and impersonal slaughter. The situation is rather like the contemporary metropolis itself in which the facelessness of destruction is periodically organized by a "berserk" multiple murderer who chooses his victims along racial or sexual lines. Both the bound time of the accumulation of capital and the dysbound time of bureaucratic torpor involve a multiplication of destructiveness even as immediate personal hostility is curbed. In both cases, the Other, though ultimately part of the self, is made to seem outside the self, thereby undercutting the ground of inner conflict. And in the process, erotic investment is lost along with hatred, leaving the self impoverished and desociated.

I have not tried for theoretical closure here,[10] and have left much that is ambiguous in these examples. To go further, to attempt a reasonably complete morphology of the dispersion of hostility occurring in the modern world, would require something of comparable scope to Sartre's treatment of group formations in his *Critique of Dialectical Reason*, and this I am not about to undertake. I have merely tried to propound the following: that what psychoanalysis calls aggression is, in fact, praxis of one kind or another; that such praxis is historically specific; that an act takes on hostile, loving, constructive or destructive qualities according to the kind of desire embedded in it and the kind of praxis that effects it; and that what appears destructive may be constructive and ultimately loving, and vice versa.

The above results from taking these matters off the psychological-biological stage and placing them on the historical stage. Because the totality and the individual are mutually constitutive, and because the totality, capitalism, is an inherently predatory society, we can no longer get away with propositions concerning the inherent predatoriness of Man. We have only men and women making history with their praxis, suffused with value and set about with desire. And those who reduce history to psychology, and violence—whether fascist or revolutionary—to the same brute instinctual force are also makers of a certain kind of history.

The central term of this work has been desire, which is the principle disclosure of psychoanalysis. The unhinging of desire in the course of capitalist history has led to the exfoliation of the individual; psychoanalysis makes us aware of the inner structure of the process and reveals the reality of desire. However, it is not desire but praxis that stands at the intersection of the individual and reality. Desire is implicated in virtually every real occurrence; however, it is only through praxis that it makes itself known. Likewise, desire may be influenced and undergo changes as a result of the impingement of reality through praxis. Psychoanalysis, which hopes to structurally modify desire, is nothing but the praxis *of* desire. Similarly, the politics of liberation may be said to be the praxis *for* desire. It is in praxis that we make choices and become moral creatures. The value of an act is judged by the quality of its praxis. But we are still at something of a loss as to how to understand this.

13

TRANSCENDENCE AND
UNIVERSALITY

Our inquiry must end on the level of praxis, of that which is to be done. And we must develop a principle of action adequate to our realization of history, one that neither ignores the individual nor forgets that the individual is a historical creature—not just any historical creature, but one living in this late-capitalist society, faced with what it has done and what needs doing to it. If there is a way, it must be a way out of capitalism.

The predatory greed of capitalism has led the world to the edge of ecocatastrophe and starvation, while its imperialism and infatuation with technology has brought us to the verge of nuclear annihilation. Confronted with such monstrosities, what is one to strive for? The society itself labors mightily to block the means of overcoming its deadliness, substituting instead an arsenal of consolations—mass culture, drugs, gadgets, an insipid fiction called mental health, material success, religious submission, or—best of the lot—a privatizing love. Yet for too many people—perhaps most—life is a daily struggle for survival against brutal conditions they have been indoctrinated to accept as natural and beyond their control. Meanwhile, the rest of the world faces death through a poverty imposed by imperialism. These are the harsh facts, which no ideologue can pretend away and with which praxis must contend. And there is a further difficulty. Socialism, which is the rational alternative to capitalist society, remains caught in the contradictions of its birth from the old order and so far has been, in any case, successfully checked in the United States. Socialism may be a lodestar, but to simply pin one's hopes to something so manifestly remote from current possibilities is to breed despair. What is needed is a map of the existing terrain, and a path, or intermediate way that begins in present reality—including the reality of a world dominated by psychological relations—and indicates the direction of emancipation.

Or a primary way—a transhistorical basis for hope. Hope may not be rational, but it is real. So long as hope exists there must be a ground for it, and something to be done with it.

Consider an infant, also a creature with praxis. The infant is a totality, not an isolated organism. The totality contains the baby, with the limits of her body and consciousness, her parents, and the immediate surround. Relative to the totality that is the whole society— or even to the totality that will be herself as an adult—she is a tiny thing. Yet by contrast to the universe, she is no more than any other human totality, only differently limited. Her limits are those of her body, which can barely pick itself up, and of her mental faculties, which can only comprehend events preverbally and in their concrete immediacy: hence, the narrow configuration of her totality. As rudimentary as the child's grasp of objects may be, she may also be presumed to have a kind of cosmic sensibility, in contact with the universe through her molecular and organismic functioning. Therefore the field of the totality at the beginning of life is mainly transhistorical; the historical, i.e., the world of cultural objects, is present from the first days but in its nascence only.

The source of hope throughout life is the experience of a reliable goodness in infancy. This becomes translated into what psychoanalysis has called good inner objects, the good Other, as a kind of loving inner companion to be mobilized in darker days to come. For the baby, however, this process takes place at the molecular level, by the warmth and sustaining pressure of being held, the contact of light with the eye, the ingestion of good substances, and, above all, the sensation of the breast in his/her mouth. The etymology is meaningful: the sense of hope is rooted in a molecular gratification that is also succor.

Hope arises when danger has been overcome through the agency of another. To the baby, who has no sense of self to preserve, danger consists of feeling overwhelmed. At the beginning of life the source of the stimulus is bodily: hunger, cold, skin irritation, and so forth. However, as her capacities begin to mature, the baby's own increasingly conscious activity becomes implicated along with that of her parent. As this takes place, she moves from the position of an organism dominated by physiological mechanism to that of a person, i.e., a historical agent.

The baby is hungry—a source of calamity—and is being fed—a source of succor. In the past few days a number of events have taken place, including the maturation of the neural substrate that controls her hand and coordinates it with her eyes. Suddenly she takes some food from the spoon and places it in her own mouth. Mother is startled, and reacts with joy. The infant smiles with delight and claps for herself. What has happened?

Mother and baby remain identifiable and linked throughout the act, yet the child has changed herself dramatically and has changed her mother as well. It is equally true to say that the mother, by being adequate to the baby's needs, has allowed the infant to change the two of them out of the danger posed by her hunger. The ground for a hope based on activity has been prepared. In other words, a *transcendent praxis* has taken place. The baby has acted consciously and has expanded that consciousness through the making of a new object— *herself*. She has in effect said: "I will not accept the food passively from you; I can, I want to, I demand to take it myself. I therefore make myself—become 'I'—refusing you." But there is a shadow side to this assertion—the distance she creates between herself and her mother: the gain won in freedom at one point becomes a loss and a danger at another. This threat must be negated, and it can be through an expansion of the self. As the self advances into an exterior individuality, a contrary movement occurs in the interior; the baby subjectively *fuses* with mother even as she *refuses* her, and adds to herself a portion containing the possibilities for fusion. As she identifies with the mother by becoming autonomous she simultaneously fantasies the swallowing of mother along with the food. The faculty of fantasy is developed negatively as a concomitant of the baby's positive advancement. Her *desire* has been set going, and with it, a caesura in the mental depths to shadow its surface burgeoning: the primary Other. Since the Other involves negating the negation that is the baby's loss of attachment, we generalize and say of desire that it is the endopsychic mark made by the negation of the negation.

The mother's adequacy is crucial here. If she loves the baby she will want the child to become herself; she forgives the baby her temerity and affirms her self-assertion, allowing the baby's desire to be shaped along the lines of love and the Other to take on an original goodness. The delight shown by the baby in her performance is a sign of the beneficence of her Other, and it is the beginnings of the secondary narcissism that rises out of the objectlessness of primary narcissism. Note also that the independence of the baby is not a move toward isolatedness but rather a heightened sociality. Resulting from love, it reproduces love in turn. Authentic independence—what we shall call individuation—neither sacrifices sociality nor occurs in the absence of desire but is simply marked by the goodness of its Other.

The baby's praxis is transcendent because the existing field has been broken without being shattered. Instead of fragmentation we see differentiation: the elements persist but are more highly articulated and bear new relationships to each other, as in the baby's richer relatedness to her mother. Further, elements appear in different dimensions entirely, opening up new possibilities as they do: with her newly created desire, the infant develops an internal dimension that articulates with her newly discovered external power. And though the desire is unrealistic and backward-looking in itself, it also ties the baby's past with her present and future and so becomes the nucleus of her imagination.

The baby's self-assertion is profoundly historical for all its transhistorical roots. It would vary according to historical locale and is itself a piece of history, a new object created in time. Through its differentiation and transcendence, however, it becomes history of a certain kind: it is *universal*. It may seem capricious to confer so grand a quality as universality onto so slight an act as an infant's feeding herself. Yet the universal inheres in the particular and is lost in the false abstraction. True science only plucks the tendency immanent in the concrete event, and that tendency which moves to encompass ever-widening organic totalities is universal. The baby's praxis widens the pre-existing field in just such a way. And the emergence of a desire that negates the separation intrinsic in the baby's refusal is therefore essential to the widening of the totality. Without desire, therefore, there would be no universality—at least as it applies to the development of the individual. But because all subsequent universalizations must be built on this one, i.e., must include the fullness of individuality in their totalities, it may be generalized that desire and the imagination are centrally involved throughout the range of universalizing acts, from the genesis of the individual person to the envisioning of a liberated society. That which is universal contains, therefore, the seed within itself to break the dichotomy between the individual and the collective, for a universalizing political solution must be true to the individual, no less than the individual must contain the collective within himself/herself. Further, since the universal contains the imaginary it cannot converge toward any homogeneous objective resolution. Specifically, no correct party line can encompass it; and the totalitarian state, which paradoxically bids to bind together the greatest number of individuals into a fused mass, is antithetical to its spirit. A universalized totality is antitotalitarian. Cultural diversity and particular imaginative solutions are more compatible with its spirit.

The baby's refusal of the spoon held by the mother is a definite assertion of freedom on her part, one specific for her level of development. It is also, in its way, a highly aggressive act. Yet to ascribe it to an "aggressive instinct" would not only be nonexplanatory, as we have seen, but would also violate its universal quality and essential freedom. There is no biological motor behind the act. Its nature lies in its own particular intelligibility. It is the differentiation within the act, not some instinct behind it, that determines the deployment of whatever energies it releases. For example, the new relation between mother and infant is also the occasion of freeing them to realize their own capacities. And the praxis itself frees up new capacities, as when the baby will learn to walk and so releases her hands for further differentiation. The "maturation" of her biological capacities should not be isolated—as bourgeois science tends to do—from the transcendent praxes within which they are realized. All are unitary processes taking place at the level of a totality and contained within the notion of universality. Similarly, the emergence of desire as the negation of separateness will, in the manifest presence of some loss of an archaic bond with the mother, only spur the development of the infant's imagination, leading to the blossoming (when other lines of development have taken place) of the symbolic faculty itself.

Transcendent praxis involves a kind of binding, one result of which is that its desire remains coupled with social reality instead of becoming alienated into neurosis. From the subjective perspective, this implies a transformation of the diffuse distress associated with the state of hunger and the passive situation of being fed. The danger of hunger becomes the pleasure of ingestion, as before; because the baby is now able to feed herself, the pleasures of eating are transferred to the sphere of active mastery. At the same time the desire of fusion draws upon the infant's success as well. Though it remains impossible and hedged with danger, it need not be repulsed, as in neurotic developments, for it has been objectified, i.e., contained in the objective act of eating and the new relatedness between infant and mother. Therefore, desire is permitted to remain, a component of hope and a stimulus to further development.

The function of desire in emancipation now becomes clearer. Desire is only an unrealistic wish: it can effect no action in itself, and is as likely to contain hatred as love. As a result, desire alone cannot make one free; indeed, it can lead one astray. But without desire, one remains in chains. It takes desire in concert, however, with rational praxis—to engender the imagination; and it takes desire to form the will. Moreover, it takes imagination and will power to achieve universality, the necessary condition of freedom. The wish to be free therefore contains the binding of desire toward universality; and on the basis of the above, we may affirm this as transhistorical.

The transcendent binding of desire may be contrasted with the situation of bound and unbound time characteristic of capitalist relations. Bound and unbound time are caught in a duality where each exists through the repulsion of the other. In a movement that everywhere reflects the historical splitting of home and workplace, labor under capitalism must exclude fantasy and desire, while playfulness is encouraged only in sharply demarcated and closely controlled preserves of subjectivity, one of which is psychoanalysis. The rationality of transcendent praxis and its desire, on the other hand, form a dialectical unity. Time is neither bound into the production of commodifiable objects nor unbound into an objectless amorphousness. Rather, it flows freely, now investing fantasy with objective seriousness—as in play—now investing the made object with fantastic quality—in what may be called the aestheticization of work. It is therefore possible to speak of a fourth order of temporality: transcendent time. Such time is not of "nature," pure and simple. Rather, it belongs to a historical creature and is therefore suffused with various limits. However, its differentiation contains a relative reconciliation of the molecular cosmic time of nature with the serial one of history.

By contrast, the bound/unbound temporal relation characteristic of capitalism involves dualistic splitting. This is recognizable in the frantic and absurd alteration of work and leisure we are asked to live by. It is most revealingly manifested under the conditions of psychoanalysis, however. Analysis mobilizes unbound time; and under such circumstances, the end of the session—which always means the resumption of bound clock-time—is regularly experienced as a savage awakening. What is most revealing about such occasions is the hatred stirred up by them. It would seem that the rigidity of the boundary itself—which is to say, the intense binding characteristic of capitalist relations—is a basic condition for the emergence of hatred. When the differentiation of transcendent praxis is replaced by splitting of one kind or another, then the abyss of separateness so induced becomes filled with hatred.

Such splits may ramify into race, gender, and national hatred, but they begin with infantile experience. The baby we have been following was loved and forgiven for the daring of her self-assertion; hence, differentiation took place. But it could have turned out differently, as in the instance of Sarah, where the mother may have become threatened and either withdrawn from the child—in which case the field would have become depleted, not differentiated—or counterattacked and force-fed the infant—in which case she would have been violated; or the baby may have given up on individuation itself and clung to the mother—in which case she would have been diminished. In none of these possibilities would the field have been transcended; quite the contrary, it would have been reduced, i.e., dehumanized, and desire would have correspondingly taken the shape of hatred, the Other of malignancy, and some form of human diminution would be under way.

We may apply the same reasoning to other situations. Whatever universality may have been contained in Hector's psychotic break, for example, was broken under the wheels of the mental-health industry. Though Hector became *transformed* in the process—into Other— nothing *transcendent* took place. That which has been broken is in more pieces than what preceded it but is not more differentiated thereby. And, as we have seen, Hector's fate was by no means accidentally related to the basic alienation characteristic of capitalist society. The increasing number of things that fill that society—or, from another angle, the "pluralism" celebrated by its apologists—are not marks of a higher differentiation, for the things are commodities, linked by the impoverishing and abstract laws of exchange, while the bureaucratic state that holds them together is, despite its amazing complexity, fundamentally antihuman, and so antiuniversal. The rule of things may therefore be very complicated; but it is by no means more differentiated than older and seemingly simpler societies. Rather, the movement of capitalist society is toward *dedifferentiation*

—marked by dysbound time, a hollowing out of social space, and, in the personal sphere, by an increasing number of desociated characters of one kind or another.

Capitalist society has lost whatever capacity for transcendence it may have embodied in its early days, during which time it was able to mobilize the desire for freedom contained in bourgeois democracy. This is the mark of its decadence and the root of its spiritual despair. Cultural despair is not a manifestation of neurosis, although neurosis is yet another element of the totality. Despair is the loss of real ground for hope, which is not a function of wealth or weaponry but of the material basis for transcendence inherent in any given situation. What the baby can do transhistorically, capital has now historically succeeded in extinguishing, whence its deadly old age.

On the other hand, American capitalist society is not totalitarian; i.e., it does not seamlessly repress the wish to be free in everyday life. True, the system of bureaucratic domination is ever at the ready to gobble up whatever desire emerges at its many points of contradiction. But omnipresence here attests to the very instability of the balance between what is bound and unbound, and also to the profound lack of gratification proffered under the aegis of dysbound time. Therefore, the possibilities for transcendence are widespread throughout everyday life; and while they are more complex and problematic than the elementary example of the baby's self-assertion, they nevertheless are composed of the same elements.

We are thus in a position to assess the radical, i.e., transcendent, quality of particular praxes. Clearly, a radical act need not be an explicitly political one, even though its universalizing quality can be consummated only at the level of all society, indeed, for the entire globe. However, as history has yielded a fragmented society, so may it be undone i.e., transcended, at the level of fragment. As personal life is a principle one of these fragments, the question of transcendence may validly be asked of it.

The elementary answer here is clear. To care for another—as in the impulse that Aide Jiminez had for patient Hector—is transcendent. Paradoxically, this is because care means accepting the other person as she/he is, in the given state of infirmity and weakness. Infirmity is no absolute but a standard relative to that of the world— in this case, productivity according to capital. Care becomes transcendent because, by affirming the indestructible value of the individual, it also criticizes the world according to whose standards she/he is wanting and so points the way toward its transformation. By staying with that person, care affirms the direction such a transformation should take—toward a community that does not yet exist.

We may venture further. Care undoubtedly derives from the transhistorical relation of transcendence between parent and infant. But it is perhaps the elementary particle of revolutionary praxis as well. Individually, the true revolutionary is motivated by a desire to universalize the care she/he received in infancy, whereas on the level of the collective, a genuinely socialist society can only be the integral, on the level of totality, of the caring relationship: "from each according to his/her abilities; to each according to his/her needs." Were that principle to become inscribed in society, replacing the current, predatory one, then true human history would, as Marx foresaw, begin. That it does not prevail is not, of course, a function of any individual will nor of any series of wills, but rather of actual, false history.

Consequently, we cannot generalize any individual caring act to a socialist outcome; too much stands in the way, and the way itself is not composed of individual forces. It is either hypocrisy or idealistic folly that preaches a politics of individual charity or claims that the model of therapy can be extended to the healing of society. States cannot be cured through harmonizing the statesmen, nor can the corporation be made benign no matter how many therapeutic workshops are offered its executives. In practice, influence extends in the opposite direction. The whole tradition of "industrial psychology"—or, from another angle, the increasing tendency of insuring psychotherapy through the employer—are essentially strategies whereby care itself is subjected to the dominating logic of productivity. In such settings, as in that ultimate travesty that is military psychiatry, the universalizing movement of care is simply reversed. True care is noninstrumental: it is posited as an end in itself, not as the adjunct to some organizational purpose. The harsh reality is contained in the paradox that care must remain humble and, so to speak, shortsighted if it is to be authentic. Once its universalizing movement gets beyond the pain of the individual, care dissolves in contradiction.

Again in practical reality, such care as attempts to be noninstrumental is meted out in bureaucratic organizations superintended by the state (or insurance companies, which comes to the same thing). We have already seen some of the broader reasons why this should be so. At the level of bureaucratic practice, the abstract contradictions at the level of political economy become concretely deadening. There

250

can be no doubt that bureaucratic practice is a violation akin to rape so far as transcendence is concerned. That bureaucracy is becoming *universal* is no comment on its *universality*, any more than the fact that a cancer takes over an organism makes the cancer a life-giving process. Yet bureaucracy cannot be indefinitely evaded; at some point, confrontation must occur.

There is temptation, but no rationality, in trying to burn it down, as Hector tried to do—and as desire, pure and unmediated, might in itself try to do. The remonstrances of Dr. Acheson on behalf of the order that Hector threatened were doubly infuriating, perhaps, for having some truth trapped within their species of logic. If funds become limited because of capitalist irrationality, a hatred of capitalism neither renders them less limited nor removes the imperative for disposing of them prudently. To burn down the abattoir of a ward or to leave the lights burning when not in use or to fail to keep coherent records or to treat one indigent patient to the exclusion of other, equally needy ones is counterbureaucratic, but not thereby transcendent. It breaks down what exists but fails to replace it with anything of greater universality; indeed, such practices only reinforce the existing order of oppression by making it seem relatively more rational.

Bureaucracy must be confronted with a transcendent rationality— a rationality that critically exposes its roots in class society and dislodges its sedimentary practice—if it is to be overcome. Dr. Acheson must be told, in effect: You cannot separate your "science" from the strangulating hospital bureaucracy; they are but different phases of one process. Therefore, the order you cherish is a false, dehumanizing one that serves to sustain your career and the particular power of the psychiatric profession. There is no universality in it, whence your theory is banal and your practice repressive, no matter how certified it is by the science of your class interest. I will not legitimize your order by degenerating into a greater irrationality than that which it represents; therefore, I will play by those rules that have the force of material necessity behind them, but I will not dignify it either. Rather, I will attack it so long as I am in range to do so, and work to see that it is overcome by a more human and universal order.

One does not talk "in effect" to a real Dr. Acheson; one speaks either in force or not at all. And the only force that will matter in the long run is an alliance of those whose labor sustains the system yet who have no voice in it. Anyone who has tried organizing within the mental-health industry—a task that includes the recruitment of patients, their families, and the community at large, for these too contribute an unarticulated labor, no less than the various echelons of mental-health workers—can attest to the formidability of the project. Scarcely anywhere else has historical inertia achieved such sedimentation. Yet to enunciate the demand already sets the alternative into motion. Furthermore, the times are ripe for these struggles, as the unending crisis of the state proletarianizes increasing numbers of health workers (including lower- and middle-rank psychiatrists) and forces them into alliances, however uneasy, with those for whom they are supposed to care.

And however difficult the fight, there can be no question of its necessity. This follows from the logic of care itself and not from any politics appended to it. It is absurd to think of caring for someone in a purely psychological way, i.e., without seeing to his/her so-called material needs. Care is given to a whole person, not just the psyche, and the person lives in the social totality, under the tutelage of the state. One should not lose sight of the differentiation here: the concrete responsibility of those taking care of the troubled is to attend to madness; and madness is so terrifying and painful a thing to face that a detour into the social and economic situation of the patient can be a tempting avoidance. However, there is no essential contradiction between being with a patient on an individual level, and organizing with fellow workers and clients against the oppressive features of the state. Indeed, the two praxes can enrich each other, for they are both movements toward universality, albeit by different routes.

In any case, it is crucial to face up to the state, to see how its bureaucracy embraces psychiatry and deadens it; to recognize its function on behalf of capital; and, of greatest importance, to struggle against it until it makes good on the promise of democracy it would like to forget.

For many who despair of caring for others under the aegis of the bureaucratic state, the intimacy of psychotherapy has loomed as a valid alternative. It is indisputable that psychotherapy can have a transcendent quality irrespective of the various ideologies under which it parades but simply a function of the possibilities for care that it offers. There is also no question, however, that to practice psychotherapy in the bourgeois world is to be enmeshed in contradictions.

As a ritual of passage, psychotherapy is a remedy for, i.e., it remediates, the split that has so crippled life under capitalism, namely, the split between the productive and the personal, the workplace and the home. Psychotherapy is that form of work—based on a free contract, remunerable, and so exchangeable in the market of capitalism —dedicated to the mending of that which is personal and nonexchangeable. From one angle, this is a crushing limitation: the business of healing souls is intrinsically a nontranscendent position from which no universality can arise. Indeed, the wretched level of existing practice in which the question of transcendence is usually secondary to that of avoiding harm follows directly from this fact. But from another perspective, this contradiction offers creative and transcendent possibilities. The simple fact that psychotherapy is remunerable opens it up to capitalist relations but does not lock it into place; i.e., it does not have to be "business." Recall that capitalist society is not yet totalitarian. The personal, being unhinged from productivity, is set loose to work out a multiplicity of particular solutions; and the overriding fact that none of these can be totalized into a political force does not deny them the property of being kindling points of desire. In other words, capitalism spontaneously generates an infinite series of potential zones of individual transcendence. Some are considered noxious and are put into the realm of the marginal— the neuroses, sexualities of deviance, criminality, et cetera and none of them is inherently virtuous. But they are points of possible freedom and belong to the domain of disorder to which psychotherapy addresses itself. If psychotherapy simply regards itself, then, as subject to professional codes, work discipline, or the standards of recognized success, it necessarily succumbs to the ways of business; if, however, it allows itself to be fertilized by the desire set loose in its object, madness, it can become transcendent. Put simply, the patient must be allowed to heal the therapist no less than the therapist the patient.

Psychotherapy must be measured not simply by the care it offers but by its attitude toward desire. The patient brings an alienated desire to the therapist, who is given the privilege of deciding what to do with it. The transcendent path in therapy begins with a certain *respect* for this desire, which is then combined with the imperative of care. Note that the implication of this position is not necessarily to foster a release of desire or even its uncritical acceptance, as such a policy is antithetical to care. Rather, the person of the patient is to be accepted, not any element of his/her being in isolation from the rest. It is an infantile therapeutics—of which we have much, particularly under the aegis of consumerist capitalism—that fetishizes desire. A transcendent therapeutics, on the other hand, begins with a respect for desire, which includes appreciation of its role as hatred in human destructiveness. It may choose, then, as a short-term strategy, to foster the suppression of desire when it adjudges the balance of forces to be such that its unmediated release will be destructive. Needless to add, this juncture often arises, especially in more seriously troubled people. But such a policy can be a short-term expedient only if therapy is open to transcendence; and even during this phase, the therapist must be unafraid of the patient's desire and open to it as an authentic manifestation of the stifled life within him/her. We have come round to considering individuation as the specific goal of a transcendent therapeutics, the terminus of the path beginning with care and respect for desire. Desire, being the voice of the transhistorical as well as of the lost possibilities of personal history, must be regarded as the truest and most spontaneous manifestation of an individuation that is trying to happen. Lost from the past, it is what wants to be born in the future. The point of greatest madness, then, is also the point wherein lies the opening to transcendence. This defines the exquisite paradoxicality of psychotherapeutics.

The logic of universality mandates a free socialist society as the goal of social development. This society can only consist of individuated persons, however; and it is the transcendent task of praxes of person-to-person contact—which include psychotherapy, but also education, child rearing, love, and so on—to foster the individuation of persons, both for their own sake and for that of the potential socialist development of society. Now it should be underscored here that individuation is not the same as that degenerate ideology of bourgeois culture, individualism. Individualism represents the wish to be free as distorted through the prism of capitalist relations. It is the credo of the isolated, predatory individual, set off from others and an embodiment of the market. Such an individual is richly rewarded by capitalist society, and so passively gains strength from that quarter. To this must be added a frantic energy—recall here our portrait of Curtis —whose source lies in the unbearable inner loneliness of individualism and the need, perpetually thwarted by its essential hostility, to reach out to others. Since these others are necessarily regarded as competitors, authorities, or victims according to the prevailing ethos, they become related to the malignant internal Other; and the energy blocked in the pursuit of intimacy becomes redirected outward in economic conquest.

Despite material gains, the self of individualism remains fundamentally weaker than that of individuation. When the individuated person draws on a genuine social power, the isolated, predatory individual becomes a particle of capital, sunk in a world order built by the labor of billions of others from whom she/he is cut off. Since these others remain Other, the life of the individualist is spectral and inhabited by living ghosts—the ghost of the proletariat, of racial others, of the other gender, of the mad—and of his/her own inner madness, the form taken by desire. The individuated person, by contrast, is sociated. Living through participation in the life of others, the inner self becomes a congregation of the Other. Internal barriers come down with external ones: the self, living through actual transcendent possibility, grows through an inner confrontation with, and an appropriation of, its Otherness; the Other will be present, not as a single looming monstrosity—as was the case for Sarah and Hector—but as an internal representation of the range of humanity itself. We will then have a sociated narcissism to contrast with the desociated narcissism of late capitalism. This should not be taken to mean that the inner world of the Other will be a precise mapping of the current stage of history or of the individual's actual practices and experiences. That kind of corrleation between inside and outside does not exist: the imagination sees to that. But the same imagination, given a life transcendentally open to the concrete social possibilities available to a person, will make of the Other a variegated tapestry within the given historical limits. For this reason, the individuated person is the rich, distinctive personality; and the isolated individual is the cipher, open to manipulation by mass culture. The isolated individual paradoxically becomes the particle comprising the mass, while the individuated one becomes, through his/her approximation to universality, the person of a distinct individuality.

It follows that individuation should not be regarded as an image of positive "mental health." The historical limits are set, and universality is only to be approximated, not gained, under existing circumstances. The degree of approximation cannot be quantified nor assigned to any particular behavior. Individuation is a bit like divine grace: no particular act can earn it—no personal acrobatics, no sexual performance, no measure of conventional success. To ascribe individuation to any behavior is to fall prey to the logic of production, here for the market of narcissism: the individual is to produce the desired behavior—say, insightfulness—then she/he is deemed formed. The trouble with such assessments is that they never go on to add "deemed by whom?" The expert in mental health? A presidential commission? Or should we return to the tried-and-tested authority of the clergy?

Freud had the decency not to legislate an image of correct mental health. (His famous pronouncement on the matter—"to love and work"—was so cryptic as to leave the door open to virtually any interpretation; indeed, the whole remark was probably made to get someone off his back.) But he left the legacy of a doctrine unable to resist conformism and moralistic penetration. I agree with Sartre: we need an existential psychoanalysis able to comprehend how the wish to be free is expressed in an individual life, and that existential freedom could be defined only in a Marxist framework, "the untranscendable philosophy for our time."[1] The notion of individuation is meant to serve this need. Individuals are fractious, fractured creatures; they are broken, and they use their scars in different ways, moving universally through their particular, unduplicable acts and showing resistance in the midst of submission. The only sure guide is to take each life concretely and to see it in light of historical possibilities.

The purpose of a transcendent psychotherapy is to help remove such barriers that hinder the person's individuation. Ultimately, this requires a confrontation with one's desire and Otherness—and, allied with this, a demand upon, and therefore a change in, the external world. The particulars of such a reconstruction—its relation to the given modalities of psychotherapy and to the range of states of disorder, not to mention a host of practical considerations—none of this can concern us here. They are materials for an entirely separate work. We can see already, however, that a transcendent therapy should be built on the dialectic of care and not on any particular external praxis of liberation. To show respect for desire and to permit it to flourish so that a confrontation can be made, consideration must be made for desire's objectless and unrealistic nature. If any program, no matter how splendid in itself, is imposed on the patient as the language of therapy, then desire will hide itself behind the object so offered and be lost to view. The reality of therapy has to be a degree of fantasy that would be fatal in everyday life. To allow this to occur, the therapist can be no one thing, no guide, no guru, but the generalized Other, the possibility of all states of otherness. This, of course, does not mean that the therapist cannot be "real" or helpful to the patient, only that in being so, the dictates of care demand for the time that the confrontation with desire be muted or held in abeyance.

The therapist must be there for the patient, accepting him/her in all his/her fragmentation and tolerating his/her hatred and spite, while at the same time representing the real hopes for individuation—that this person could become other than what she/he is—and realizing the historical as well as transhistorical limits to which individuation can be taken in any instance. The work of therapy requires then a delicate and uncommon mixture of qualities: critical capacity, an almost maternal acceptingness, and, in the end, the strength to bear forgiveness. If true growth is to occur, the hatred that has been locked away in desire will have to be forgiven. But forgiveness itself can take place only where care has established an adequate foundation.

Can psychotherapy be a radical praxis? We seemed to answer yes by positing for it a transcendent possibility. But the matter of historical limits stalks this question. Psychotherapy becomes transcendent by building on the possibilities inherent in the care of the individual. Care, we observed, was immanently critical and predicated upon the hope for a true community. But for all that, care cannot escape the public/private split of capitalism. It may heal that split within the individual and *release* her/him for further praxis, but in itself it remains bound to the individual side of the divide and retains whatever transcendent character it has through accepting its limits. If a therapist, for example, were to organize his patients into a working, public association, the universalizing qualities of care could readily be swept away by the domination inseparable from their highly asymmetric relationship. But one does not have to imagine such an eventuality; it has already happened many times, in fact, whenever a powerful and original therapist has attempted to build a school in his name. The invariable result of such ventures—and one thinks here not just of the school of Freud and its subsidiaries but of those of Jung, Reich, Perls, et al.—is a flowering of the authoritarianism latent in the therapeutic relationship, associated with puerility of the followers and a general decline in the level of discourse. The lesson to be drawn from this history is not a psychological one but rather the ultimate subordination of psychology to the capitalist totality it is structured to ignore. However, to combine psychotherapeutic practice with a serious critique of capitalist relations means the introduction of a consciously socialist spirit; and to the extent that this attitude manifests itself in the fine structure of day-to-day practice, so will desire be deprived of the unstructuredness demanded for its emergence.

There is no such thing, therefore, as a Marxist psychotherapy. At

257

best we can have a psychotherapy compatible with Marxism or radical practice—a transcendent therapy, one predicated on the movement toward universality. The point is not whether such a therapeutics covertly prepares people to see and act in a socialist way. In any case political orientation is shaped outside the therapist's office and is best left there for all accounts. Rather, it is to keep a certain line of development open in society, in the conviction that what is "best" for individuals, i.e., their free individuation, is best for the totality. History will be fought out, as before, at the material level of class. It does not take a very deep look to establish that the struggle has for some time been going against labor, and the Left in general; nor is there much likelihood of the trend reversing itself in the near future. However, neither the retreat of the Left nor the insufficiency of therapy (or any other personal praxis) to effect direct political change suggests that what takes place psychotherapeutically is historically negligible. On the contrary, the whole direction of radical praxis is at stake.

The issue is whether one waits passively for "objective" conditions to ripen or—what amounts to the same thing—puts one's trust blindly in a vanguard party as the agent of revolutionary change as opposed to actively structuring everyday life and participating in the social struggle from whatever position in which one finds oneself. To take the former course is to invite nothing to happen or to create the preconditions for a future society that will make one yearn for today's capitalism, with its sloppy contradictoriness. The march of bureaucratic domination passes through human inertia. Bureaucracy is never simply imposed; rather, it is always created at the actively passive point of acquiescence.

And from the other side, radical practice cannot be ceded to another without dissolving. The only worthwhile, i.e., universal, goal of revolution is self-determination and self-management. This means a society structured along the lines of face-to-face interaction rather than a society of massified otherness; and it means that the revolution is or is not being prepared in every minute particular of daily existence: the ways babies are held or love made or speech spoken or work conducted. To be sure, great social changes are consummated on a mass level, often surprising to the participants, who suddenly find themselves drawn into large-scale group actions that convulse an entire society. But the mushroom that springs up in a day is the product of a mycelium that prepared itself long before the event; and the great visible movements of history are likewise the products of billions of individual, invisible precursors. These precursory acts are themselves organized as well as chosen actively and, to a certain extent, freely. And since each succeeding phase of society retains much of the character of the old no matter how much it may also transcend it, the degree to which freedom and universality imbue the precursory activities of everyday life will determine the character of the future.

History is not a determinable process obeying an iron economic law but is made in the zone where desire and praxis interact to give birth to new events. Because desire is of the imagination, and so disjoined from necessity, history contains a degree of indeterminacy. But what is indeterminate from the objective side is manifest to the participants as an essential freedom. And since desire cannot link itself to objects, it remains unappeased even by transcendent praxis; moreover, it is negated even at the moment of revolutionary change and so lives on as a new source of demand. There is no fixed path, then; the choice of object, i.e., praxis, lies open to freedom, and with it, the historical outcome.

The victors in history are those whose desire is best harmonized with material givens. Reaching beyond, but never so far that they cannot pull themselves along, they remain guided by a transcendent belief that mobilizes actuality by calling on memory and, in so doing, generates the future. Historical time is the creation of a transcendent desire acting on materiality. Capital had this quality once, and bureaucracy succeeds by keeping others from seizing it now that its master is senile. Nonetheless, desire remains to haunt capital no less than its inexorable material contradictions.

It is for ths reason that the ideas advanced here may prove helpful and not merely quixotic. In any case, one must struggle to justify even a hint of revolutionary optimism in times such as these. As capital dies it seems determined to take the world along with it. The age of scarcity that we are now to endure as a result of capitalist folly threatens us with the hateful aspect of desire that eventuates in racism and fascism. Meanwhile, the limited mind and mean spirit of those in power are given godlike dimensions through control of the means of nuclear annihilation.

Nonetheless, capital is doomed, no matter how the Right props it up in the short run. Its empire totters, and nature will no longer pay the price for ruthless exploitation. As capital ceases to expand, it must die. Our task for the dark time of its agony is to survive and to create the best possible conditions for the future. We cannot afford the luxury of despair but must look without flinching and struggle all the more resolutely. The question now is not the reconstruction of one corner of the bourgeois world called psychoanalysis but a fresh look at the centerpiece of the radical tradition itself, Marxism.

Certain Marxists may claim that I am trying to mystify history by ascribing so basic a function to a nonrational force such as desire, one, moreover that seems to fly in the face of materialism by being unable to attach itself to any object in the world. And it must be admitted that I am not a very good Marxist, but one of the oft-rejected anarchistic, or humanistic, type.[2] I am so, however, with reason. The issue is not whether desire fits into Marxist dogma but whether it exists—and if it exists and palpably plays a major role in shaping events and is not reducible to ordinary material influence, then is it not a mystification to leave it out? Besides, what is Marxism in its revolutionary heart but the most salient, the purest manifestation of desire in the modern world, and the concrete embodiment of universality on the widest scale? Marxism is the historical integral of all those forces that, arising negatively out of capital, seek to overthrow it. It is—or should be—therefore the praxis *for* desire.

Capital may be characterized as a system of domination through its entrapment of the object world in a web of false reason: Blake's Urizen. We have seen how desire arises negatively out of this conjuncture. It follows that Marxism has to appropriate desire, both to overcome capital and to avoid lapsing into the worst features of what it bids to overcome. Marxism, in short, must become transcendent if it is not to become bureaucratic; and transcendence is the pressing toward freedom. But who is to say what freedom is? Who can legislate it for us or pin down its indeterminacy, born of desire and begetting desire in turn? If desire is understood as the striving for an object that cannot be named, then infancy is desire's point of origin in the individual. But this same individual will never come to exist except in the free society, which must be desire's point of realization for the species.

POSTSCRIPT

How do you know but evr'y Bird that cuts the airy way,
Is an immense world of delight, clos'd by your senses five?

APPOINTMENT DIARY OF A RADICAL PSYCHOANALYST

The book is approximately three-by-five inches and has a spiral metal binding. Each week of the year is spread out on a page of its own, the days properly laid out next to each other. Each day has a grid of lines for the hours. Orthogonal time binding. The cover is of black plastic made to simulate leather. One year the book was lost for a while. Hell to pay.

*   *

Is an immense world of daylight, clos'd by your senses five?

8:00 A.M.   SARAH

8:50 A.M.   JANE

9:40 A.M.   CURTIS

Drive to hospital. Where is Hector? Where is Frank?

11:30 A.M.   CONFERENCE WITH RESIDENTS. Subject: the iniquity of psychiatric discourse. Reading from Karl Marx.

It is not the consciousness of men that determines their being, but, on the contrary, their social being that determines their consciousness.

After the conference I am accosted by W, one of the sharpest residents. He loved the class, but the more he loves it the worse he feels. He accuses me. How can I go on, year after year, sowing doubt in their minds, shaking the foundations of what they have been taught not to question—and have no real alternative to offer, only a socialism that nobody believes in any more? I explain patiently about prefigurative politics, the transcendence of small acts, determinate negations, the value of making a critique from

261

amidst the world and not above it. He nods. I go on to speak of the unfree labor of billions that supports our thought and of how our praxis must move to liberate that labor if it is not to become sterile and academic. Utopianism is only a moment in true socialism, which in its fullness is the source of vitality. He tepidly agrees. Then I realize I have been haranguing again. I remember that I am a psychotherapist, too, and inquire whether anything new has happened to him. He flushes uncomfortably. Yes, he has been offered a job on the new ward they are setting up to expedite commitment. Just last week we had called it the Eichmann Service. He's afraid he's going to take it: it's really pretty humanely organized, the pay is so good, his analysis is so expensive, his kid's nursery school costs so much, his debts are so great . . . but he is worried that he will be selling out. A flash of anger. My best student, the only one who really understood Adorno. I try to remember what I wrote about forgiveness. Can I forgive—who? Specter of Quesalid. I look at my watch: already late for the committee meeting. I tell W to make an appointment to discuss his dilemma further. I forgive myself.

1:00 P.M. CURRICULUM COMMITTEE. Agenda: forthcoming merger with Hospital X; request by the drug-abuse service for core teaching time in the first-year program. They act like big shots since their giant Grant came through. It's where psychiatry is heading. What's the matter, don't you want to keep up with the times? This is a pragmatic profession.

their social being determines their consciousness clos'd by your senses five

2:30 P.M. PAPERWORK. Junk. Wheeling and dealing. I hang around too long and have to drive downtown in a hurry. Don't want to be late for the patients. More meetings coming up. Miles to go before I sleep. The expressway is cut deeply through black rock. Massive icicles hang from severed underground streams. There is the dead dog again. A whole week. Poor bastard. No one crosses the expressway, no vulture will find you. Buildings blind-eyed with desertion are ready to fall into the canyon. Turn on the radio. A man sings, of brotherhood, the voice inexpressibly rich and deep. It is Paul Robeson and the "Ode to Joy." My eyes well with tears.

APPENDIX
NOTES
INDEX

APPENDIX

As the form of this work left no room for an adequate critical engagement with particular psychoanalytic thinkers, I have decided to append two brief confrontations with theories that parallel some of the main themes of the text. The aim is not to be comprehensive, either with respect to the range of current psychoanalytic thought or to the actual weight and texture of the *oeuvre* confronted. Such would have to be the province of an entirely separate work. Instead, I have tried to indicate only some of the direction such a work might take, along with a few substantive points. The purpose of these critical vignettes is mainly to aid the reader in differentiating some of the central concepts of the present study from other closely related themes that have lately been the subject of considerable interest.

A NOTE ON KOHUT

Heinz Kohut is widely known within psychoanalysis as the progenitor of "Self Psychology," the central thesis of which is that narcissism is a whole separate line of development to be set alongside the sexual instincts, and that the outcome of healthy narcissism is the formation of a stable, integrated mature Self.[1] Alone among the Freudians, Kohut was able to sense the need for a revision in psychoanalytic discourse as a result of the structural shift toward pathological narcissism in late-capitalist society. His success in articulating a shift in the paradigm without rupturing either the basic logic or the social relations of the psychoanalytic profession has made Kohut the John Maynard Keynes of Freudianism. This is either his glory or his shame, depending on the point from which one views him.

Kohut has shown skill in adapting psychoanalysis to contend with a changing world in which fragmentary self-experience increasingly becomes the norm. He has done so as the quintessentially liberal reformer, swathing the fractured self in the categories of humanism. On balance, Kohut has been somewhat more progressive than the classical Freudian, particularly in his concept of aggression and destructiveness (SS–615–659). And he has succeeded in prying the dimension of narcissism loose enough from the traditional drive-defense model of Freudian discourse to permit some clinical generalizations to be made that are both useful and open to social mediation—for example, in the concept of the "selfobject" (AS–26–27 and passim), which closely resembles that of the *Other*, advanced in this work; or, indeed, in his whole characterization of psychoanalysis as a discourse based upon empathy (RS–303–305), in other words, as something intersubjective and so social at the core.

So far, so good. However, Kohut the humanist now has a serious problem on his hands, for humanism contains within itself a universalizing motion whose intrinsic aim is socialism, the overcoming of all forms of domination and heirarchy. This can be seen clearly in Kohut's own central value, empathy. True empathy requires a genuine recognition of the other; it can be carried out only between those who can "see things the other's way," a capacity that must be based materially if it is not to become trivial.

Kohut never confronts this question head-on; however, the actual texture of his writing leaves little question that it is the trivial, narrowly psychologistic sense of the term he has in mind. The social order posited by his intersubjectivity is merely the existing class society; and the empathy he preaches is without transcendence, being merely that of the professional who cozily strokes those who share his values and ignores the rest of history. Kohut is a liberal, true, but he reminds us that liberalism draws on the liberatory promise of capitalism to reproduce capitalist domination.

Needless to add, there is nothing overt or intentional in all this. Kohut can have his humanism and his professionalism, too, through a timeworn expedient that he never tires of championing. Kohut reminds his readers again and again throughout his writings that what he is doing is part of *Science* and that it is therefore loaded with technical, value-free operations and concepts.[2] After all, anyone who can write the following need not be bothered with the relationship between pathological narcissism and the alienation of capitalist society:

> *Psychoanalysis can deal with the obstacles that stand in the way of empathic comprehension just as other sciences have learned to deal with the obstacles that stood in the way of mastering the use of the observational tools—sensory organs, including their extension and refinement through instruments—they employed. (RS–144)*

He can stop the search for social causes at the tried-and-true level of the mother-infant dyad and refer all deeper mysteries to the arcana of instinctual cathexis and the wondrous ways of the ego.

This is not to say that Kohut, who seems to see himself in the Mosaic tradition, can refrain from speaking out on matters of social concern. When he does, however, the scientism is once again apparent, this time decked out with a filigree of false humility. According to Kohut, psychoanalysis lacks the "scientific equipment" of social psychology, history, and sociology. And because of this, the psychoanalyst

> *would also not be able, unaided, to do justice to a general comparative examination of the changing social factors that are correlated to the changing psychological disorders encountered by various generations of depth psychologists. (RS–270)*

This statement is too disingenuous to be circumspect. Nor can we seriously believe that these other disciplines are in any condition to offer penetrating insights into the problem of history and psychology. Rather, Kohut's disclaimer must be read as an apologia for the craven incapacity of psychoanalysis to transcend its bourgeois essence, a move that would have to begin with the unthinkable step of examining its class bias.

On the other hand, what Kohut actually does say about social issues could stand an infusion of some sociological expertise, or at least some elementary intelligence. Consider the following: We are exhorted to overcome

> *the deeply ingrained value system of the Occident (pervading the religion, the philosophy, the social utopias of Western man) (that) extols altruism and concern for others and disparages egotism and concern for one's self* (SS–619)

Since Kohut considers narcissism to be, like sex, one of the great life forces, its suppression can retard progress and lead, in extreme instances, to horrors such as nazism. Kohut sees his mission as one of leading us out of this darkness:

> *I think that the overcoming of a hypocritical attitude toward narcissism is as much required today as was the overcoming of sexual hypocrisy a hundred years ago. We should not deny our ambitions, our wish to dominate [sic], our wish to shine and our yearning to merge with omnipotent figures. [For] if we learn to acknowledge the legitimacy of these narcissistic forces . . . we shall be able . . . to transform our archaic grandiosity and exhibitionism into realistic self-esteem and into pleasure with ourselves, and our yearning to be at one with the omnipotent selfobject into the socially useful, adaptive, and joyful capacity to be enthusiastic and to admire the great after whose lives, deeds, and personalities we can permit ourselves to model our own. (SS–620)*

At one level, this may be read simply as a promise to ease the lot of prospective disciples. But its asininity goes much further and is based on two quite characteristic tendencies of psychoanalytic thought through the sharing of which Kohut proves his bona fides, since all has a semblance to heresy. One is the old specter of biologism, for only by raising narcissism to the level of a force of nature with his pseudoscience can Kohut let it rain down on us an imperative—one, moreover, that can in principle be freed from historical contamination (so that "the wish to dominate," et cetera, can then be read as natural and therefore good for us). The other tendency we have also met with: an inability to assess what is true in a historical situation. Kohut here goes one better than Freud, who at least recognized that capitalist society was rapacious, even if he then tried to explain this away psychologically. Now we simply have it turned on its head: the ideology—religion, et cetera (and here one would have to include socialism, as one of the "social utopias")—that has arisen to check, usually unsuccessfully, the rapacity of the system is neatly substituted for the reality it tries to negate. We are then asked to believe that the basic tendency of capitalist society—an order based upon predatory individualism—is the "ingrained value system" of altruism.

But there is no further point in tracing the logic of Heinz Kohut. Whatever the logic, the aim is clear: to keep psychoanalysis up-to-date without changing its class position; and to salve the conscience—and the Selves—of its practitioners and clientele. His attempt to do so has brought the radical discourse of Freud to the level of the moral philosophy of Dr. Norman Vincent Peale: a psychology for winners.

Appendix

A NOTE ON LACAN

Our survey concludes with a brief look at a line of psychoanalytic discourse that explicitly takes desire as a leading term. Jacques Lacan—and a considerable body of French practice influenced by him—has developed a formidable reading of Freud that avoids the kind of Cartesian split responsible for monstrosities such as the theory of the ego. Accordingly, Lacan has germinated an anti-theoretical theory of deliberate ellipticality and paradox, a theory like a room full of mirrors, designed, so it seems, to keep exegesis occupied for all time. This has the distinct virtue of preventing the reduction of Freudian thought to a common-sense psychology. However, it also makes the explication of Lacan's notion of desire a boundless project, one that would require the reconstruction of the entire colossus of his antitheory for a serious examination.

In lieu of this, we shall opt for a parsimony that merely asserts the following: Lacanian theory is constructed along two main axes: that of structural linguistics, dominated by the logic of the *signifier*, so that the neurotic symptom, and the unconscious in general, is "structured like a Language"; and that of a Hegelian conception of intersubjectivity that regards the self as constituted in a dialectic with others. Desire, then, which is Lacan's interpretation of Freud's notion of *Wunsch*, or wish, may be approached from two angles:

Desire is an effect in the subject of the condition that is imposed on him by the existence of the discourse [i.e., psychoanalysis], to make his need pass through the defiles of the signifier;

and,

man's desire finds its meaning in the desire of the other . . . because the first object of desire is to be recognized by the other.[3]

Desire is therefore primarily intersubjective and is carried forth on the plane of the Imaginary according to Language. Desire, for Lacan, is the mediation between the need for objects and the demand placed upon the other person, specifically, the analyst. Desire cannot be reduced to either demand or need but is based upon the wish for recognition, i.e., for self-constitution. As such, desire seeks the annihilation of the other person as an independent subject and so is related to the objectless world of primary narcissism. Hence, desire is real, and a need, but not a real need. Rather, it is an impossible state of longing dimly expressed in actual demands. The work of analysis consists of bringing desire to consciousness.

It is clear that Lacan's concept of desire resembles that advanced in the preceding pages. Indeed, if one could equate need with the transhistorical, and demand with the historical, the equivalence would become even more exact. Lacan's example, in fact, was influential in my own questioning of received psychoanalytic dogma and encouraged me to strive for a more radical appreciation of what Freud was trying to say. That the two views of desire converge is related then to a common understanding of what Freud disclosed, and what psychoanalytic praxis again and again reveals, that is, a nameless imaginary striving at the center of self-experience. Desire is, in fact, the primary datum of psychoanalysis.

However, Lacan's ideas do not converge with the historical/transhistorical dialectic that animates the present work. From another angle, he remains with Hegelian idealism instead of doing with it what Marx did and what is being attempted here in a Marxian spirit, i.e., to situate desire and the unconscious in the real, historically developing life of people. Without such a root, Lacan's theory becomes a brilliant but groundless display of fireworks; it mystifies language and ends after all by committing the same kind of Phallocentrism as did Freud—for example, by making the Phallus the ultimate signifier of desire; or by ensconsing the "name of the father" in a timeless structure instead of regarding it as a historically mediated element of the totality.[4]

It might be added that Lacan's rococo theorizing seems less a search for the truth than a priestly assertion of mystery. Once again the radical project has been debased, and by one who touched upon a genuinely emancipatory discovery.

NOTES

PREFACE

1. Cf. in this regard Michael Schneider, *Neurosis and Civilization*, trans, Michael Roloff (New York: Seabury Press, 1975); Bruce Brown, *Marx, Freud, and the Critique of Everyday Life: Toward a Permanent Cultural Revolution* (New York: Monthly Review Press, 1973); Russell Jacoby, *Social Amnesia: A Critique of Conformist Psychology from Adler to Laing* (Boston: Beacon Press, 1975).

1 THE LAMENTATIONS OF QUESALID

1. Claude Lévi-Strauss, "The Sorcerer and His Magic," in *Structural Anthropology*, 2 vols., vol. 1, trans. Claire Jacobson and Brooke Grundfest Schoepf (New York: Basic Books, 1963–1976), 1: 167–85.

3 BABEL: A FANTASY

1. In Franz Mehring, *Karl Marx: The Story of His Life*, trans. Edward Fitzgerald (Ann Arbor: University of Michigan Press, 1962), p. 60.
2. The first of the "Theses on Feuerbach," in *Writings of the Young Marx on Philosophy and Society*, ed. and trans. Loyd D. Easton and Kurt H. Guddat (Garden City, N.Y.: Doubleday, 1967), p. 400.
3. Georg Lukács, *History and Class Consciousness: Studies in Marxist Dialectics*, trans. Rodney Livingstone (Cambridge, Mass.: MIT Press, 1971).

4 LOVE AND MONEY

1. Sigmund Freud, *Studies in Hysteria*, in *The Standard Edition of the Complete Psychological Works of Sigmund Freud*, 24 vols., translated from the German under the general editorship of James Strachey, in collaboration with Anna Freud, assisted by Alix Strachey and Alan Tyson (London: The Hogarth Press, 1953–1974), 2:305. (*The Standard Edition* will henceforth be designated by *SE*, followed by volume number.)

5 CONCERNING TOTALITY

1. Carl E. Schorske, "Politics and Patricide" in Freud's *Interpretation of Dreams*, in idem, *Fin-de-Siècle Vienna: Politics and Culture* (New York: Knopf, 1980), pp. 181–205.

2. Otto Fenichel, "The Drive to Amass Wealth," *Psychoanalytic Quarterly* 7 (1948): 69–95. Cf. also Norman O. Brown, *Life Against Death: The Psychoanalytical Meaning of History* (Middletown, Conn.: Wesleyan University Press, 1959).

3. Karl Marx, *Capital*.

4. This is not necessarily a Marxist insight. Cf. Alfred North Whitehead, *Science and the Modern World* (New York: The Free Press, 1967).

5. Cf. Harry Braverman, *Labor and Monopoly Capital: The Degradation of Work in the Twentieth Century* (New York: Monthly Review Press, 1975).

6. Joel Kovel, "Mind and State in Ancient Greece," *Dialectical Anthropology* 5, no. 4 (in press).

7. For two recent, quite diverse critiques, cf. Russell Means, "Fighting Words on the Future of the Earth," *Mother Jones*, December 1980, pp. 22–38; and Russell Jacoby, "What Is Conformist Marxism?" *Telos* 45 (Fall 1980): 19–44.

8. The notion of totality does not admit of ready-made comprehension. As a cardinal concept of dialectical thought, totality is more than the "whole which exceeds the sum of its parts"; nor is it equivalent to any of the terms of General Systems Theory. Totality conveys a reciprocal motion: the whole is in the parts and constitutive of them, even as it is defined by their aggregation. The concept is used variously by Hegel, who saw in it a closed ontological system, the unity of Reason with history; Marx, who saw it as the superordinate reality of class society, driven onward by the split-off energy of the proletariat; Lukács; and Adorno. The definition that corresponds most closely to the sense used in this work is that of Sartre:

> A totality is defined as a being which, while radically distinct from the sum of its parts, is present in its entirety, in one form or another, in each of these parts, and which relates to itself either through its relation to one or more of its parts or through its relation to the relations between all or some of them.

Jean-Paul Sartre, *Critique of Dialectical Reason, Theory of Practical Ensembles*, trans. Alan Sheridan-Smith, and ed. Jonathan Rée (London: NLB, 1976), p. 45.

Sartre goes on to state that totalities revert to an inert condition (the "practico-inert") unless synthetically unified by historical activity: *totalisation*. Dialectical reason is "the very movement of totalisation" (*Critique of Dialectical Reason*, p. 46). This kind of activity is conveyed in the notion of *praxis*, a principal concept of the present work. Totalisation—a term that shall not be employed directly in this work—is therefore intended as an element of the concept of praxis employed here.

It should also be noted that person (or "personalities") are totalities on their own, even as they are also parts of the totality of the society. Freud intuited this relationship in his theory, although he never explicitly developed it.

Cf. also Herbert Marcuse, *Reason and Revolution: Hegel and the Rise of Social Theory* (Boston: Beacon Press, 1960); Susan Buck-Morss, *The Origin of Negative Dialectics: Theodor W. Adorno, Walter Benjamin and the Frank-*

furt Institute (New York: The Free Press, 1977); and Theodor W. Adorno, "Sociology and Psychology," *New Left Review* 46 (November-December 1967): 67–80, 47 (January-February 1968): 79–95.

6 DESIRE AND THE TRANSHISTORICAL

1. Freud, *Beyond the Pleasure Principle*, SE, 18: 3–66.

2. István Meszáros, *Marx's Theory of Alienation* (London: Merlin Press, 1970).

3. Freud, "The Unconscious," SE, 14: 159–216.

4. René Spitz, "Transference: The Analytical Setting and Its Prototype," *International Journal of Psycho-analysis* 37 (1956): 380–85; D. W. Winnicott, "On Transference," *International Journal of Psycho-Analysis* 37 (1956): 386–88; H.W. Loewald, "On the Therapeutic Effect of Psychoanalysis," *International Journal of Psycho-analysis* 41 (1960): 16–33.

5. Colwyn Trevarthen, "Communication and Cooperation in Early Infancy: A Description of Primary Intersubjectivity," in *Before Speech: The Beginning of Interpersonal Communication*, ed. Margaret Bullowa (Cambridge and New York: Cambridge University Press, 1979), pp. 321–47.

6. St. Augustine, *Confessions*, trans. R.S. Pine-Coffin (Baltimore: Penguin, 1961), p. 28.

7. Freud, *Civilization and Its Discontents*, SE, 21: 59–148.

8. It is true that Freud, in *Beyond the Pleasure Principle*, tried to extricate himself from the trap of dualism with the notion of the Nirvana Principle as the ultimate agency of the instinctual forces. This may be seen as a manifestation of Freud's genius warning with his bourgeois tendencies. The same cudgel was later taken up by Herbert Marcuse in *Eros and Civilization: A Philosophical Inquiry into Freud* (Boston: Beacon Press, 1955) and, with lesser success, by Norman O. Brown in *Life Against Death*. However, the case of Freud's psychoanalysis can best be weighed by its practical results: in real situations, both clinically and politically, psychoanalysis gravitates toward the dualism intrinsic to its practice as a bourgeois profession. Moreover, the theory of Nirvana cannot escape a quietism that denies the realities of human activity.

9. Freud, *Future of an Illusion*, SE, 21: 3–58.

10. Freud, "Dostoevsky and Parricide," SE, 21: 175–98.

11. Marx, *The Eighteenth Brumaire of Louis Bonaparte*, in *Karl Marx and Frederick Engels: Selected Works* (New York: International Publishers, 1968), p. 97.

12. Cf. note 8, chap. 5.

13. Freud, "Formulations on the Two Principles of Mental Functioning," SE, 12: 213–26.

14. Marx, *Capital: A Critique of Political Economy*, ed. Frederick Engels, 3 vols. (New York: International Publishers, 1967), 1:35.

7 RICH GIRL

1. Wilhelm Reich, *Character Analysis*, trans. Theodore P. Wolfe (New York: Simon & Schuster, 1970).

2. Freud, "Instincts and Their Vicissitudes," *SE*, 14:109–40.

3. Cf. Appendix for a discussion of Heinz Kohut's work. Cf. also Otto F. Kernberg, *Borderline Conditions and Pathological Narcissism* (New York: J. Aronson, 1975).

4. Kernberg, *Borderline Conditions and Pathological Narcissism*, p. 229.

5. Christopher Lasch, *The Culture of Narcissism: American Life in an Age of Diminishing Expectations* (New York: Norton, 1979). Cf. also "Symposium on Narcissism," *Telos* 44 (Summer 1980): 49–126.

6. Freud, "Remembering, Repeating, and Working Through," *SE*, 12: 145–57.

8 DESIRE AND THE FAMILY

1. Cf. Lloyd de Mause, "The Evolution of Childhood," *History of Childhood Quarterly* 1 (1974): 503–606.

2. Stanley Diamond, *In Search of the Primitive: A Critique of Civilization* (New Brunswick, N.J.: Transaction Books, 1974).

3. Marx, *Capital*, 1:71.

4. Edward Shorter, *The Making of the Modern Family* (New York: Basic Books, 1975).

5. Philippe Ariès, *Centuries of Childhood: A Social History of Family Life*, trans. Robert Baldick (New York: Knopf, 1962).

6. Christopher Lasch, *Haven in a Heartless World: The Family Besieged* (New York: Basic Books, 1977).

7. Peter Schrag, *Mind Control* (New York: Pantheon Books, 1978).

8. Paul A. Baran and Paul M. Sweezy, *Monopoly Capital: An Essay on the American Economic and Social Order* (New York: Monthly Review Press, 1966)

9. Jacques Donzelot, *The Policing of Families*, trans. Robert Hurley (New York: Pantheon Books, 1979).

10. Freud, *The Ego and the Id, SE*, 19:3–68.

11. David J. Rothman, *The Discovery of the Asylum: Social Order and Disorder in the New Republic* (Boston: Little, Brown, 1971).

12. Michel Foucault, *Madness and Civilization: A History of Insanity in the Age of Reason*, trans. Richard Howard (New York: Pantheon Books, 1965).

13. A.B. Hollingshead and F.C. Redlich, *Social Class and Mental Illness: A Community Study* (New York: John Wiley, 1958).

9 THE VIGILANTE

1. Max Weber, "Religious Rejections of the World and Their Directions," in idem, *From Max Weber: Essays in Sociology*, ed. and trans. H.H. Gerth and C. Wright Mills (New York: Oxford University Press, 1958), p. 335.

2. Freud, "The Unconscious," *SE*, 14: 159–216.

10 THE ADMINISTRATION OF MIND

1. Max Weber writes, "The state is an association that claims the monopoly of the *legitimate use of violence*, and cannot be defined in any other manner"

(italics Weber's). In Weber, *From Max Weber*, p. 334.

2. Max Weber, "Bureaucracy," in *From Max Weber*, pp. 196–244.

3. Peter Schrag and Diane Divoky, *The Myth of the Hyperactive Child: And Other Means of Child Control* (New York: Pantheon Books, 1975). Cf. also Eli Messinger, "Ritalin and MBD," Health PAC Bulletin 67 (December 1975).

4. Iván D. Illich, *Medical Nemesis: The Expropriation of Health* (New York: Pantheon Books, 1976).

5. For the best study of this difficult concept, see Karl Figlio, "Sinister Medicine," *Radical Science Journal* 9 (1979): 14–69.

6. John Ehrenreich, ed., *The Cultural Crisis of Modern Medicine* (New York: Monthly Review Press, 1978).

7. James R. O'Connor, *The Fiscal Crisis of the State* (New York: St. Martin's Press, 1973).

8. Marx, *Capital*, 1:35.

9. Cf. Joel Kovel, "The American Mental Health Industry," in *Critical Psychiatry*, ed. David Ingleby (New York: Pantheon Books, 1980), pp. 72–101.

10. Marx, "Theses on Feuerbach," in *Writings of the Young Marx on Philosophy and Society*, p. 401.

11. This is not to say that no one cares in the larger context. The authorities do, greatly, because worker laxness is a prime cause of the declining productivity that plays so large a role in the economic crisis of capitalism. It is on the immediate level that no one, supervisor or supervisees alike, can be made to care, hence the goofing off. That this is a form of worker resistance is indisputable. Cf. Richard C. Edwards, *Contested Terrain: The Transformation of the Workplace in the Twentieth Century* (New York: Basic Books, 1979).

12. Cf. Ernest G. Schachtel, "On Memory and Childhood Amnesia," in *Metamorphosis: On the Development of Affect, Perception, Attention, and Memory* (New York: Basic Books, 1959), pp. 279–322.

13. Sudhir Kakar, *Frederick Taylor: A Study in Personality and Innovation* (Cambridge, Mass.: MIT Press, 1970).

14. Harry Braverman, *Labor and Monopoly Capital: The Degradation of Work in the Twentieth Century* (New York: Monthly Review Press, 1975).

15. The literature is enormous. For an anthology along Marxist lines, see Armand Mattelart and Seth Siegelaub, eds., *Communication and Class Struggle*, vol. 1 (New York: International General, 1979).

16. E.P. Thompson, "Time, Work Discipline and Industrial Capitalism," *Past and Present* 38 (1967): 56–97.

17. E.P. Thompson, *The Making of the English Working Class* (New York: Pantheon Books, 1964).

18. Herbert I. Schiller, *The Mind Managers* (Boston: Beacon Press, 1973); and *Mass Communications and American Empire* (New York: A.M. Kelly, 1970).

19. Mattelart and Siegelaub, *Communication and Class Struggle*, 1:64.

20. The work of Erving Coffman contains the classic account of this kind of intrusion, which renders paranoia an adaptive defense in the administered world. Cf. Erving Goffman, *Asylums: Essays on the Social Situation of Mental*

Patients and Other Inmates (Chicago: Aldine Publishing Co., 1962).

21. M. Harvey Brenner, *Mental Illness and the Economy* (Cambridge, Mass.: Harvard University Press, 1973).

22. Braverman, *Labor and Monopoly Capital.*

23. Cf. M.M. Gill and P.S. Holzman, eds., *Psychology versus Metapsychology*, Psychological Issues Monograph no. 36 (New York: International Universities Press, 1976).

24. "All objectification is a forgetting." Max Horkheimer and Theodor W. Adorno, *Dialectic of Enlightenment*, trans. John Cumming (New York: Herder and Herder, 1972), p. 230.

25. Nancy Chodorow, *The Reproduction of Mothering: Psychoanalysis and the Sociology of Gender* (Berkeley: University of California Press, 1978).

26. Cf. Paul Mattick, *Marx and Keynes: The Limits of the Mixed Economy* (Boston: Porter Sargent, 1969).

11 THE MENDING OF SARAH

1. Joel Kovel, *A Complete Guide to Therapy; from Psychoanalysis to Behavior Modification* (New York: Pantheon Books, 1976).

2. Freud, "Analysis Terminable and Interminable," *SE*, 23:209–254.

12 DESIRE AND PRAXIS

1. Freud, *Beyond the Pleasure Principle.*

2. Freud, "Instincts and Their Vicissitudes."

3. Marx, *The Eighteenth Brumaire of Louis Bonaparte.*

4. Freud, *Civilization and Its Discontents.*

5. Marx, *Economic & Philosophical Manuscripts*, in *Karl Marx: Early Writings*, trans. T. Bottomore (New York: McGraw-Hill, 1964), p. 161.

6. William Blake, *The Marriage of Heaven and Hell*, in *The Poetical Works of William Blake*, ed. John Sampson (London: Oxford University Press, Humphrey Milford, 1925), p. 248.

7. Marx, *Economic and Philosophical Manuscripts*. Cf. also Mészáros, *Marx's Theory of Alienation.*

8. Jean Baudrillard, *The Mirror of Production*, trans. with introduction, Mark Poster (St. Louis, Mo.: Telos Press, 1975).

9. Freud, *Beyond the Pleasure Principle.*

10. A fuller account would have to include the fact that there is obviously a "natural" tendency in people to take pleasure in aggressive activities. Little children love to play "roughhouse," and even to bite; and the pleasure taken by adults in sports such as prize fighting cannot be dismissed as a purely historical phenomenon. Just as obviously, the rage, et cetera, invoked above as the consummatory act of various hostile praxes, must have a transhistorical substratum. The "aggressive capacity," then, is an inherent biological part of our species life and functions, as does the sexual apparatus, as a kind of condition of human development. Unlike erotics, however, the aggressive capacity does not become a configuration of desire, and hence is no instinct, for the simple reason that it cannot in itself conserve an object. It does, however, provide

praxis with one of its basic tools and is, as observed above, mobilized by desire when the latter turns to hatred. At such points aggression enters integrally into instincts such as sadism, et cetera.

13 TRANSCENDENCE AND UNIVERSALITY

1. Sartre, *Critique of Dialectical Reason*, p. 822.
2. The same can be said for Marx—and was said by Marx himself. For evidence that he was right, see José Miranda, *Marx Against the Marxists*, trans. John Drury (New York: Orbis Books, 1980). Also cf. Murray Bookchin, *Post-Scarcity Anarchism* (Berkeley: Ramparts Press, 1971); Raya Durayevskaya, *Philosophy and Revolution* (New York: Dell Publishing Co., 1973).

APPENDIX

1. The body of Heinz Kohut's writings are contained in the following books: *The Analysis of the Self: A Systematic Approach to the Psychoanalytic Treatment of Narcissistic Personality Disorders* (New York: International Universities Press, 1971); *The Restoration of the Self* (New York: International Universities Press, 1977); and *The Search for the Self* (New York: International Universities Press, 1978). References to these will be keyed AS, RS, and SS, respectively.
2. An excellent critique of Kohut's scientific pretensions is that by Edward Jones, "Critique of Empathic Science: Heinz Kohut's Psychology of the Self" (Ph.D. diss., Northwestern University, 1980).
3. Jacques Lacan, *Écrits: A Selection*, trans. Alan Sheridan (New York: Norton, 1977), pp. 264, 58.
4. Lacan, *Écrits*, pp. 288, 67.

INDEX

Aeschylus, 198
aggression:
  as biology vs. praxis, 237–41
  as instinct (Thanatos), 13, 14, 34, 78, 79–80, 94, 232, 233, 246
alienation, 189, 205, 206, 218
  artists' portrayals of, 129–32
  of desire, 72, 81–83, 84, 85, 113, 122, 169, 177, 178, 200, 212, 214, 246–47
  as outcome of capitalism, 116, 126–29, 202, 236, 248
  self-, 47, 99, 126, 177, 200
  as social reality, 47–49
Ariès, Philipe, 114
armoring, 97
artists:
  alienation depicted by, 129–32
  cultural domination and, 182
Augustine, Saint, 77–78

badness, 74, 77
Bartleby (Melville), 131–32
behavior:
  neurological explanation of, 24–25
  as product of labor, 33
Berkman, Alexander, 239
Blake, William, 28, 97, 100, 146, 151, 164, 169, 194, 204, 207, 227, 233
body, as condition in historical development, 233–34
breakthrough concept, 221
bureaucracy, 142, 249, 258
  as capitalist institution, 169–71, 173, 199
  depersonalization of, 136, 170, 173, 176, 177, 178, 240, 248
  desire in shaping of, 199, 259
  dysbound time of, 178–79
  of mental-health industry, 146–48, 150, 153–56, 158, 171–72, 173–74, 176, 177–79, 251–52

rationalizations of, 169–71, 177, 178
transcendence and, 250–52

capital, 259
  as inherently self-expanding, 199
  as social relation, 186–87
capitalism, 52, 53–60, 61, 107, 242
  abstraction under, 53, 56, 183–84
  artists as critics of, 129–32
  dedifferentiation under, 248–49
  desensualized world of, 53–54, 180
  desire alienated under, 72, 81–83, 84, 85, 113, 122
  family under, 110–27
  fundamental irrationality of, 54, 58, 59
  living human labor vs. dead machine labor under, 121, 199–200
  mass culture under, 181–90
  monopoly, 120–21, 180, 182–83, 201
  neurosis under, 125–29
  pathological narcissism and, 103–4, 123–25, 200–201
  revolutionary attacks on, 59–60
  sexual liberation under, 101–2, 113–14
  society reproduced under, 58–59, 122
  splitting of, 55–59, 82, 84, 112, 116–17, 119, 125–26, 202, 247–48, 253
  superalienation of insane under, 127–28
  total administration of society under, 120, 121, 169, 185, 200, 201
care, as transcendent, 249–50, 252, 257
child, as pure consumer, 121–22
child/parent differentiation, 12, 13, 15, 90–91, 93

child/parent differentiation, (*cont.*)
  merger with mother in, 197–98
  Other and, 98–99, 100, 123–25, 190, 244–45, 248
  transcendence and, 244–47, 248, 250
child rearing, consolidation of industrial capital and, 113, 114–15
civilization, instinct vs., 66, 79–80, 232, 234, 237
class structure, 73, 111, 112, 133
  internalization of, 57, 58
commodity, 188
  defined, 173
  fetishism of, 112, 187
  narcissism and, 125
community, 206
  capitalism and loss of, 116, 117, 205
  socialization and, 111, 113, 115, 205
  symbolic, in therapy, 205
consciousness, 66, 235
consumption:
  artificial stimulation of, 121–22, 183
  neurosis of, 106–7, 108
culture industry, 183, 184, 185–86, 201
  narcissism of, 187–89
  see also mass culture

death, 50
  meaning given to, 64, 135
Descartes, René, 183
desire, 69–85, 108, 192, 193, 199, 259
  administration of, 83, 180–81, 187, 190
  alienated, 72, 81–83, 84, 85, 113, 122, 169, 177, 178, 200, 212, 214, 246–47
  dualism and, 78–80
  emancipation and, 247
  emergence in infants of, 244, 245, 246–47
  forgetting and, 195–96
  gratification of, 74, 82
  growth and, 196–97
  hatred as negation of, 74–75, 99–100, 101, 104, 129, 180, 214, 248
  illusion in realization of, 197
  intersubjectivity of, 72–74
  naming and, 71–72, 80, 81, 193, 194

as narcissistic, 216
  Other and, 72, 74, 99, 104, 109
  praxis as negation of, 235, 236
  psychoanalysis as discourse of, 69, 72–74, 84, 105, 141–42, 207, 212, 214–15, 224, 226, 231, 232, 241, 253–54, 256
  sensuous immediacy of, 75–76, 77, 82
  sexual fantasies and, 101–2
  subjectivity and, 194–95, 215
  use of term, 71
  working class and, 200–201
diagnosis, 159, 176
  historical in, 221–22
  mental illnesses enumerated in, 156–58, 161–62, 164, 165
  needs of bureaucracy for, 154–55
  patient split from madness by, 150, 165
Donzelot, Jacques, 123
Dostoevsky, Feodor, 79, 128, 141–42
drugs, 175
  see also psychotropic drugs
dualism, 31–32, 78–80, 232, 233
  dialectical monism vs., 66, 78
  differentiation in, 80

education, 175, 176
ego, 11, 13–14, 15, 19, 20, 119, 189, 223
  adult, in analysis, 24, 69, 209, 217
  praxis vs., 236
Engels, Frederick, 32
Eros, *see* sexuality
evil, 79–80
exchange relations, 183, 195, 248
  in capitalism, 54, 55–56, 173, 239
  in mental-health industry, 165, 167–68, 173
  in psychoanalysis, 213–14, 224, 253
family, 98, 106, 108–27, 182, 187, 214, 216, 225
  archaic, 110–11
  capitalism and administration of, 119–20, 122–23
  desociation of, 124–25
  economic functions removed from, 110–12, 121
  emotional demands on, 116–18, 119, 120, 122

history of, 110–16
origin of, 63, 110
family therapy, 21–22
fascism, 184–85, 238–39
forgetting, desire and, 195–96
forgiveness, 223–24
Foucault, Michel, 128
Freud, Sigmund, 19, 20, 23, 24, 32, 37, 38, 39, 70, 71, 103, 107, 115, 124, 165–66, 193, 212, 256
   ambivalence toward society of, 79
   analytic method of, 26, 69, 105, 217, 218
   dualism of, 66, 78–80, 189, 232, 233
   father figure postulated by, 45, 52
   human beings viewed as totalities by, 61–62
   instinct theories of, 34, 65, 94, 232–34, 237
   legacy of, 6, 8, 10, 14–15, 22, 25
   mind as concept of, 48
   spirit of discoveries of, 16–17, 47
   subjectivity as viewed by, 194–95
Frick, Henry Clay, 239
Fromm, Erich, 19

generation gap, 122
goodness, 74

hatred, 77, 197, 198, 240
   as negation of desire, 74–75, 99–100, 101, 104, 129, 180, 214, 248
   neurosis and, 214–15, 223
   splitting and, 248
health, contradictions of, 172
health-care industry:
   bureaucratization of, 173–74
   legitimation role of, 172–73
   see also mental-health industry
Hegel, Georg, 78, 213, 235
historical:
   Freud and, 61–62
   twofold aspect of, 62–63
historical/transhistorical conjunction, 61–66, 124–25, 171, 213, 254
   desire and, 69–72, 75–76, 78, 80–81, 200, 234
   naming and, 63–64, 71
   as system of negations, 62
   theses about, 64–66
   time and, 179–80

history, 84, 151, 212, 250, 260
   as chain of human reproduction, 47–48, 58
   desire in shaping of, 192, 259
   sensuous human activity in, 32–33
Hobbes, Thomas, 111
hope, 243–44, 247, 249
Horney, Karen, 19
hostility, 237–40
   praxis and, 238–40, 241
"human nature," 34, 64, 65, 75
Huxley, Aldous, 24

id, 11, 13, 15, 20, 119, 189, 193, 194
identification, 196–97
imagination, 234, 245, 246, 247, 255
   historical/transhistorical conjunction and, 63, 71, 72
immediacy, 22, 195, 212
   sensuous, of desire, 75–76, 77, 82
individualism, 33, 34, 111, 115, 201
   as bourgeois ideology, 55, 58, 61, 71, 126, 172, 216, 254–55
   capitalist splitting and, 55, 58, 84, 116
   individuation vs., 254–55
   narcissism and, 216, 255
individuation, 245, 254–55
   as therapeutic goal, 222–23, 254, 255–58
infants:
   hope and, 243–44, 247
   innocence of, 100
   as prestructured, 70
   self-assertion of, 244–47, 248
   totality of, 243
   see also child/parent differentiation
innocence, 100
instinct, 13, 14, 20, 94, 232–41
   civilization vs., 66, 79–80, 232, 234, 237
   compulsion to repeat and, 65, 232–33
   desire and, 234, 236
   gratification of, 234–35
   praxis and, 236–41, 246
insurance companies, psychiatry and, 9, 16, 62, 158, 224

Jackson, Hughlings, 11
Jung, Carl, 151

Index

Kafka, Franz, 168, 174

Lacan, Jacques, 207, 232
language, 17, 20, 72
  see also naming
Lasch, Christopher, 118, 123
Lévi-Strauss, 3–4
libido theory, 193
love, 74–75, 99
Lukacs, Georg, 33

Madame Bovary (Flaubert), 182
Marcuse, Herbert, 223
Marx, Karl, 29–30, 55, 70, 78, 118,
  176, 226
  capital described by, 186–87, 199
  commodities as viewed by, 112, 173
  history as viewed by, 63, 80, 233,
    250
  praxis as viewed by, 32, 66, 235–36
Marxism, 64, 65, 260
  revolutionary theory of, 59–60
  totality of history as proper realm
    of, 60, 83–84
mass culture, 100–101, 181–90, 205
  contradiction in, 186
  high culture vs., 182
  ideology of, 184
  popular (spontaneous) culture vs.,
    182, 184, 186, 188
  relations between psyche and world
    altered by, 187–90
  supermessage of, 185–87
  technology and, 181, 183–84
mechanization, 115, 121, 199–200
Melville, Herman, 130–32
"mental health," 174, 255–56
mental-health industry, 144–81, 201,
  250
  bureaucratization of, 146–48, 150,
    153–56, 158, 171–72, 173–74,
    176, 177–79, 251–52
  case conferences (Grand Rounds)
    in, 158–62, 164–65
  commodity relations in, 165, 167–
    68, 171–72, 173, 206
  dysbound time and space of, 179,
    180
  family controlled by, 119–20, 122–
    23
  funding of, 175
  in nineteenth century, 127–28

mental illness, as myth, 33–34
Me theory, 15–16, 19–20
Meyer, Adolph, 8
mind, nature and society severed from,
  48, 56
"minimal brain dysfunction," 171
Moby Dick (Melville), 130
money, 187
  sensuous character of, 53
  symbolic equivalents of, 45, 56–57
  time bound to, 56, 108

naming, 33
  desire and, 71–72, 80, 81, 193, 194
  as transformation, 63–64
narcissism, 10–14, 103–7, 210, 216–
  17, 223, 245
  as archetypical emotional disorder
    of late capitalism, 103–4, 123–
    25, 200–201
  of culture industry, 187–89
  defined, 104
  description of, 10–11
  desociation in, 223–24
  empty sensibility of, 106, 107, 187,
    212
  as historical development, 106–7,
    187
  schematizing of, 11–13
  sociated, 255
  transhistorical in, 104–5
nature, 48, 56, 64
  instinct and, 65, 232, 233, 237
neurosis, 49–50, 210, 217, 249
  alienation of desire and, 212, 214,
    246–47
  under capitalism, 125–29
Nietzsche, Friedrich, 76

Oedipal relations, 12, 124–25, 233
  in patriarchy, 197, 203
  in psychoanalysis, 203
"one-dimensionality," 223
Other, 67, 101, 102, 103, 179, 181,
  215, 234, 240, 243
  in analysis, 105–6, 256
  child/parent differentiation and, 98–
    99, 100, 123–25, 190, 244–45,
    248
  desire and, 72, 74, 99, 104, 109
  exchange principle and, 165, 167–
    68

in individualism vs. individuation, 254–55
mass culture and, 187, 188
mental health and, 174, 177
praxis and, 238, 239

Pasolini, Pier Paolo, 185
patriarchy, 18, 195, 197–99, 232
Oedipality and, 197, 203
violence toward women in, 197–98
Plato, 57, 58, 76, 78, 183, 226
pleasure principle, 31, 32, 81
Poe, Edgar Allan, 129–30
political economy, 60, 65, 82–85, 183
as cold and objective, 82–83
desire severed from, 84, 85
praxis, 28, 32–33, 133, 200, 205, 223–24, 235–41, 242
defined, 53, 66, 235
history and, 63, 81
instinct and, 236–41, 246
psychoanalysis as, 223–24, 226, 241
revolutionary, 249–50, 257–60
see also transcendence
private life, public life vs., 38, 48–49, 214
production:
domestic life and, 110–12, 115
neurosis of, 106–7
of people, 108
praxis vs., 235
Proust, Marcel, 133, 179–80
psychiatry:
bourgois stupidity in, 175–76
crisis of, 8–10
function of, 174–75, 177
patient as object in, 176–77
scientific management in, 180–81
System and, 176–78
see also mental-health industry
psychoanalysis, 202, 208–27, 247
analytic reasoning in, 208–9
biologization of, 232, 236–41
as bourgeois ideology, 61, 62, 204, 214, 231
casing of individual in, 231
contracts and scope of, 140–42
critique of, 16–34
as discourse of desire, 69, 72–74, 84, 105, 141–42, 207, 212, 214–15, 224, 226, 231, 232, 241, 253–54, 256

exchange relations in, 213–14, 224
faith role in, 211, 218–19
historical consciousness in, 33, 47–49, 61, 189, 231–32
individuation in, 222–23
influence question in, 225–26
Marxist, 202, 226, 257–58
material events in, 221–23
as mechanism of social reproduction, 48, 51, 231
metaphor for, 46
moment of emptiness in, 69, 105
parents blamed in, 17, 106
as praxis, 223–24, 226, 241
predicament of, 47, 202–4, 206, 217–18
reconciliation of radical position and, 202, 207–8, 252–60
as reconstruction of infantile transactions, 69, 209
scientific detachment in, 21–23
true speech in, 224, 226
unbound time of, 107, 109, 114–15, 119, 178, 180, 187, 247–48
psychology:
modern era as age of, 125–26
second nature of, 33–34
as sensuous human activity, 32–33
psychosis, 103, 149, 151, 155, 161, 210
psychotherapy, 204, 205–7
radical, 252–60
scientific standardization in, 206
in supermarket society, 205–6
transcendence and, 252–54, 256–57
psychotropic drugs, 24, 157
mental-health industry in emphasis on, 142, 150–51, 155–56, 157, 162, 163
as substitute for real care, 142, 150–51, 155–56
public life, private life vs., 38, 48–49, 214

Quesalid, 3–4, 6

rationality, 76, 77
rationalization, capitalist, 169–71, 177, 178, 180
reality principle, 31, 32, 81, 85
Reich, Wilhelm, 78, 97
repression, 15, 46, 72, 77, 129

repression (*cont.*)
under capitalism, 82, 83, 85
desire and, 71, 78–79, 101, 218
subjectivity and, 195, 215
revenant, 195
Roots, 186

Sartre, Jean-Paul, 81, 152, 167, 176, 240, 256
Schorske, Carl, 52
self-splitting, 44–45, 51, 74
alienation and, 47, 49
under capitalism, 55–59
class barriers and, 57
reappropriation and, 46
sexuality, 94, 101–3
capitalism and liberation of, 101–2, 113–14
as instinct (Eros), 34, 78, 79, 80, 101, 232, 233, 236–37
Shorter, Edward, 113
socialism, 30, 242, 254
space, dysbound, 179–80
state, 117, 158, 183, 225
contradictions embodied in, 168–69, 172–73
family in struggle with, 110
intrusion into health care of, 173–74
labor in creation of, 168
psychiatry and, 8, 9, 62
subjective life, outer world severed from, 38, 52
subjectivity, 194–95, 202, 215, 247
subject/object differentiation, 32, 70–71, 215, 235
superego, 14, 124, 189

Taylor, Frederick W., 180, 181
Thanatos, *see* aggression
"thing-presentations," 66, 165–66
Thompson, E. P., 181
time, 179–80
bound, 56, 107, 108–9, 119, 178, 180, 187, 240, 247–48
child rearing and, 114–15
dysbound, 178–79, 187, 240, 249
transcendent, 247
unbound, 107, 109, 114–15, 119, 178, 180, 187, 247–48
totalitarianism, 246, 249, 253
totality:
defined, 53

of human beings, 61–62, 243
transcendence (transcendent praxis), 244–60
capitalism and, 248–49, 253
care as, 249–50, 252, 257
in child/parent differentiation, 244–45, 246–47, 248, 250
psychotherapy and, 252–54, 256–57
time and, 247–48
transference, 15, 74, 105–6, 109, 203, 218, 219
transhistorical, 34, 233
defined, 63, 64
see also historical/transhistorical conjunction

unconscious, 66, 204
collective, 151
universality, 29, 245–58
individual/collective dichotomy and, 246
revolutionary praxis and, 249, 250
socialist society and, 254
unreason, 76, 77, 78
utopianism, 65

Vietnam War, 135–36, 175, 240
violence, 79–80
toward women, 197–98

Weber, Max, 135
women, 18, 115, 182, 232
capitalism and inferiority of, 118–19, 120
personal freedom of, 114
violence against, 197–98
"word-presentations," 66, 165–66
work:
aestheticization of, 247
praxis and, 53
self-splitting and, 55–56
workplace, 113, 181–82
home and family severed from, 84, 115, 247, 253
imperatives of production vs. desire in, 83
as nonpsychological mind, 54–55

Yeats, William Butler, 27

A NOTE ABOUT THE AUTHOR

Joel Kovel is the author of *White Racism* and *A Complete Guide to Therapy* (Pantheon). He is a trained physician, psychiatrist, and psychoanalyst. He is currently on the faculty of the Albert Einstein College of Medicine, where he is Professor of Psychiatry and Director of Residency Training at the Bronx Municipal Hospital. In addition he is Visiting Professor of Anthropology at the Graduate Faculty of the New School for Social Research in New York City.